Riding Into the Heart of PATAGONIA

Praise for Riding into the Heart of Patagonia . . .

"This book begins as one kind of epic—a novice horseback rider in her 30s, making her solitary way across one of the world's great wildernesses. That would be reason enough to read this absorbing account—but at the end it morphs into something even deeper, the story of her participation in the glorious nonviolent struggle (conducted largely from the saddle) to stop the damming of Patagonia's great rivers. An adventure in the truest sense of the word." — Bill McKibben, author of *Wandering Home*

"Nancy Pfeiffer writes with an easy going, conversational grace, with pithy aphorisms tossed in to spice things up. *Riding into the Heart of Patagonia* is a story of a cultural landscape that is changing rapidly as all cultural landscapes are changing. It is a must read for those of us who have experienced adventure ourselves, and equally important for those who can appreciate the awakening on a physical journey, without necessarily seeking the hardship itself." — Jon Turk, author of *The Raven's Gift*

"Saddle up. These gutsy journeys will not only take you into the wild, tangled, changing heart of Patagonia, but also lead you deep into its soul. Pfeiffer is extraordinarily spunky and tough, but it is her gentleness, astute observations, and seasoned insight that will make her story resonate long after you have warmed up by the fire." — Jill Fredston, author of *Rowing to Latitude*

"Patagonian people are proud of where we come from. It isn't often we find foreigners who understand and experience this amazing wild place we call home as we do, almost becoming one of us. I met Nancy at a reading of her book here in Patagonia. The words and the feelings she shared touched me deeply. It didn't matter the language or the audience, I felt a connection that goes beyond race or nationality. Her's is a story of one who has lived the way we do, the way our parents and grandparents did." — Samuel Niklitschek Foitzick, Ensenada Valle Simpson, Patagonia, Chile

NANCY PFEIFFER

Riding Into the Heart of PATAGONIA

Bink Books
Bedazzled Ink Publishing Company • Fairfield, California

978-1-945805-67-7 paperback

Cover Photo
by
Fredrik Norrsell

Back Cover Photo
by
Ignacio Grez

Cover Design
by

DESiGNS

Photo credits:
Fredrik Norrsell
Ignacio Grez
Nancy Pfeiffer

Folk Literature of the Tehuelche Indians. Jahannes Wilbert, Karin Simoneau. Estados Unidos : University of California, 1984. Story on page 14.

Bink Books
a division of
Bedazzled Ink Publishing, LLC
Fairfield, California
http://www.bedazzledink.com

To the people of Patagonia

Photograph by Fredrik Norrsell.

Patagonia

I long to belong
to this place and its wind
I could be that old woman
on the back of a horse
And flash a toothless grin
at strangers passing by
I could live in this place
raise chickens and sell sheep
I could be of this place
Yet, never like those
who know this place
and no other

Photograph by Fredrik Norrsell.

Passing an abandoned *campo* along the Rio Baker.

Table of Contents

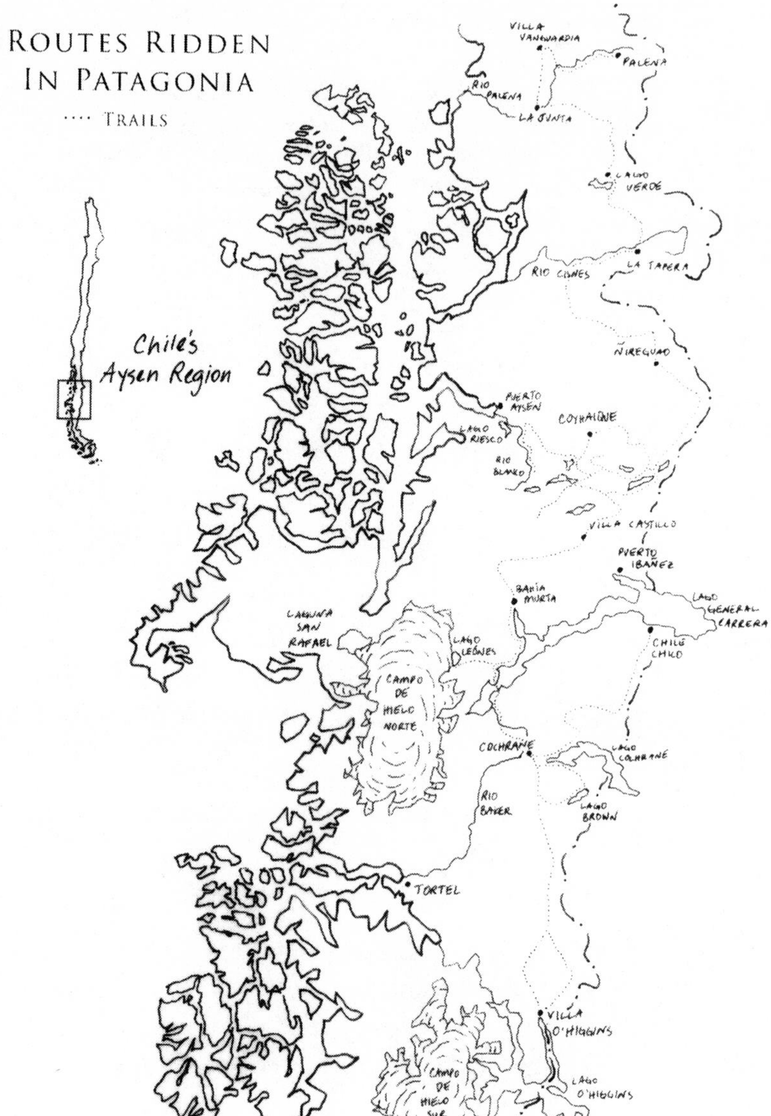
ROUTES RIDDEN
IN PATAGONIA
···· TRAILS
Chile's Aysen Region
VILLA VANGUARDIA
PALENA
RIO PALENA
LA JUNTA
LAGO VERDE
LA TAPERA
RIO CISNES
ÑIREGUAO
PUERTO AYSEN
COYHAIQUE
LAGO RIESCO
RIO BLANCO
VILLA CASTILLO
PUERTO IBAÑEZ
BAHIA MURTA
LAGO GENERAL CARRERA
CHILE CHICO
LAGUNA SAN RAFAEL
LAGO LEONES
CAMPO DE HIELO NORTE
COCHRANE
LAGO COCHRANE
RIO BAKER
LAGO BROWN
TORTEL
VILLA O'HIGGINS
LAGO O'HIGGINS
CAMPO DE HIELO SUR

Map by Rachel James

Chapter 1

La Semilla (The Seed)

Patagonia 1993

A MAN APPROACHED on a horse. His mount, a rusty red beauty, sported the short-trimmed mane and neatly squared-off tail of a well-kept mount. Colorful handwoven saddlebags tied behind a sheepskin-covered saddle held groceries from town. The man wore goatskin chaps, a woolen poncho, and the jaunty black beret typical of the region. Crinkles around his eyes spoke of years of squinting into the sun. This man and his horse belonged to this place in a way I could only dream of.

He paused on the banks of the rain-swollen river to stare at us, a group of college students up to our knees in mud and dwarfed by huge backpacks. Wet and hungry, we had been stacked up on the wrong side of the river for days, our next food supply a few kilometers away on the other side of the torrent. He looked perplexed. We had tents. We had expensive rain jackets. We obviously had money, but we had no horses.

"*¿Por qué no tienes caballos?*" he asked as he rode into the river. The strong current piled up around his horse's belly. The man gently lifted his feet from the stirrups and placed them on the horse's rump so as not to wet his boots, as his horse strode confidently through the rushing water.

That moment, I knew. I wanted to travel this country like the people who lived here. I longed to know this place as only one on horseback can. Having ridden horses only a few times in my life, I knew practically nothing about them. This was irrelevant. There was a thirteen-year-old girl inside of me who desperately wanted a horse.

I HAD COME to Patagonia as a mountaineering instructor for the National Outdoor Leadership School (NOLS), an international nonprofit that teaches wilderness and leadership skills to young people. For months my colleagues and I had been traversing the mountain ranges of the Aysén Region of Chile with a group of college students, teaching them to read a map, live in a tent, dry their clothes, and be responsible for themselves and each other. Mostly we were letting nature do the teaching. Wilderness, the great equalizer, didn't care if you were rich or poor, if you lost your coat you were going to freeze.

While we often hiked on the same trails the locals traveled on horseback, I lived each day in my own little *gringo* community, insulated from the lifestyle of Patagonia.

That year, I stayed in Patagonia long enough to watch early spring pass into late summer. On our last morning, the friends I had lived and worked with for the last several months gathered on a windy ridge high above the NOLS base camp. We stood in intermittent rain and sun, while just to the west heavy rain fell from dark clouds. Broad bands of color arched across the sky as a double rainbow stretched from horizon to horizon. One of the senior instructors, Scott, told us the legend of the *calafate*:

> Koonek, the old sorceress of the tribe, was too weak to continue migrating with her people. So they built her a sturdy hut, and Koonek remained there alone. That fall the birds moved away. Somehow, the old woman survived the long winter. When the birds returned, Koonek blamed them for leaving her in such solitude, but the birds could not have stayed as there was no food for them in winter.

The sun shone brighter and the rainbow intensified. Our little band huddled together against the chill as Scott continued the story.

> "From now on, you will be able to remain here, and you will have shelter and food," Koonek told the birds. When the hut was opened, the old woman had changed into a beautiful, thorny bush with bright yellow flowers. In the fall the same bush bore sweet, purple fruit, and the birds never needed to leave again. Today it is remembered that he who eats the *calafate* will always return.

After hearing the story, we solemnly passed around a handful of *calafate* berries that had been ripening all summer. I placed a dark, juicy berry into my mouth and let the sweetness of the whole summer sink into my soul.

THAT YEAR I returned to my home in Alaska, but I had vowed to come back, and I did. For three more seasons I hiked, kayaked, and climbed mountains in Patagonia, bringing groups of young people with me. But something was missing. I was still traveling like a foreigner. Worse yet, I still lived like one. My *gringa* impatience and the futile desire to bend the world to my will followed me everywhere.

Sergio and Veronica, the caretakers of the NOLS *campo*, were my closest contacts with the Patagonia ranching life that so intrigued me. My Spanish was still so poor I understood little of what they said, but I sensed they knew the things I needed to learn, lessons that would run far beyond saddling horses and shearing sheep.

BACK HOME IN Palmer, Alaska, a town famous for its giant mountains and giant cabbages, I began taking horseback riding lessons. My classmates were thirteen-year-old girls. I was thirty-eight. Twenty-five years earlier, I had been one of those horse-crazy girls, bugging my parents endlessly about getting a horse. I grew up in suburban Denver and a horse was the furthest thing from what my parents needed or wanted in their lives. To my bitter disappointment they had the common sense to say no. Fortunately, I wasn't thirteen anymore, and I was far from suburban Denver.

In riding class, I learned to brush coats until they shone, cinch a saddle, and pick rocks out of a horse's hooves. I walked in circles in a ring. My first horse, Yukon, was a big, brown gelding. He was old and gentle, and probably everyone's first horse. Yukon stopped hopefully at the gate every time we went by.

"Keep him moving. Give him direction," my teacher urged me.

With practice and persistence, I prompted Yukon into the laziest of canters. I was hooked. Moving in unison with another living thing delighted me.

In the barn one Saturday, confused by the array of leather and metal tack before me, I looked to my classmates for help.

"What bridle do I put on Yukon?" I asked.

A cute girl stepped forward, grasping a bridle and holding back a tiny giggle. Later, she caught her reflection in a window, and I overheard her say, "I can't stand my hair."

Looking at her lovely, long blonde hair, I wanted to say, "Don't worry, you won't always feel like that." I had been that girl, awkward in my own body, completely assured that everything about me was wrong.

In high school, a misguided guidance counselor suggested I consider working in a bank. The possibility of spending my life indoors in a tiny box counting money horrified me. At the same time, I almost laughed out loud. Let's see, I thought, I am terrible at math, I can't sit still, I hate being indoors, and I abhor dressing up.

It took me years to understand. The guidance counselor hadn't even remotely known who I was, and mountain guide was not on her list of prospective careers for young women. Someday there would be a place for me. At nineteen, I found that place—Alaska.

A couple of months after my first riding lesson, I graduated to a sweet dun mare named Carmel. By then I had earned the right to rent a horse by the month, and my world opened up. I basked in the aroma of freshly hayed fields mixed with the sweet, acidic scent of over-ripe cranberries. Carmel and I trotted along dirt farming roads, kicking up mounds of fallen birch leaves. We explored the trails through valley cottonwoods, hillside birch, and hilltop spruce, occasionally coming across huge glacial erratic rocks standing in the woods like messengers from another era. Mostly we searched out hay fields where we could gallop.

The Matanuska Valley still held a rich rural flavor. Palmer's main street reminded me of the small town in Montana where my grandparents lived when I was a child, a place where kids could ride their bikes to town for an ice cream soda.

A year later, as Carmel and I galloped through recently hayed fields, the "termination dust" of the first snowfall on the mountains reminded me that the seasons were changing. But that wasn't all. Scattered across the valley, the original colony homes, along with the wooden barns and pastures that had once dominated the landscape, were rapidly being replaced by suburban houses and shopping malls. It reminded me of the Denver suburb I had fled. Change was everywhere. It was happening in Patagonia, as well.

A *calafate* seed was growing inside me. The idea was simple: return to Coyhaique, buy a horse, and head south. The reality was a bit more complicated.

Secretly, I doubted my ability, as well as my sanity. Why is it that I insist on doing things that other people never even think about?

I often get asked, "Did your family do things outdoors?" What people want to know is, "How did a girl from suburban America end up living in Alaska and climbing mountains for a living?"

"Yes, we did." I'd recount weekend trips to local ski areas and summer car-camping vacations in the West. What I had neglected to say was that we didn't pursue outdoor activities in a way that takes over your life, makes you want to live in a tent a hundred-and-eighty days a year, or makes you crave wilderness to the point that anywhere within a hundred miles of a road feels cramped.

MY FIRST DAY at summer camp—was I eight? Was I ten? I don't know, but I recall that the prospect of spending a week in the woods sounded like heaven. I was ushered to my cabin by some nameless, faceless young camp counselor. A red squirrel was chattering away in the tree just outside the door. I stepped outside. It was gathering pinecones and bombarding me with them from the treetops. As it scampered off to the next tree and the next, I followed.

Before my parents were out of the parking lot, a lost camper alert had been sounded. A girl was missing.

"I wasn't lost," proclaimed the skinny blond girl firmly seated on her bunk in front of her counselor and the camp director.

"You need to stay in here until we all go out together," the camp director explained. "If you need to go to the bathroom in the night, you must wake up your counselor to go with you. Do you understand?"

I understood all right. This wasn't heaven. This was jail, and I was going to hate it here!

That experience may have been my first inkling that I was somehow different, as well as my first blatant understanding that I had darn well better pretend that I wasn't. I tried to get along, do my arts and crafts, and never chase squirrels again.

It didn't work.

BACK IN PALMER, I was well into making plans to return to Patagonia when I met an acquaintance in the grocery store.

"What are you doing this fall?" he asked.

Could I say it out loud? "I am going to buy a horse and ride across Patagonia by myself." That sounded both pretentious and crazy.

"Uh, going back to Patagonia?" I mumbled.

"Oh, to work for NOLS," he said, not overly interested.

I said nothing. By not denying his assumption, he would at least think I was off to do something productive, like work for a living.

I envy people who are great self-promoters. I am not one of them. National Geographic wouldn't be sponsoring this expedition. Besides, I didn't want the world watching my escapades on TV.

Over tea, I told my friend Cathy, what I had in mind.

"Aren't you afraid?" she asked.

Was I afraid of driving myself crazy? Maybe. Afraid of boring myself to death? Possibly. However, I knew what she meant: Aren't you afraid of the men? My answer to that was absolutely not.

"The people of Patagonia are respectful, even shy, especially with foreigners," I explained. "Women hitchhike into town to get groceries." I didn't go into the rest of the story, which was that I felt safer and more looked-after in southern Chile than I did in my own hometown.

That fall, I did it. I left Alaska for Patagonia, taking with me a horse first-aid kit far more comprehensive than the one I brought for myself, a pair of new saddlebags, some horseshoeing tools I didn't know how to use, and way too much excess baggage in worries and uncertainties.

RETURNING TO PATAGONIA was exactly how I pictured it. Veronica saw me as I stepped off the bus at the *campo* gate.

"Hola," she hollered from the porch. "*Pasé a la casa.*" She invited me into her cozy blue house and gave me a *beso* on my cheek. I had missed the Chilean tradition of greeting and parting with a kiss.

Her hair was shorter now—the unruly ringlets of a slightly younger woman had been replaced by loose dark curls.

"*Sienta sé,*" she said, pointing to a comfortable, worn sofa. Sergio's father, an even older man than I remembered, sat silently behind the woodstove.

Veronica filled a gourd with *yerba maté* and added hot water from the kettle on the woodstove. She took the first, often bitter, taste of *yerba* herself, and spit it into the sink. Next she passed the *maté* my way. As I sipped the stimulating herb at the center of social life in Patagonia, time rewound.

That illusion was shattered when Veronica's son, Humberto, wandered into the house. No longer a small, round child wedged into the saddle in front of his dad, he looked all grown-up in his navy and gray school uniform.

When the gourd was empty, I turned the gourd so that the *bombilla*, the silver straw used to strain and sip the tea, was pointed in Veronica's direction and handed it back to her.

"How old is Humberto these days?" I asked in my rusty Spanish.

He was now seven, and in the first grade. Veronica told me that she hitchhiked with him to school in Coyhaique every morning, hitched home alone, and then back in to get him at three. She must have seen the look of disbelief on my face. This was a hardship I could barely imagine.

"We are fortunate," she said. "We live close enough to town that I can bring Humberto to school each day. It is much harder for many families. Often when the children reach school age, the woman has to move to town, while her husband stays and runs the *campo*."

I knew that many families either maintained two separate houses or sent their children to live with relatives, or even to boarding schools. Despite the hardship, every child goes to school. Still, I couldn't help but think about what a simple thing like a school bus could do for my friend. In Alaska, I live at the end of a dirt road, slightly farther from town than Veronica, who lives along the main highway. A bus arrives daily at the corner, picking up the two school-age children who live on my road.

As the *servidor*, Veronica refilled the gourd and passed it to Sergio's father, who participated in the *maté*, but said nothing. Even years ago, I hadn't understood a word he said. Was it because my Spanish was so poor or had he been suffering, even then, from the dementia that had now left him mute?

Out the window I saw Sergio coming from the upper *campo.* He tied his favorite dun mare, Reflauta, to the fence post and joined in the *maté* session. Sergio had the kind of round, boyish face that never seemed to age. His easy manner of greeting me made me feel like I had never left. He had already asked around about a horse for me.

"It may be difficult to find a good horse," he told me. "You must know someone. A horse that is advertised could be lame or wild."

Only a few hours into my trip, my enthusiasm could not be squelched. "I will find something," I assured both of us.

Days blurred together. I hitched the twelve kilometers into town daily. In the last decade, cars had replaced horses, and Coyhaique, the capital of the region, had become a bustling community. I looked longingly at the few horses still tied in the empty lot at the edge of town, but I figured their owners, people from the *campos* buying supplies in town, did not want to sell the horses they were using.

Although the streets were full of noisy automobile traffic, Coyhaique was still the kind of place where a walk down Calle Prat, the main street, could result in running into a half-dozen people I knew. I spent my days visiting tack stores, veterinary offices, and talking to anyone I could think of who had anything to do with horses. At the end of each day, my feet hurt from pounding the cement sidewalks, and I was no closer to finding a horse.

At the *campo*, Veronica and I made empanadas, and I talked incessantly to Sergio about horses. None of Veronica's other friends came into her house and talked endlessly to her husband. Socially, women talked with women about women's issues. Men talked to men about horses. But it was well understood that *gringos* were different. Here, I was unusual, but I was accepted.

A lead on a horse took me to the nearby village of Balmaceda, where I tromped all day in the cold, dry wind and dust. I had been told his place was a cement house that could not be seen from the road and that there was a wooden gate with a big rock nearby. None of the houses were visible from the road. Every one, of course, had a wooden gate, and there were many large rocks.

Almost a week into my journey, I had yet to find one horse for sale. The next day, I took the bus back to Balmaceda and went looking a second time for Señor Muñoz. Trudging from house to unoccupied house in the Patagonian wind, I saw myself as I must have looked from the outside—a tall, skinny *gringa* snooping around empty houses, her face hidden by a whirlwind of blonde hair. Then I noticed a small wooden signpost near a bridge I had crossed multiple times. It read: Puente Muñoz. A cement house set far back on the property was barely visible behind a cluster of *alamo* trees doubled over by the wind. The gray cement blockhouse was empty like all the others. I looked around and hollered in the direction of the barn. No one answered. The last bus to Coyhaique was at four-thirty. I was about to leave when a battered blue pickup truck pulled in.

I strode up to the truck, and before the man could open the door, I blurted out, "*Señor Flores me invitió a ver el caballo de Señor Muñoz.*"

For the past two days, I had been practicing my introduction: Señor Flores has sent me to look at the horse of Señor Muñoz.

"*Allá esta,*" he said, punctuating his words with the uniquely Patagonian mannerism of pointing with his lips. The man began unloading boxes from the truck as if a crazed-looking *gringa* showed up every day looking for a horse. I snuck around behind the house. Sure enough, a small, dark horse stood saddled near the corral. His long, dreadlocked mane spoke of a horse that no one cared for, but I loved the way it blew in the wind. He was older than I had imagined. His feet looked terrible, and he had a sore on his hind leg.

I stepped into the stirrups, which fit perfectly, and settled myself into the soft sheepskin saddle. When I asked him to go, he took off with the good Chilean horse walk of an animal accustomed to working hard. A sweet and willing horse, he had obviously learned a long time ago that it was best to do what people wanted without complaint. Overjoyed to be in the saddle at last, I took a quick trip around the dilapidated barn, but I knew he was not the horse for me. I couldn't imagine making this poor old guy march across Patagonia.

Once I was on the bus, I took heart. At last I had ridden a horse that was for sale.

Back at the *campo,* Sergio had put an advertisement for me on Radio Santa Maria, looking for a horse. The radio station aired messages three times a day, connecting a quarter-million square kilometers of rural Patagonia, letting people without telephones know who was coming to visit, who was ill in Coyhaique, and who had what to sell or trade. Sergio's ad produced a lead. A man named Carmen Vásquez was selling a horse.

After hours of searching, I found Vásquez' small backyard apartment. He talked loud and fast with the heavy accent of the *pobladores*—people who have lived on remote *campos* all their lives, talking mainly with each other, dropping their esses (making *muchas gracias, mucha gracia*), and slurring their words (making *una mes, ume*).

When I didn't understand him, he talked louder. I tried to tell him I was a foreigner, not deaf, but I mispronounced the word for deaf, *sordo*, and told him I wasn't *zurdo*. I doubt he knew why I told him I wasn't left handed, which ironically, I am. At times like this I desperately wished I had studied harder. My high school Spanish and a few years of kayak guiding in Mexico weren't going to get me far in rural Patagonia.

Somehow, we managed to make plans for him to pick me up at seven-thirty the next morning, a time I thought no one in Chile would be awake.

At seven-thirty a.m. he honked at the *campo* gate. He wanted to borrow a saddle from Sergio. His plan was that I would buy the horse and ride it back. There were a couple problems with that idea. One, I might not buy his horse and I didn't want to be stuck hitching with a saddle. The second problem, which I didn't have the Spanish to explain, was that the NOLS director had informed me that I needed to have any new horse checked out by a veterinarian before I brought it onto the *campo*. We left with a saddle.

Barely outside of the *campo* gate, the conversation turned to my marital status.

"*¿Estás casada?*" he asked. This line of interrogation caused every joint in my body to tighten. The fact that the sturdy woman sitting beside me was his wife made me only slightly more comfortable.

I answered in single syllables. At other times I would have faked incomprehension of the question, but that day, I needed to understand Spanish. He wanted to set me up with one of his friends.

"My boyfriend wouldn't like that," I lied through my teeth.

Whatever I thought of Señor Vásquez, I liked his horse immediately. The deep red *colorado* walked right up to me. His pasture was nothing but a damp, fenced-off peninsula in a lake. His feet didn't look bad compared to the other hooves I had seen. He was skinny, but it was early spring, and I figured good feed would fatten him up a bit.

Señor Vásquez saddled him and asked for the whip. I hadn't brought one and had no intention of buying a horse that I'd have to whip. He stepped up on the stirrups and set himself down hard in the saddle. The *colorado* bucked and lunged as Señor Vásquez pranced around on him. Then it was my turn. Apprehensive about riding a horse I had just seen buck, I slid my toes into the stirrups.

"Lento, lento," his wife hollered from inside the rough lean-to where she was tending a fire.

Was it for lack of confidence in me or in the horse that she wanted me to go slowly?

"¿Esta manso?" I asked. Just a few days earlier I had learned the important difference between the word *manso*, which means tame, and *mañoso*, which denotes ill tempered.

"Si, si, muy manso," she assured me from behind the wall of sticks.

The skinny *colorado* actually seemed to enjoy moving. We trotted around some downed trees, and then I nudged him into a gentle, willing canter. I felt like he was asking me to buy him and get him out of there.

Sitting beside the fire, in a shelter that kept off the worst of the elements, we passed the *maté*. The bus to Coyhaique would pass in a half hour. If I was not on it, I would be hitchhiking with a saddle. Trying to pretend that I wasn't in a hurry, I sipped my *maté* and chatted.

"I will return with a veterinarian this afternoon," I said. Having no idea how I would accomplish that, I headed for the bus.

By some miracle, I returned that same day in a car with a veterinarian. The vet picked up the horse's feet and muttered, "*hongos.*"

My sweet horse had a foot fungus from standing in the wet pasture. He picked a small white grub from the horse's coat and held it out for me to examine.

"Parasitos," he said.

My horse had parasites. These little *bichos* were the reason NOLS required a vet check before bringing any new animals to the *campo*. Worst of all, the vet explained, the reason the horse was skinny was that he couldn't eat properly because of his teeth.

The *colorado's* fate was sealed when the vet, who had made me stumble though complicated questions in Spanish all day, said in perfect English, without breaking his pleasant conversation with Señor Vásquez, "Do not buy this horse."

In his car, he told me, again in Spanish, "I have another possibility. A friend of mine is selling a mare."

I wasn't excited about traveling with a mare. I suspected that free-ranging stallions would be common where I was going. I had seen the power and violence of horse sex only once. It wasn't anything I wanted to deal with on the trail.

Then the vet said, "She might be pregnant."

That wasn't appealing either. I didn't even know how long a horse's gestation period was, let alone what I would do with a baby horse.

"We might as well go look," I said.

Riding around in a car with the vet was a pleasant experience compared to hitching the roads alone. Just outside of town we stopped to open a gate. Well-kept grounds surrounded several tourist cabins. In the back of the property a corral contained both the *yegua* and the stallion she had recently mated with. At least if she was pregnant, she was not very pregnant, I thought, as if one can be not very pregnant.

She was a *tobiano*, a black and white paint, a rare coloration here. Well taken care of, she had a short-cropped mane and squared-off tail, and her feet were in fine shape. For a light-colored horse, her coat was impeccable. If I bought her, I doubted she would ever be this clean again. A dainty heart had been recently branded on her muscular butt.

The veterinarian lifted each leg, bending her fetlock tight against her upper leg in several positions. Running his hands down her front legs from withers to hooves, he talked with the workers in a rapid-fire Spanish I did not understand, but he seemed satisfied.

The workers threw a saddle on her for me. I stepped into the stirrups and settled onto her back. She fidgeted, dancing a little sidestep motion I was unaccustomed to. I figured she was just interested in getting away from the stallion, so I took her on a tour of the property. She settled down. Far from eager to walk in mud and dirty her pretty feet, she was a city girl in my opinion, but I figured a few hundred miles would cure her of that. I was interested.

She even came with a veterinary certificate and ownership papers, something no one else had offered. If I got accused of having a stolen horse, this girl would be certifiably mine.

Looking far into the future, I hoped these fancy papers would help me get her into Argentina. Patagonia is neither a country nor a state, but a loosely defined region shared by two countries. Nearly 600 kilometers south of Coyhaique, the glaciers on the western edge of the Southern Patagonia Ice Field ooze into the Pacific Ocean. The eastern side of the same ice field calves directly into Lago O'Higgins, a thousand-square-kilometer lake extending into Argentina. At that point, all of Chilean Patagonia is composed of water in either its liquid or frozen form. If I intended to ride the length of Patagonia, I would need to get my horse into Argentina.

Before roads were constructed in Chilean Patagonia, going through Argentina was the only way to travel north to south. *"Entre gauchos no hay fronteras,"* a common Patagonian saying, means, "Between local cowboys there are no borders." But, for me there would be. In the 1960s the Chilean version of the Department of Agriculture made transporting livestock between Chile and Argentina illegal. But I could worry about all that when and if I got to the southern end.

"I've got a horse!" I hollered to Sergio from the doorstep. Five minutes later, my horse—a black and white *tobiano* mare—stepped from a truck parked in front of his house. I had a brand new responsibility.

The next morning, sipping coffee on the front porch, watching my very own horse graze was like living a dream. A thin, low-lying valley fog flowed over her withers and down around her hooves. She was Pegasus without wings. Her coat, a blended patchwork of white, gray, and black, reminded me of clouds before a heavy rain. *Nimbus, como las nubes cuando va a llover.* "Nimbus, like the clouds when it is going to rain." That would be her name. It sounded a bit pretentious, like a long pedigree, but I liked it. With what I knew of her personality, she would love it too. She could be Nimbus for short.

That afternoon, Nimbus and I went for our first real ride. We joined up with Sergio and headed to the upper *campo,* looking for the cows. It was late October, and the first flowering plants of the spring were beginning to bloom. Each new scent brought a long-forgotten name in Spanish bubbling to the surface of my mind. *Notro*: Clusters of bright red flowers and large, brilliant green leaves, the first tree to burst into bloom in the spring. *Michay:* A prickly bush with leaves like holly, now dressed in small, orange blossoms. *Calafate*: Yellow flowers hiding sharp thorns would become December's sweet dark berries and a legendary invitation to return.

Screeching *tero-teros,* a southern lapwing as common and raucous in *campo* land as gulls on the Alaska coast, dive-bombed us, protecting their nests. Once we were in the deep woods, I heard the familiar call of the *chucao* singing out its name, *chucao tapaculo.*

We found the cows at the uppermost part of the *campo.* Looking out over the rich, rolling land below, Sergio and I discussed my horse's color. Was she a *tobiano*, a true paint, or *manchado*, a white horse with dark patches? Nimbus's spots were far too large for her to be considered an *overo.* The paint-splatter spots of an *overo* drip off a horse's haunches like tiny raindrops. Like the Inuit with their multitude of words describing snow, Patagonians make fine distinctions between the things that matter in their lives. I longed to understand the subtle differences that others could see. Someday, if told to pick the *potrillo zaino estrallita* from a herd, I hoped to return with the right horse, a young, almost black male with a rusty tinge on his nose and a small white star on his forehead.

The cows were content, and no new calves had been born. We started downhill. With Sergio leaning back in the saddle, his horse strode down the fall line. Nimbus did zigzags, picking each step carefully and trying to avoid the steepest sections. We soon fell behind. I had never ridden down anything this steep, and I thought her reluctance was just part of the city-girl attitude she would need to outgrow. Sergio's verdict on my new horse was different.

"The way she is walking means her knees are not good," he said. "Maybe you should trade her."

Trade her? The words smacked me in the gut with a log. What? How? It had taken two weeks of hard work to find this horse. How could I trade her, and to whom?

I didn't doubt that there were things *campo* people knew that veterinarians did not, but I had watched the vet pick up each leg, fold it back hard on itself, and stare into Nimbus's eyes, looking for any sign of pain. Could the vet have made a mistake? Could he have purposely steered me wrong? I did buy the horse from a friend of his. My mind was a kaleidoscope concerning what had happened in the past. The horse I bought and already loved was somehow deficient. But no ideas came to me about what I should do about it now.

"She may have been used in the rodeo," Sergio said, interrupting my thoughts.

In the Chilean rodeo horses and riders push two-year-old cows along a wooden fence. The goal is to check and turn the animal four times, eventually pinning it against a padded part of the fence. Horses dance sideways along the fence, crossing their front legs. I had felt it. That crossover step was the motion Nimbus did when I first climbed on her.

"Sometimes horses miss and plow into the fence with their knees," Sergio told me.

The look of horror on my face must have said it all.

He softened his words. "You never know, maybe it will be years until her knees get really bad."

It didn't matter how it had happened. The fact was my new horse wasn't perfect, maybe not even good enough. I sensed that Sergio's concept of time was different than mine. Selling this horse and buying another was a real option in his world. My *gringa* brain just couldn't accept starting over, pounding the streets again, looking for another horse, trying to sell this one, knowing her knees were bad. Besides, the NOLS director had let me know I was welcome to stay for two weeks, until I could launch my expedition. I had already overstayed my limit. The entire way to the valley bottom scenarios flooded my mind, but no solution came to me.

At the base, a message was waiting for me from the NOLS director. I suspected that he was either going to inform me I had overstayed my welcome and needed to leave or someone had canceled a contract and he wanted to offer me work. Either way it was going to be bad news for my expedition.

NOLS had been good to me by providing a launch pad for my journey. If the school needed an instructor, agreeing to work would be the least I could do. On the other hand, I had planned this trip for years. I had already abandoned home and work and friends. I was here, and I had a horse, albeit an imperfect one.

I could not bail on my trip because I was scared or unsure about my new horse without losing face. But accepting a job would be a normal, sane choice that mainstream America would support.

The director offered me work.

I turned it down.

I was going and I needed to go soon, before anything else came up. But first, I needed a saddle. New saddles were more expensive than horses. Horses reproduce themselves. Saddles had to be carefully made by hand.

Sergio told me of a neighbor, Señor Foitzick, who might have a used saddle for sale. The story of the Foitzick family was part of the history of Coyhaique.

Between 1910 and 1920, Chileans, some of whom had been living in Argentina for years, began to colonize the Coyhaique area. They came into the country and established homes, trails, towns, and schools without the central government in Santiago knowing of their existence. By 1920, there were 155 households in the Coyhaique area. Chilean government officials, fearing that if Chile didn't populate Patagonia, Argentina would, leased huge tracts of land in the southern regions to large cattle companies.

When the company men arrived, they found the land already occupied by a strong, independent breed. The cattle companies fenced off what it considered to be their land and warned the locals that cutting the fence would be a violation of the law.

One of these early settlers, Juan Foitzick Casanova, had had his eye on a piece of land inside the company's fence. Señor Foitzick simply built a bridge over the fence and settled his family on the other side.

The company also prohibited new houses from being constructed within its holdings, so neighbors collectively built houses in a single night. The homes were naturally nestled into whatever protection the landscape offered from the Patagonia winds. By the time the cattle company owners noticed a new house, the residents would simply claim that it had been there all along. Their sudden appearance earned these homes the name *casas brujas* (witches' houses).

In Argentina and other parts of Chilean Patagonia, *estancias,* large tracks of corporate-owned ranch land, the legacy of the original cattle companies, are more the norm. However, to this day, the style of agriculture in the Aysén Region is primarily small family farms, and Laguna Foitzick and the land around it is still in the hands of the Foitzick family.

Nimbus and I rode off to talk to Señor Foitzick. Riding, even beside the road, was delightful compared to dragging myself around on foot. No longer a person without a horse, I understood the pity that had once been directed at me.

The road indicated on Sergio's hand-drawn map branched into smaller and smaller roads, eventually ending at a closed gate. The *gringa* in me was not inclined to open the gate, ride through, and close the gate behind me as is the local custom. Trails are the same as roads here, and they often run right through people's yards. It is expected that if you have business there, you will enter, if not, you won't.

In Juan Fotzick's cluttered kitchen, lace doilies and old photographs adorned a house that had been occupied for generations. We drank *maté* and talked about his land and his horses. He did not have a saddle for sale. He owned one saddle, the one he used every day.

In the end, a friend loaned me a saddle for my journey.

Next, I needed a rope to tie my horse at night. In every garage in my neighborhood in Alaska there was plenty of unused rope. The ingrained North American mentality that there is always a little extra of everything was still strongly within me. Ropes, like everything else in Chile, were owned by someone who had a specific use for them. There was no "extra" anything lying around. Half a day's shopping later, I owned a rope. I would need to take good care of it.

One evening, everything was done. The sunlight spread in long silver fingers beneath the clouds that were always present to the west. Nimbus was grazing in front of the house. On a whim I jumped on her bareback. Moments later, we were galloping around the now-green pasture. Pure exhilaration pulsed through my body as we bounded over open, undulating terrain. All her power was my power. She ran like she wanted to run, and I felt the expression of my joy within her.

I was finally mentally ready to go.

As if watching an old, black-and-white, slow-motion movie, I can still see myself leaving the *campo*. I looked back at Sergio and Veronica waving from the yard. After closing the heavy wooden gate behind me, I stepped up on onto the left stirrup and swung my right leg high over the overstuffed saddlebags that contained all of my current life's belongings. We headed off down the dirt road across the street.

Chapter 2

Los Lecciones (The Lessons)

THE "STREET" WAS the Carretera Austral, the main highway through Patagonia. The continued creation of an all-Chilean north-south road had been one of the most hotly debated issues in Patagonia for twenty years. Unbeknownst to me, the situation was intensifying.

It was early November, springtime in the rain shadow of the Andes. While the rich valley bottomland was greening up, the mountains were still thickly snow covered. Except that snow line was headed upward instead of down, I had traveled to the other side of the world and found a place much like where I'd come from. This could have been the Matanuska Valley fifty years ago. For once in my life I was in exactly the right place at the right time.

As I traveled through the fertile grazing land of the Simpson Valley, a desperately needed sense of space slipped into my soul. *Alamo* trees, tall, fast-growing poplars planted by the homesteaders as windbreaks, marked the farmhouses scattered across the pastoral landscape.

By afternoon I was walking, claiming Nimbus was tired, while in reality it was my butt that was sore. Poorly packed gear kept bouncing out of Nimbus's saddlebags. Unable to find a secure place for the hardback books, horse-grooming tools, and spare sunglasses I had far too many of, I stuffed them into my own pack.

An ancient red truck slowed nearly to a stop. A gray-haired couple stared at me through the cracked windshield of what was likely the first automobile they had ever owned. Mortified, I saw myself through their eyes, not as a woman on an expedition headed for the southern end of the continent, but as an overloaded, disorganized *gringa* walking down the road, leading a perfectly good horse.

By late afternoon, Nimbus tugged on the lead rope, letting me know that it was time to go home. How could I tell her that her sweet pasture was a thing of the past? Every night from now on we would need to look for a new place with decent grass. What I didn't know yet myself was that behind me was also my own last night of uninterrupted sleep. For the next month, I would wake up several times every night to check on and move my horse.

That evening we camped in a small, trashy pull-off with barely enough grass for the night. Trucks rumbled by and dust settled onto my tent. My reality was a poor match for my dream of galloping off across Patagonia on horseback. The next day, unable to face another night beside the road, I marched Nimbus toward a nearby lake. I wasn't headed south, but I didn't care. A pattern for my journey was already being set.

A few graying giants, the skeletal remains of a once great forest, stood like sentinels around the lake, their comrades lay fallen, sinking into the soil. It was hard to believe that early explorers had described this now-open grazing land as an "exuberantly vegetated forest."

In the 1930s and '40s, Chilean laws designed to populate the province had given title to settlers who cleared and fenced their land. With no mechanized way to open the country to agriculture, the pioneers turned to fire. Spurred by the relentless Patagonia winds, blazes raged up mountainsides into country that would never be good grazing. Fires burned out of control through the winter, destroying homes, towns, and schools.

Beside the lake, tall fronds of bamboo grew in feathery clusters. A few kilometers to the west, the same plant flourished in impenetrable mats. During my NOLS courses, fighting my way on hands and knees through the dense foliage of western Patagonia had given me a measure of empathy for the pioneers who had wrestled homesteads from this verdant valley by whatever means they could.

Fifty percent of Aysén's native forest has been lost or damaged by fire, yet nature's ability to heal herself amazed me. When I arrived at camp, I hiked up a small hill overlooking the lake. A stand of *Notro* trees bent permanently downwind, red flowers flaring to leeward like trees on fire, contrasted with the soft pink of wild rose, the pastel purple of lupine. The delightful scent of a dozen different flowers and the soft sound of wavelets on the shore brought me sweet serenity. With my senses already bursting, a flock of chattering *cachañas,* twenty lime-green parrots, landed in a blazing-red tree.

Back at camp, cows were in the kitchen, trashing plastic bags, stomping my precious potato flakes into the dirt. I ran cursing at the beasts. My state of contentment, my fragile conception of my own competence—shattered.

The next day, a shortcut took me down a rough two-track dirt road with dozens of gates. At each, I got off Nimbus, opened the gate, walked her through, closed the latch behind me, and remounted my horse. If a single gate were to be locked, it would mean turning around and losing the entire day's travel.

While stopped at yet another gate, a man on horseback galloped up to us, wool poncho flapping, black cap perched on his head, hand outstretched. He rode a gorgeous *alazán,* a red horse with a few white under hairs showing through.

He greeted me with a handshake. "Visitors usually stop at the house," he informed me in Spanish.

I had not seen a house, but in the distance was a clump of *alamo* trees. Begging forgiveness for my rudeness, I said, "*Permiso. Soy extranjero,*" as if it weren't obvious I was a foreigner.

When he asked where I was headed, I told him the name of a nearby lake. I was not ready to tell anyone I was riding this horse to Cochrane.

"I will show you the way," he said.

Suddenly, I was riding with a *gaucho,* the name given in the early 1900s to the itinerant horsemen of Argentina. We blazed through *campo* land and forest at a pace I had not traveled before. All too soon he deposited me on a gravel road and rode off with a wave and a grin.

The day wore on. Ahead of me, barbed wire fence lined both sides of the road. Wishing we had camped in the open country we had just passed through at a trot, I examined each wide spot in the road for a place big enough to camp a night with a horse. A man was closing a *campo* gate.

"Is this your *campo*?" I asked.

"No, I only work here. Why?"

"Oh, I was just looking for a place to camp," I said, trying not to sound desperate.

"I have two friends, Cantadilla and Juana, who live just down the road. You could stay there," he told me, describing his friends' house in detail. "Very friendly folks," he assured me.

I thanked him and trudged onward. No stranger passing by had ever asked to stay at my house. I would not be asking Cantadilla.

I inspected every slightly more spacious spot between the fence lines. Nothing wide enough appeared. I marched onward. It was getting late, and the low sun behind me produced an amazing light show. The brilliant bands of a Patagonian rainbow ended right at Cantadilla and Juana's place. I decided to stop. One cannot afford to pass up rainbows.

Maybe the illusion of colored light cast by the setting sun that led me here was just a coincidence, but Cantadilla and Juana's house was indeed a pot of gold. A place to camp, fresh cow's milk, homemade bread, and, best of all, new friends.

That evening a neighbor stopped by to buy some cheese from Juana and stayed to talk.

"Children these days are so much smarter than their parents," he told me. "Take for example my daughter who lives in the city. She can talk on the phone, change the baby's diaper, and open the mail all at the same time." He patted his head and rolled his tongue counterclockwise.

Everyone burst out laughing, but I asked in all seriousness, "Is it really good to do three things at once?"

"Oh, in today's Chile it is necessary," he assured me.

On my trip, I had been purposely concentrating on one thing at a time. I didn't read while I ate. I didn't brush my teeth while I packed, and I felt saner than I had in years. If multi-tasking was essential even here in Chile, how had I survived my life in the United States?

If serendipity is the development of events by chance that leads to a brilliant discovery, this evening had been exactly that. As I slipped into sleep, a new confidence accompanied me. I would be taken care of. I would meet the people along the way who would teach me the things I needed to know.

The next morning, I headed off in the direction of a southbound trail that was clearly marked on my map. On my way I met a man carrying a chainsaw on the road.

"Can you get to La Horqueta from here?" I asked.

"*Si, si,*" he said. "It's a great trail, wide like a road."

I thanked him and hurried off.

We climbed into the *lenga* forest on a broad, well-maintained trail. Each tree, with its high, twisted branches, told an individual life story, making the lodgepole woods of my youth resemble a cluster of boring clones. Years of fallen *lenga* leaves had left the soil so acidic that only *lenga* and a few mosses could grow, making for open wooded country that was a delight to travel through. Ancestors of this southern beech tree had grown sixty-five million years ago on the supercontinent Gondwana. The *Nothofagus* family was ripped apart by continental drift. Patagonia's *lenga* has cousins in New Zealand and Tasmania. This was my favorite forest on earth. But there was one problem: Grass. Camping with horses was about one thing—grass, quality and quantity.

Nimbus understood better than I did that the cool, damp understory of the forest lacked anything resembling good fodder. Tossing her head and swishing her tail, she let me know she was ready to go back to the lowlands. She, I was learning, was a strong-headed little girl, but I am also a willful female, and we had not yet come to an understanding.

We were off the road system and in the wild country I loved, when Nimbus planted her front feet and refused to move. Giving her a strong kick, I told her what I wanted. Complete with a youthful bucking fit, Nimbus and I had our first war. I won. I knew I had to. Still, punishing my horse left me shaken. If the last grass was indeed behind us, I had blown it, and I knew it.

Half an hour later, I stumbled upon what I took as deliverance—an open meadow and a tumbled-down corral. The grass was short and barely green at this altitude, but there was grass.

I was halfway through cooking dinner when Nimbus looked up. Her eyes ablaze with *mal* intent, she laid her ears back flat along her head and, hobbles and all, jumped the log wall of the broken-down corral. To my astonishment, she galloped down the trail in hobbles faster than I could run without. Boots unlaced, I stumbled behind her.

My poor girl was sweating and lunging. Pursuing her just made her run faster, but I couldn't stand letting her out of my sight. At last her pace slowed. I lagged a bit farther behind. Exhausted, she hung her head in defeat. I slipped the rope over her neck, undid the hobbles, and led her back to camp.

I have a long history of talking people into expeditions they are unsure about. At least my human companions are able to say, "No, Nancy, I do not wish to go on your crazy adventure," and they frequently do. Poor Nimbus did not have that option. I had bought her. However, she had just made her statement. She did not want to go on this trip. What was I to do now?

Tucked inside my little pyramid-shaped nylon shelter, I dozed fitfully. Outside, sleet was turning to snow. I felt sorry for Nimbus out in the storm. Part of me realized I was being ridiculous. Chilean horses spend the entire winter outside in the rain, wind, and snow, a barn an unheard of luxury. Her life with me was, in this way, no different than if she were still back in her pasture.

As I lay awake listening to snow pelt the nylon walls, I wondered how I could return to NOLS and explain that I had given up on my expedition because my horse did not want to go. When I finally slept, I dreamed of carrying a boyfriend around on my back and of being able to talk to horses.

The early morning sun melted the piles of snow that had drifted in around the trees, changing both the scene outside my tent and my mood. I did not want to give up on my expedition, but I had no idea where the trail went from here. Leaving Nimbus to graze what grass she could find, I took off on foot.

A tremendous amount of work had once gone into this old ox-cart road. Log bridges made of now-rotten timbers hung swaybacked over deep chasms, a certain death trap for a horse punching through. Soon, I was scrambling over a downed log every six feet. This trail hadn't been maintained in years.

Curiosity and hardheaded stubbornness drove me on. Crawling through deadfall on my belly, I could see the Rio Blanco, the valley that would lead us at last toward La Horqueta, and from there, southward. But this was not a route that could be done with a horse.

Retreating down the long road I had come in on, I met the same man, again carrying a chainsaw.

"That trail should take about five hours," he said.

I had been gone for two days.

"It is covered in downed trunks," I informed him.

"*Pero, los caballos saltan*," he said.

I tried to picture a horse jumping the hundreds of logs I had crawled over—maybe his horse but not mine. On a whim I asked, "How long since you traveled that trail?"

"*Veinte años*" He said.

Twenty years. Was it possible that the trail on my map had not existed for decades?

Then I remembered a conversation with Sergio. "There are three kinds of trails in Chile: Those that exist on the map but do not exist in reality, those that exist in reality but are not on the map, and those that are located more or less where they are shown on the map." Praying for the third kind, I took off in the direction of another trail two days away.

A week into my trip, I could still see the backside of the mountain where the NOLS *campo* was located. We had been traveling in a circle. Was I subconsciously afraid to leave?

That night, with more than thirty kilometers behind us, our longest day so far, I believed we were finally on our way to La Horqueta. Camp was set up, and dinner in the making when an old man appeared on horseback. Smartly dressed in a gray wool vest, he sat upright on his horse, but as he drew near I noticed he was even more ancient than I had thought. The deep wrinkles of a hard outdoor life lined his face, but the expression worn into his face told of years well spent. He was hard of hearing and responded to my greeting with a heavy *poblador* accent through several missing teeth.

"Is it OK that I camp here?" I asked, assuming this was his land.

He looked at me, raised his bushy gray eyebrows, and said nothing.

Did he not hear me? Was my Spanish that poor? Did he not understand my question, or was it the concept he was unfamiliar with?

Finally, he spoke. *"¿Estás sola?"*

This again. Yes, I was alone.

"¿Con ese caballo?" he asked with astonishment and obvious disapproval.

"Yes, with a horse. Yes, I am alone with this horse."

"Where is your companion?" he asked.

That remark struck a chord so painful my brain clamped shut. That question, I wasn't ready to discuss with him or anyone else, in any language.

"There are sheep here," he told me.

There were sheep nearly everywhere. Did he think the sheep were going to be a bother to me or that I was going to be a problem to the sheep? I was doing my best to understand him, but I could catch only a few words at a time.

"What about your husband? There could be thieves. There might be mountain lions."

A smile frozen to my face, I fumbled with my stove for something to do. I suspected that the biggest danger I was faced with was the reaction of people like him convincing me that this entire trip was, indeed, a bad idea.

All I understood was that whatever I was doing was not OK, and no, I could not sleep anywhere there were sheep. His response baffled me. I had never been kicked out of anywhere in Chile before. The man lifted his eyebrows again and made a "follow me" motion with his head as he turned his horse away.

Was I supposed to pack up my things and travel however far it was to this man's house for the night? Packing alone would take me an hour. I was exhausted. Besides, I couldn't imagine convincing Nimbus that packing and moving now was a good idea. Plus, when I got to his house, there would surely be sheep. It wouldn't be appropriate for me to put my tent up in his yard and fall asleep. Hours of drinking *maté* and attempting to explain myself would be involved before I would be set up in a spare bed or on the couch. Here in camp I was half an hour from rest.

More than just language stood in the way of understanding. This man had been brought up in a time and place where women did not do things like this. For better or worse, I had been raised to think I could do anything I darn well pleased.

Social etiquette said I should accept his hospitality, but I couldn't muster the energy. I shrugged as if again I didn't understand, and he rode off. I was exhibiting a bold-faced lack of manners, and I knew it.

I lay awake, wondering for the third time in a week whether this whole trip was, indeed, an exceptionally bad idea. Too disturbed to sleep, I pulled out my hardcover copy of *The South American Sketches of R.B. Cunningham Graham* and began reading. Accidentally, I turned to the story, "The Captive" published in 1910. Graham was retelling a story about a woman taken prisoner while traveling alone on horseback.

> "As I was saying, she might have gotten away—said my friend—only the mare of her *tropilla* had recently foaled, and either she was hard to drive or the maternal instinct in the woman was too strong . . ."

Was it possible that the Patagonia in Graham's book was the country the gentleman I had just met had grown up in? These people, old men who had lived in this country all their lives, were exactly who I wanted to meet. Yet, here I was at last in Patagonia, without enough Spanish to be polite and too exhausted and cranky to care.

Before I could fall asleep, another man approached on a horse, this time, a stylishly dressed younger man on a leggy *colorado*. Not wanting a repeat of the evening's events, my first reaction was to slink into my sleeping bag, to hide like a fugitive, my only crime being that I was a woman traveling alone. But it was obvious I was camped here. I decided on the friendly approach.

"*Buenas noches*," I sang out, hopefully giving him the option of stopping to talk or saying, "*Buenas noches*," and traveling on. He stopped to talk, but stayed astride his pretty cinnamon colored gelding.

"*¿De donde viene*?" I asked where he had come from.

"*La Horqueta*," he answered.

At last, proof that this trail went where I wanted to go.

"It's a good trail. I will be coming through tomorrow with my groceries; we can travel together," he told me, as if what I was doing was the most natural thing in the world.

The next morning, I sat drinking coffee in the sun, waiting for the man from La Horqueta. By what felt like noon, he had not shown up. Could time actually move at a different rate in Patagonia, or was two cups of coffee and my *gringa* impatience getting the best of me?

When the sun was well overhead, I saddled Nimbus, and we headed off on our own. An obvious trail cut through straight lines of pine trees.

As a solution to the rampant erosion caused by fires in the mid-twentieth century, the Chilean government had given subsidies to farmers to plant forests of fast-growing, non-native lodgepole pines. The result was this extended expanse of trees all the same age, standing at attention in neat, orderly rows.

In this land of impressive hardwoods, no one has much use for these fast-growing, soft-wooded trees. The problems caused by the monoculture of pine plantations are now being realized, but things change slowly in Chile. As I rode through that sterile, artificial forest, some pine plantations in Patagonia were being removed, while new ones were still being subsidized.

Not far into the pine plantations, the man from La Horqueta rode up behind me. An attractive *Patagon* with long, thin legs, tall riding boots, and a colorful scarf around his neck, he was dressed for town. His horse, too, looked festive with its bright green hand-woven saddlebags filled with groceries. He had expected me to wait for him. I felt like the impatient *gringa* I was. One with his horse, I got an education watching him ride. At our first gate, he reached forward, opened the gate from astride his horse, and ushered me through. I watched as he nudged his mount alongside the gate, swung it closed, and slipped the wire-loop back over the fence post. This was a trick I needed to learn.

The trail, wide and unobstructed, dropped steeply to the river. The Rio Blanco had just enough glacial water in it to give it a soft, milky blue color. I leaned back in the saddle as Nimbus picked her way down. This was the steepest hill we had encountered so far. The man from La Horqueta waited for us at the bottom.

His horse traveled the flat, verdant pastureland in the valley bottom with the smooth, fast, Chilean horse walk that would take me years to master. Nimbus and I had to break into a bouncy trot every so often to keep up. When we did, my butt flew up off the saddle and came down hard. At our first stream crossing, Nimbus plunged in like she had done it all her life. Maybe she wasn't such a city girl after all. I wished she could tell me her story.

By late afternoon, the volcanic pinnacles of Pico Blanco, which had been white with the previous night's snow, shone black along the skyline. I had been in the saddle for hours. I suggested we stop for *maté*.

In an open, grassy place beside the river, a lone shade tree beckoned. I hopped off and dug into my bags for the things I would need: *yerba*, a gourd, and the *bombilla*. I had enjoyed *maté* in other people's houses, but I was nervous about being the *servador*. Would the water be the right temperature, the *maté* not too bitter, the *bombilla* stay unclogged?

The man from La Horqueta was leading his horse to a good place to graze. For the first time, I realized that this man who moved through this country on horseback with a far greater ease than me walked with a lopsided gait. Like the mythological Greek centaur, a creature both man and horse, a good horse was this man's grace, his speed, his efficiency, his ability to work and live in this country.

I showed him my map. He didn't know what the lines meant, but he understood that I did. It helped explain how I was getting around in a country I did not know.

Instead of starting a fire to make hot water for the *maté,* I pulled out a lightweight backpacking stove and boiled water almost instantly. I had him perplexed.

"Don't you miss your family?" he asked.

I wasn't sure if he meant my mother and father or the husband and kids I don't have.

"S*í, a veces,*" Yes, sometimes, I answered, thinking that would cover both options.

"¿No te aburro?" he asked.

The literal translation, "Do you not bore yourself?" struck deep within me.

The answer to that was much too complicated to explain in Spanish. I hoped I would get bored less and less as I adjusted to the quiet rhythm of life on the trail. I wanted to let the lack of external noise seep in, to let silence quiet the internal noise as well. Perhaps, boring myself was exactly what I was craving.

This man was the *cuidador* of La Horqueta *campo* and caretaker of three hundred cows.

"The owner lives in Balmaceda and doesn't come by often," he told me. "Once every two weeks I travel this route to buy food in El Blanco and visit my mother."

This man, I thought, could teach me a thing or two about solitude.

A few hours later, I decided to camp in a delightful spot beside the river. Again, I had him perplexed. He always rode to La Horqueta in one day, but with a nod and a wave he headed home.

I woke up by the river to the kind of spectacular morning that reminded me that my entire life's experiences, and all my decisions—good and bad—had combined to place me here in Patagonia on this particular springtime day, and that life was perfect just as it was. I traveled without a watch. With no desire to be anywhere else, I drank coffee and stretched. I hung around, reading and writing in the sun until the shadows grew small.

I counted on my fingers, starting with the last far-off date I could remember, the day I had landed in Chile. My birthday had been coming up and today was the day.

Was my lack of internal calendar a Freudian slip? If you don't know it's your birthday, do you still turn forty?

I jumped on Nimbus and galloped barefoot and bareback beside the river, unbrushed blonde hair blowing behind me. I don't think Nimbus understood this pointless running in circles, but she caught the spirit. I gave her a gentle squeeze with my right leg and felt her turn left. That was it, the change of lead that my riding instructor in Alaska had been talking about. I tried it again, doing figure eights in the field, feeling her respond to my touch, matching the rhythm of her switch every time. My seat never left her bare back. It felt like magic and one thousand pounds of personal power.

I set her free, and she made no effort to leave. It is said in Patagonia, "If you have a *caballo* (a gelding) you have the same horse every day. But, if you have a *yegua* (a mare) you have a different horse every day." She liked this place and its fat, green grass just fine. It dawned on me like a revelation: A few days ago on that high mountain pass, she had run away from a place she did not like, and I had taken it hard. "Don't take things so personally." I had heard this all my life from the people closest to me. Now I was learning it from a horse.

As a thirteen-year-old gymnast, I had learned to throw backflips. I hadn't stuck with formal gymnastic training. The tension of competition had put knots in my stomach. Still, I loved the feeling of hurling my body through time and space, landing exactly how and where I expected. All through my twenties and thirties I continued to throw backflips in parks and on beaches. I intended to throw backflips in my forties, as well.

On a flat, grassy bench beside the Rio Blanco, I gathered my breath, snapped my mind into that place of perfect concentration, that place where solo rock climbers and big wave surfers go, that place where nothing is capable of going wrong. I took a powerful running start, did a round-off, and threw a backflip so high and powerful I had to recover with a backward roll. Afterward, my mother's voice broke in:

"You could have landed on your head in the middle of nowhere with no one to pick up the pieces." I hushed her and all other cautionary voices. Today, I needed to feel foolish and young.

Late that afternoon I felt the urge to travel on. With the sun already far past its apex, I loaded Nimbus.

All too soon our lovely trail ended with a steep drop into La Horqueta valley, the first of a series of easterly flowing valleys that drained the expansive glacier-covered peaks to the west. While the lowlands were turning green, the high mountain passes between them were still deeply snow covered. These passes, the man from La Horqueta had assured me, were impassable on horseback, even in the summer.

With nowhere else to turn, Nimbus and I camped alongside the only north-south route available, the Carretera Austral. The highway, still called by some the Carretera Presidenté Pinochet, was pushed through by President Augusto Pinochet's motivation to connect the country and secure Chilean Patagonia from the influence of Argentina. Construction of even this winding dirt road was a major feat, and the project was still incomplete. Some 370 kilometers to the south, the *carretera* ended 100 kilometers short of the village of O'Higgins. About 420 kilometers in the other direction, it ended, once again on the shores of a long, narrow fjord. From there, a combination of roads and ferries circumnavigated the most rugged, densely forested sections of coastline to link up with the rest of Chile's road system.

As I turned southward on the Carretera Austral, the region of Aysén boasted 110 kilometers of paved road. The section of highway I was traveling was undergoing Chile's attempt to up that number. While the peaceful *lenga* forest was just out of reach, dust, noise, and loose plastic were everywhere. Even worse, road construction in Patagonia included hundreds of men with shovels all staring at me.

The wind blew grit into my teeth and eyes. Nimbus got edgier as the day wore on, panicking at every piece of fluttering debris, unfamiliar noise, and sudden movement. I tried to keep her under control, but I was in the same state myself. "If one more person shouts or honks in my general direction I am going to scream!" We were a dismal sight, a worn-out *gringa* in filthy clothing alternately riding and leading an unmanageable mare down a dusty road.

My slow pace over the last several days meant that I was at the end of my rations. My hummingbird metabolism clashed violently with lack of food. With the foundation of Maslow's hierarchy of needs crumbling, it was impossible for me to think of anything else. I pushed for the tiny village of Cerro Castillo, hoping to get there before stores closed for *siesta*.

I didn't make it.

Villa Cerro Castillo was named after the peak that towers above the town. Castle Mountain is a heavily eroded volcano with rugged basalt columns rising an impressive two thousand meters into a clear blue sky. As I marched toward town, the base of Cerro Castillo's spires were hidden by a layer of blowing grit.

When I arrived in the collection of square blocks that is Villa Cerro Castillo, the few stores on the main street had their lights off and doors closed. There was no movement anywhere. Near the edge of town, I saw a woman ahead of me. She walked up to the door of a small shop and rang the bell, something that would never have occurred to me. The owner, a short woman with shoulder-length hair, came to the door and happily opened up for her. I slipped in before the door could close. The store sold mostly cookies and candy, but food was food, and I was hungry.

Somehow the storekeeper, Eva, intuitively gathered the critical information about me. I was alone, on a horse, and famished. Soon, I was sitting behind her woodstove, and she was putting a steaming bowl of broth with a floating sheep vertebra in front of me. My hands, cracked and filthy with the dust of the last few days etched into the creases, looked like those of a sixty-year-old *poblador*. Unconcerned with what my vegetarian friends back home would think, I picked up the bone and began gnawing on it.

A chubby three-year-old boy bounded in and plopped onto Eva's lap. I assumed him to be her son. He was her grandson. How old could this woman be? Her skin was smooth and her laughter light. Certainly not much older than me.

A calendar hung on the pale green wall behind the woodstove.

"*¿Que día es hoy?*" I asked.

"*Diez de Noviembre*," she said.

Tenth of November. Ah, hell. I'd miscalculated. This horrible day on the *carretera* was my real birthday. Deciding not to say or do anything about it, I returned to my soup.

Eva offered to put me and Nimbus up on an extra piece of land she owned. My imagination took me to a green pasture beside a gently flowing brook, while Eva led us to an abandoned lot bordered by houses on three sides. However, after helping Eva fix the fence, it was home and it was heaven. I washed clothes, bought food, and took a bath in a bucket inside my tent.

In the evening, I closed the gate behind me and walked over to visit with Eva. So this was what life without a horse felt like. Funny, already I could barely remember a time when I did not need to look after my horse.

After a few days' rest, I packed up and headed south again. Not ten minutes into my day, a big sign proclaiming *Cueva de Las Manos* caught my eye. The glitzy sign seemed a bit touristy, but archeological sites fascinate me, so I turned left in search of the Cave of Hands. The signs got smaller and older, taking me down one back road and then another until I found a hand-painted scrap of wood that had fallen off a fence and was lying in the road, leaving me with no idea which direction it had originally pointed. I decided to ask at the nearest house.

Andrés Vargas opened the door. Once he understood what I was looking for, he tossed on a coat and motioned for me to follow. We walked down a narrow trail leading to a two-hundred-foot overhanging cliff with a spectacular view of the entire Rio Ibáñez Valley. Painted in black and red were hundreds of outlines of hands. Most of the handprints, some higher up the wall than any normal person could reach, were of adults. But on one low section of overhanging wall, dozens of children's handprints were neatly lined up.

Similar paintings have been found in indigenous sites from the American Southwest to Australia and Europe. This painting with hands struck me as a universal first self-expression. In kindergarten, I, too, had dipped my small hand in paint and put its impression on paper.

Andrés showed me a rectangular-shaped painting with softly rounded edges. "*Moler,*" he said, making a grinding action with his hands. Why would a grinding stone be depicted, but not horses? Then I remembered these paintings were between five thousand and eight thousand years old. The ancient inhabitants of this land had hunted on foot. Horses hadn't come into their culture until the mid-1600s.

Photograph by Fredrik Norrsell.

Handprints at Cueva de Las Manos.

Historians believe that the original horses of Patagonia were all descendants of a few mares and stallions abandoned by the Spanish conquistador Pedro de Mendoza in 1536, when he was expelled from the shores of the La Plata River by the indigenous population of Argentina. By the mid-1600s the horse had transformed Tehuelche culture.

The Tehuelche were so much a part of the country that the word *pampas,* used today to describe the land in arid eastern Argentina, is Tehuelche for flat. Although a few traditions and many of their words live on, there are virtually no Tehuelches left today to tell us the story. By 1896, the influx of Europeans and their diseases had reduced the population to about five hundred individuals. The conquest of 1897 killed off the last remaining Tehuelches.

The screeching of *bandurrias* brought me back to the present. Dozens of prehistoric-looking buff-necked ibis with their long curved beaks were nesting in the cliffs. I had no idea that these birds that pick for fish and bugs along rivers and hang out in flat farmlands were cliff nesters.

A big, square stucco structure dominated the valley below the cliffs. "What's that building?" I asked Andrés.

"It's an old residential school," he told me. "Early settlers sent their children to live there for the school year. It's abandoned now. This area is going to be a park. One day soon that building will be a visitors' center.

MORE THAN TEN years later, I would return to the *Cueva de Las Manos* to find a small ranger station sitting where I had pitched my camp. In a four-wheel-drive van with friends from the States, the distance from town would seem so short, straightforward, and well marked. Domingo Vargas, Andrés's son, would be working as a ranger. After paying a small entry fee, he would take us up to the paintings and show us around. Later over *maté,* I would ask about the old school. "One day soon it will be a visitors' center," Domingo would reply.

AFTER A NIGHT camped above the old residential school that would not become a visitors' center any time soon, Nimbus and I headed south through the most open country we had traveled so far. Sedge grasses clumped together to hold onto scant soil and moisture mixed with circular mats of florescent-red *herba negro* brush in bloom. Forced by the terrain farther east than I had anticipated, I traveled off the edge of my map.

This wasn't the first time I had journeyed without a map in Patagonia. In my NOLS-instructor days, we had often traveled into the areas marked S.V.E. (*Sin Visibilidad Esterioscopico)*. Rumor has it that southern Chile was flown over to be mapped on one particular day. Everything under clouds that day was marked S.V.E., leaving huge blank spots on the map. No one cared. The cloud-covered regions were high in the mountains. Nobody went there anyway.

As Aldo Leopold once wrote, "Of what avail are forty freedoms without a blank spot on the map?" I moved by asking myself, if I lived in this country how would I get my animals around? The path of least resistance usually led to a trail. I didn't know exactly where I was, but I knew vaguely where I was going, which is better than I often do in my life.

Nightfall found me camped on the edge of a tremendous cliff. In one day of moving generally westward, I had traveled from desert-like *pampas* to thick, verdant rain forest. From the sunless depths of the forest floor, I could hear the elusive *huet-huet*—a larger version of the *chucao tapaculo*, and another one of Darwin's discoveries—calling out its eerie name.

The next day, after a long, hard, circuitous day in the saddle, I camped a vertical quarter-mile away at the bottom of the same cliff. I was beginning to suspect that progress, like time, was defined differently in Patagonia.

Somewhere ahead of me the Rio Sin Nombré drained a tremendous amount of country. I would need a bridge to cross that river. The next day, I asked the few people I saw about the existence of a *puente*. Their contrasting answers confused me. I have bad Spanish days the way other people have bad hair days, but I was exasperated. What was so hard about my question? Was there, yes, a bridge, or no, not a bridge?

It wasn't until I arrived at the river and found a red and white swinging cable bridge wide enough for two horses to pass that I knew I would not have to double back several days' worth of riding. Years would pass before I'd understand why I had not comprehended the peoples' answers. A *puente* is a bridge built for automobiles, while a *pasarela* is the swinging cable variety used primarily by livestock. Two of the people I had asked had answered my question literally, no there was not a *puente*, while the third had understood my meaning and answered, yes, there was a way to cross the river with my horse.

As I traveled west, the vegetation should have been getting healthier and greener, instead it was getting thinner and poorer. Something wasn't right. Gray dust blew from between spindly clumps of grass. Then I remembered . . . the volcano. When Volcan Hudson, only forty kilometers north of us, had exploded on August 8, 1991, the wind had been blowing south. A three hundred square kilometer area had been covered with volcanic ash and pumice up to a meter deep.

By afternoon we were traveling through buried farms. Fence lines that once stood four feet tall were now stubby rows of sticks a few inches above the ash. The few animals around simply stepped over them, a tiny inconvenience in their search for food. *Campos* had been abandoned or sold, no doubt cheap. The place looked like a previously inhabited moonscape.

Nimbus and I stopped for long periods whenever we found good grass. Nimbus was showing no signs of becoming skinny. In fact, people usually complimented me on the fact that my horse was "*bien gorda,*" but like me, she was a witch when she was hungry.

Again, we were traveling slower than I had expected. Figuring we were still several days from the next town, I also made use of whatever food the land had to offer. *Dihueñe*, small, round mushrooms that grow on *lenga* trees, fried with butter and onion made a delicious addition to the last of the spaghetti sauce. *Nalca*, a prehistoric-looking plant with a single huge, spiny leaf supported by a meaty stalk the size of a man's arm, when stripped of its spines and dipped in sugar, made a tasty desert. I wasn't the first to use *nalca* in hard times. Indigenous people, as well as early homesteaders, knew *nalca* as an appetite suppressant.

Nimbus and I stopped at an abandoned house for a long break. Wild roses grew out of the broken windows of a large, gray, wooden structure. The grass around the old house was already coming back thick and green. A wooden swing hung from an old apple tree. The tree was still producing, but the apples were small, few, and too bitter to eat. What had the people who lived here been like? Where had this family gone?

The garden was overgrown with weeds. The house would have to be gutted. Too many years of allowing whatever grew outdoors to grow inside had passed. Resting in a sweet smelling field of blue and purple lupines, deep into my fantasy about living in that old, wooden house, I let myself drift into an afternoon nap. The long-abandoned garden produced lettuce and cilantro in abundance, and laughing children climbed the apple tree.

That evening, I settled Nimbus into the best spot of grass I could find, a patch only about twenty square feet and a bit thin. It would have to do. The previous night, I had slept to the soft swoosh of the Rio Ibáñez flowing around the silvered trees left standing when the river changed its course during the eruption. The night before, I had enjoyed the almost imperceptible lapping of waves on the shore of Lago Alto. That night the babbling of a small brook lured me into dreams.

The faintest hint of light was in the sky when I awoke to move Nimbus to better grass. I had overslept. Stumbling outside, I forced my eyes to focus. An empty halter lay on the ground. I shook myself to awaken from my nightmare. The halter still lay there . . . empty.

I peered behind the nearby bushes, but in my heart I knew Nimbus had been gone for hours. We hadn't closed a gate behind us for days. Hoof prints wandered around a bit as if searching for grass, and then headed decisively north. I took off after her. Fortunately, it is not hard to track an animal in pumice.

My mind started its all-too-familiar whirlwind which usually ends in, "my life is a disaster." Why would anyone who had a good job with good pay, a comfortable home, and three meals a day choose to be hungry, stinky, and dragging a reluctant mare across Chile? Walking a lonely road at five-thirty in the morning, carrying an empty halter is this the highest form of accomplishment I can produce in my life? I should send myself home to write a thousand times on the blackboard: "I will not do crazy things."

A few hours into my search I realized this could be an all-day affair. In my panic I had brought no food, no water, no extra clothing. I kept walking.

Chapter 3

Perseverancia (Perseverance)

AHEAD OF ME a van was stopped in the middle of the road. Visions of Nimbus hit by a car flashed through my mind. The family in the van had not hit a *yegua tobiano*. They were picking *nalca* to sell in town. They had not seen a black and white horse. Later, I saw a man moving a handful of cows. He had not seen a *yegua tobiano*.

"But, she has been here, and not long ago," he said, bending down to examine her tracks in the pumice. "She will be down there." He pointed to the valley bottom, a place that seemed to me like an eternity away. "That is where my animals always go when they run away."

The man and I walked together down the pumice-covered road, kicking up small puffs of ash with every step until he turned his cows out into a pasture full of half-eaten bushes.

"Stop and take a rest at the house on your way back. My wife will be there if I am not," he said, pointing by pursing his lips back up the road behind us.

The small, yellow house a few kilometers behind me had to be his. It was the only occupied house I had seen in days. I had never knocked on anyone's door and informed the woman of the house that her husband had invited me for tea. If I was going to invite myself in, I had better know his name.

"¿Como té llamas?" I asked.

"Me llamo Feliz," he said.

How curious, this man who lived on a *campo* full of ash was called Happy. There were so many things I wanted to know. What had it been like when the volcano exploded? What was it like to live on this *campo* smothered in ash when all of his neighbors had abandoned theirs? I suspected this man called Happy had a kind of perseverance I could barely imagine. From where did he get it?

Promising to stop by later, I kept walking. I noticed a herd of horses in the distance. There wasn't a *yegua tobiano* in the bunch.

Far away I saw a light colored horse. Sure it was Nimbus, I saw dark markings that were not there. Behind every bush, I saw a *tobiano* mare. I was always wrong.

In my mind's eye, I saw myself haunting this road for weeks, asking every neighbor within a hundred kilometers if they had seen a *yegua tobiano*, becoming known as the stupid *gringa* who lost her horse. By late afternoon, I hadn't eaten for twenty-four hours. I had no horse and no plan.

I had no food and no water, and I was already a long way from camp. The terrifying question, what if I don't find her, kept creeping forward in my mind. How far could I go in this direction and still make it back to camp? Would I actually turn around without my horse?

Deep inside, I knew the answer and it scared me. During desperate times on long mountaineering trips, I had tapped an immense well of physical energy. I would walk all night. I had done it before.

Near the abandoned house where Nimbus and I had stopped the day before, the rear end of yet another black and white horse stuck out from behind a bush.

This time, it was her!

I crawled onto her back, buried my face in her mane, and wrapped my arms around her neck in a huge hug. Nimbus, my sweet, sweet, Nimbus. Her body relaxed underneath me. She, too, was happy to be found. Instantly I forgave her for leaving me. Who could blame her for wanting to eat sweet green grass?

Instantaneously, all misgivings about who I was and what I was doing with my life vanished. The world was immediately beautiful and my journey, once again, a grand adventure.

But now what? It was late, I was miles from home, and I had no saddle. I gave her a little squeeze with my knees. She started walking. I reached around her neck and tied the lead rope to both sides of her halter, and we were off. Back on the road, Nimbus, still casting her vote for going home, turned resolutely north. I pulled her head southward with equal determination. She turned south, but walked like she was dead. At this rate we wouldn't get home before midnight. I turned her north and she trotted. I urged her a little; she galloped. When her energy was high, I turned her south again, but this time I kept her at a trot. It worked.

Without the saddle my body ached for the kind of riding I had seen the *gauchos* doing. They never trotted with the English-style posting—one and two and up and down—that I did. The locals sat perfectly level, their upper bodies still, while their hips and legs swung back and forth to the rhythm of the trot. It was a mystery to me, but more than anything, I wanted to ride like that, and today I was riding home, saddle or no saddle.

A whole day without food and water had made me bold, and my encounter with Feliz had piqued my curiosity. At the front gate of a yellow clapboard house with purple lilac bushes miraculously blooming beside the front door, I tied Nimbus to the fence post with her head up. I couldn't let even my Nimbus eat the precious little grass that grew in their yard.

A big woman answered the door with a welcoming smile. She wore red basketball shoes laced up her ample ankles and a green sweater that did not match her flowered skirt.

"*Pasé,*" Susana said, and without asking why I was there, she settled me into the most comfortable spot directly behind the woodstove.

I wanted to ask about the volcano. What was it like the night fire shot into the air? And how did it feel to have all your neighbors move away, to leave you here with your husband on this barren ground with cows that eat bushes? But one does not come in the door asking questions. First, there is *maté* to drink.

Susana put fresh *sopaipillas* and homemade cherry jam in front of me. The cherries, she informed me, came from the tree that, despite the volcano, still bloomed outside the window.

"Did you know the volcano was coming?" I asked at last.

"We did because we live close. We saw the ash plume and the fire shooting into the sky at night. Then the ash really started to fall. It didn't stop for a week. Days passed when you couldn't see the sun. It accumulated over three feet thick. People's roofs caved in. We went to live with my sister for three days, but then we came back," Susana told me. "We used to have sheep. They all died from the ash. Now we have cows. Cows can eat bushes."

A picture of three young boys hung on the wall.

"One is in Cerro Castillo," she told me, "and one is working on a remote *campo* up valley. The youngest one is herding goats in California."

"Do you hear from him often?" I asked.

"Oh, yes, he called us just last year," she said. "He will be coming home soon, only another year and a half."

Again, I suspected that time somehow moved differently in Patagonia.

It was common for young men to leave their parents' *campos* to work in the States for a few years. If they were lucky and frugal, they could earn enough money to return and start their own farms. Some of these young men ended up working on good ranches, where they were well paid and respected. Others did not. Sometimes these men were looked upon and treated as illegal aliens, but they were working legally and most couldn't wait to get home. Their opinion of the outside world, or at least the United States, was formed by these experiences. I hoped Susana's son was on a good ranch.

Feliz had been born on this *campo*, as was his father before him. Susana had lived here since her wedding day. No mere volcano was driving them off their land.

"Doesn't it get lonely without neighbors?" I asked.

"Oh, yes, but the grass will come back, then the neighbors will as well, at least those who have not sold out," Susana said.

"When will that happen?" I asked.

"Oh, things get better all the time. Ten years will help, and in thirty, forty years this place will have grass this high," she said, pointing to halfway between her red sneakers and the hem of her flowered skirt. Susana was not a young woman.

I looked again at the photo of the boys on the wall. Would they also come back with the grass? It was obvious that the future of this land and the rebound of abundant life on this *campo* was not for her generation, but the next.

I didn't want to leave Susana's comfortable home, but I needed to get to camp by dark. I excused myself, sure that someday I would make it back for a visit, bringing with me a big loaf of sweet bread to share.

We kept up a good trot. Nimbus also realized the serious need to get home soon. Of course, camp had even less of the same sparse grass that Nimbus had abandoned the night before. At the end of a long day of walking and trotting without a saddle, there was no part of my body that didn't hurt. Selfishly, I wanted to crawl into my sleeping bag and call it a night, but it was obvious what I needed to do. I packed camp, loaded Nimbus, and went another seven kilometers. Well after dark I set up camp in a wet, bumpy, buggy, miserable spot beside a swamp, but it had that one important commodity of camping with horses: Grass.

At the next town, Bahia Murta, the silhouette of an old church broke the skyline. The weathered wooden shingles on the steeple matched the gray of the clouds. Surrounded by a cute picket fence and fields of blooming lupines, the old church called to us to take a break. The gate was open and inviting.

Photograph by Fredrik Norrsell.

The old church at Bahia Murta.

On a beautiful summer evening in 1977, a tremendous landslide upstream on the Rio Engaño had sent a torrent of water, mud, and broken tree trunks raging through the town of Bahia Murta. The flood destroyed several houses and picked others up in their entirety and deposited them downstream. Somehow, some say miraculously, it missed this church. Rumor also has it that the church bell rang by itself in the night to warn the villagers. As I looked around at the three or four remaining houses, it was hard to believe that the village had once been a town of a thousand people.

On the outskirts of the old village, I camped on a beach where finely ground volcanic ash produced the softest sand I had ever felt between my toes. The turquoise-blue waters of Lago General Carrera, the second largest lake in South America, stretched into the distance. The scene could have been the Caribbean. That evening as I walked the beach, the sunlight slid under a layer of clouds at the mouth of the river, turning the Rio Engaño to liquid silver. My sleeping bag laid out on the shore, I slipped into a soft sleep, soothed by the gentle lapping of waves. Little did I know that I was destined to return to the church at Bahia Murta, and I would not be alone.

The next day, I crossed the Rio Tranquilo on a steel and concrete bridge. Six years earlier, I had stood on the banks of the Rio Tranquilo, with an overloaded backpack and a dozen NOLS students, watching a man on horseback cross the river. That moment had changed the course of my future. Today, a new gravel road wound westward to within twenty miles of the Pacific coast. A short drive—if, of course, you had a car—could get you to within a few hundred meters of the same glacier our NOLS group had taken a month to reach.

The people of the town of Rio Tranquilo and the *campos* to the west had been anxiously awaiting this road for decades. In 1993 I had stumbled upon faded markers in the woods flagging the intended route of what some claimed would one day soon be a road.

I had always dreamed of returning to this valley on horseback, but the freshly laid gravel of the new road would be horrible for my horse's feet. Furthermore, I had no desire to walk a gravel road through what once had been wilderness, leaving me to return by the same route, eating the dust of whizzing automobiles.

I needed to buy food. Not wanting to make a spectacle of myself, I unloaded Nimbus on the outskirts of the town of Rio Tranquilo and walked in. The food selection in the only small shop I could find open was slim, as usual. Once again, my diet would consist of pasta, tomato paste, cookies, and white bread.

When I returned, an old man in a tattered blue sweater and a pair of worn-out mud boots was walking slow, contemplative circles around my disheveled pile of gear.

"Buenas tardes," I said, announcing myself and claiming that odd-looking pile of junk, in what turned out to be his yard, as mine.

Antonio greeted me with a huge smile. The mystery was explained. It was a *gringa.*

"Is it okay if my things are here?" I asked.

"Si, pero adentro," he said as he started to pick up my gear and carry it inside his fence.

It was obvious I would be staying awhile. Antonio insisted on carrying the saddle, even though he was much older and smaller than I am. He led me to a two-room shack. People in rural Patagonia don't usually have the kind of excess we are accustomed to in the United States, but this man struck me as poor.

In Alaska, I had lived for seven years in a twelve-by-twelve-foot cabin most people would call a shack, but the difference between Antonio's home and mine was striking. Every niche of my small cabin was crammed full: climbing gear, skis, more clothes than a person should own, sleeping bags, tents, pots and pans, artwork, and piles and piles of books. Antonio's possessions included a sink for the water he let run constantly, a bench by the woodstove for us both to sit on, a pot, a bowl, a spoon, and a knife. In the other room I could see a wooden bed neatly made up with heavy woolen blankets. No books, no television, no radio; for entertainment he looked out the window.

Antonio was fifty-nine, although he struck me as older. He was still fit, but decades of hard work making a living cutting trees were etched into his face and hands. Here was a man who could tell you about wood.

Ciprés, which grows in the wetter regions in the far west, is good for fence posts. It doesn't rot, but it can take more than a year to dry. *Coihue,* the evergreen version of *lenga,* grows just to the west and is used for hardwood floors, tables, and axe handles. Antonio stoked the small firebox of his stove with *lenga.*

"*Lenga* is good firewood. It burns a long time," he told me.

I had long desired a Chilean-style, wood cookstove for my cabin in Alaska, but if I were burning spruce in a firebox that small I would need to stoke it almost constantly.

"What do you think about the new road?" I asked.

"It's wonderful," he said. "You can drive nearly to the coast. Best of all, everyone is working!"

I couldn't help noticing that he didn't have a car to drive to the coast, nor was he working, but I kept my mouth closed. Like many of his neighbors, Antonio had never been anywhere overrun with cars and roads. The few people I had met who had been to Santiago or even the U.S. had a different opinion.

"It's terrible, too many roads, too much noise," they all agreed, but the idea of that kind of development ever happening in Patagonia remained unfathomable.

In the 1970s, the construction of the trans-Alaska pipeline cut a road through 270,000 square miles of northern Alaska, effectively cutting nearly in half the biggest chunk of unmolested wilderness left in the United States.

The road into the Rio Tranquilo Valley was cutting the wilderness I loved into smaller and smaller chunks, but I kept my viewpoint to myself. While my strong feelings about wilderness were deeply ingrained, I also held firmly to my conviction that as a visitor here, it was not my place to decide.

In locations where news travels mostly by word of mouth, inaccurate information can become rampant. I had heard that a Canadian mining company was looking for a place to put an aluminum processing plant, and Patagonia, with its huge, free-flowing rivers, was a prime candidate to placate the world's hunger for cheap electricity.

"Have you heard anything about anyone wanting to put an aluminum processing plant in this valley?" I asked Antonio.

"No, but that would be good, too," he said, making a split-second decision.

I didn't agree, but I had no idea if the stories I had heard were even true. I also didn't believe environmental issues eight thousand miles from home would have anything to do with my life.

Almost 1,500 kilometers north of Rio Tranquilo a company called Endesa was busy damming Chile's second largest river, the

Bio-Bío. I had heard about the controversy behind damming this world class whitewater river, but—like everyone else—I had plenty of things on my worry list. My priorities were: Grass for my horse, a place to sleep, keeping myself dry when it rained. Still, I felt a sense of urgency about this trip. How many other horse trails would be replaced by roads a year from now? One locked gate, one "no trespassing" sign, and my journey would be over. Patagonia was changing. I had no idea how fast.

I hadn't traveled an hour out of Rio Tranquilo when I saw a sign announcing, "La Hacienda." That's odd, I thought, most people don't have a sign on their house.

"Pasé, descansa un poco." A young guy on horseback invited me in for a rest. Thinking he was the boy of the family, I was surprised when he introduced me to his wife, Llorena, and their three-year-old daughter, Valentina. Llorena wore clean, fashionable jeans, a brilliant green T-shirt, and a bright, inviting smile. Beside her I felt old, travel worn, drab, and dirty. Valentina, a cute little girl with straight dark hair and huge brown eyes, peaked at me from behind her mother's jeans.

Their house was small but also exceptionally bright, cheery, and clean.

"I love it here," Llorena told me. *"Todo esta tranquilo aquí."*

I understood, the quiet country life grabbed me as well. I noticed a small washing machine in the corner.

"It is amazing," I said. "You have electricity and running water way out here."

"Oh, this isn't even the *hacienda*," she said.

Fabio and Llorena were the *cuidadors* of someone else's fancy estate. The *hacienda*, a huge house made of stone and glass, sat conspicuously on the shore, a motorboat tied to the dock. Excessively extravagant, it dominated the landscape. Fortunately for me, the kind of opulence many people envy never appealed to me. I wouldn't trade my simple cabin in the woods in Alaska for anyone's mansion.

"The *dueño* lives in Santiago and comes down maybe once or twice a year," she said. "We get to live here by this gorgeous lake all the time. The best thing is that each day we get to do everything with our daughter. The *dueño* has his priorities all wrong. Our life is the best possible life."

I doubted much of the world would see it my way, but I agreed with Llorena.

The next day I marched up a side valley into the mountains. Once again, I would not be traveling south, but I was beginning to care less and less about some arbitrary definition of progress. I needed to get away from the dust and noise of the *carretera.*

Deep in the Leones Valley, dozens of perfect campsites beckoned. Each one had plenty of grass, easy access to the river, and views of glaciers spilling into the valley. I chose one and settled in.

Nimbus wandered away during dinner. I no longer panicked about such things. There was a gate not far behind us. When I went to retrieve her, Elvira was out in her garden. We talked over the fence like neighbors. She and her friend, Sophia, were running the *campo* while her father was in the hospital in Coyhaique. To my surprise, neither of these women, who have lived nearby all their lives, had ever been to the head of the valley.

"Want to come with me tomorrow?" I asked, ecstatic about the idea of having companions.

"Oh, no," Elvira said. "We have way too much work to do. Some other day."

The next day, as I trotted up valley, miles of spectacular scenery rolled easily by. I understood that it was the culture of excess I came from that had produced the remarkable combination of time and money that allowed me to travel up this valley for the simple, pure joy of it. On this perfect Patagonia spring day, guilt easily slipped away.

Miles into the valley, well beyond where anyone lived, I came across a sign announcing money available to improve road access to the area. Oh, Elvira will be thrilled, I thought. She can finally go see the lake, if, of course, she can find a car. Meanwhile, I felt deeply content to be in this valley in what I was just beginning to understand was a very special time in Patagonia's history.

The terrain got steeper and the forest denser. At the end of the trail, I tied Nimbus in a grassy spot and took off on foot. I needed to get to that lake the same way, in my previous life, I had needed to get to a summit. Cresting one rocky ridge after another, I realized there could be hundreds of these old moraines. This desire to push on had gotten me into serious trouble before. I didn't want to leave Nimbus tied too long in the woods. This was wild country. A tied horse would be easy prey for a puma.

However, the late November days were long. My heart pushed oxygen through my body as I hurried along, glad that kind of drive was still in me.

Suddenly, Lago Leones and the immense glaciers of the Campo de Hielo Norte, the most northerly ice field in the Southern Hemisphere, burst into view. Mount Haydes, a 3078-meter glaciated giant, rose impressively from the far end of the lake. Fifty kilometers to the west, the San Rafael Glacier flowed down the other side of the same ice sheet, discharging icebergs into the Pacific Ocean.

Eighteen thousand years ago, the Northern and Southern Patagonian Ice Fields were one humongous ice sheet, and the entire verdant valley we had just traveled through was locked beneath a mile of ice. A huge piedmont lake far larger than Lago General Carrera drained east into the Atlantic. The explosive melting of the Baker River basin split the ice fields, and the giant glacial lake at its base turned its flow westward to the Pacific. Today, at only four percent of its original size, these two Patagonia ice fields constitute the third largest fresh-water reserve in the world. Five hundred square kilometers of Patagonia's ice fields have disappeared in my lifetime. Climate change—actually, change of all types—was happening fast in Patagonia.

As I began my descent to the shore, a large brown animal watched me from the woods. What was a horse doing so deep in the dense forest? Then I noticed antlers and big ears like a mule deer. It was a *huemul.* Thick, furry, one-pronged antlers and the distinctive dark V on his face gave him away as a young male.

He froze. I froze. Both of us were unsure whether we had been seen. In more than half a cumulative year in the wildest parts of Patagonia, I had seen exactly one track and one scat of this elusive, endangered animal.

The Tehuelches had seldom entered the depths of the forest to hunt, leaving the *huemul* amazingly docile and innocent. In the early 1920s, the *huemul's* first contact with settlers and guns quickly led to the endangered species list. Subsisting on a fraction of its former domain, the *huemul* was protected in the 1980s.

Knowing that having two eyes close together gave me away as a predator, I tried not to fix my gaze upon him as I wandered in his general direction. A glimpse of his tawny coat in the late-afternoon sun reminded me it was past time for me to turn around, but I simply wanted to be with him. Eventually, he slipped quietly into the brush. I was still unsure if he knew he had been spotted. I rushed back to Nimbus, excited to tell Elvira about the *huemul.* On second thought, maybe I shouldn't tell anyone.

The next morning, rain was coming down in a deluge. My tent rattled in the wind. I had no desire to go anywhere, but my linear North American brain reminded me I had just taken two extra days to go up a valley that did not lead south. Late in the day, I set off into the storm. I hadn't made but a few kilometers in a southerly direction when a small man in a bright yellow raincoat stopped me on the road.

"¿Por qué tu viajas en un día como esté?" he asked.

"Porque, voy a Cochrane," I said, as if simply going to Cochrane was a good enough reason to be traveling on this kind of day.

"?Por qué no te quedas aquí?" he said, nodding in the direction of his house, a waiting woodstove, and another round of *maté.*

"Gracias," I said, explaining that I had a friend waiting for me in Cochrane.

A month earlier I had told my friend, Samuel, my trip to Cochrane would take a month and I would look him up as soon as I arrived. A month had already gone by and I was still a long way from Cochrane. But the truth was, there was not a person on the planet concerned with my whereabouts that day.

At the next bend the brunt of the Patagonia wind hit me hard in the face. Here, smack in the middle of a set of latitudes known as the Roaring Forties, westerly winds roar around the globe unimpeded until they hit their first and only landfall—Patagonia. I had made a mistake. Horizontal rain came in sheets. Wind worked water in through every opening in my rain gear. Soon, I was soaked up to the knees and down to the elbows. At first, small icy trickles, then streams of cold water, ran down between my breasts. Eventually, the storm pushed cold water through my Gortex and into every pore of my body. A familiar pre-shiver tightness welled up between my shoulder blades.

"Porque soy tonta," was what I should have told the man in the yellow rain coat. Because I am foolish, because I am *gringa,* because I think I am so important that the world cares what I do today. So what

if I had traveled only a little more than an hour? So what if I took yesterday off and drank tea all morning? Only a fool would travel in this miserable weather.

I thought of turning around and trying to find his house. Every step forward made it less likely that would happen. An occasional trot helped keep both of us warm, but I wondered how long my body could keep pumping out the needed calories. I needed to eat. In order to eat I needed to cook. In order to cook I needed to find a sheltered spot. The word *porfiado* stepped to the forefront of my mind. *Puro porfiado*, pure stubbornness, had gotten me into this, and now pure stubbornness would have to get me out. Native people all over the world understood how to remove themselves from physical pain and toil by singing and chanting. As windy mile after cold, windy mile dragged on, I made up a rough song in Spanish for Nimbus.

"*Que buena la yegua. Que cruce los río. Que saltan los tuncos.*" What a good mare, who crosses the rivers and jumps the logs. *"Esa yeguita tan bonita,"* I sang to my beautiful little mare. It seemed to work. Nimbus kept moving. Maybe she, too, understood that our other option was freezing.

Late in the day, we found a protected place to camp behind some giant *coihue* trees out of the wind.

The next day we arrived in the small village of Puerto Bertrand where I had a friend who ran a guide company. As I walked through Jonathan's garage, which was filled with neatly organized shelves of outdoor equipment, and into a kitchen wallpapered with maps, I stepped directly back into the culture from which I'd come. Within moments we were sitting at his kitchen table, maps spread out before us, beers in hand. We talked easily in English. River running, mountain climbing, love of the world's wild places, we had a vocabulary in common. How long had it been since I had spoken without first deliberating? How long since I had discussed anything except the cows?

"Right here you can cross the Baker River on a swinging bridge," he said, pointing less than a day's travel farther south. "From there you can ride beside the Colonia River and stay off the *carretera* all the way to Cochrane."

"That's great," I said, "but I would have to cross the Baker again to get to Cochrane."

Thirty miles downstream, the Baker would look like the Mississippi.

"There will be a barge that can take horses right where you need to cross."

Later that afternoon, I made myself useful patching rafts. Tourist season was still a month or two away, so we labored in an easy, unhurried manner. As in every other household in Patagonia, when neighbors stopped by, work ceased and a *maté* session began.

Jonathan's mother was visiting from the States. We ate good food and chatted easily in English. Inside the house was like living with an American family. Outside, a quaint Patagonian village and a tranquil lake with a backdrop of snow-covered mountains were only footsteps away.

Only a block from Jonathan's doorstep, I sat on a giant, rounded granite boulder beside the Baker River. The sun bore down intensely on my shoulders. Upstream the turquoise waters of Lago General Carrera flowed quietly into Lago Bertrand. From where I sat sunning myself—my near hypothermic episode already a faint memory—the Rio Baker poured out of Lago Bertrand and flowed deep, blue, and strong all the way to the Pacific Ocean. I daydreamed of casting off in a small boat and following the river's powerful flow to the sea. It would be a decade before I would feel the power of the Baker beneath my hull.

Puerto Bertrand boasted three hundred residents on a good day. I considered making it three hundred and one. I could ask if Jonathan would hire me for the summer. But I could feel it, my pull, like that of the Baker, was still flowing powerfully southward.

On the next sunny day we flung the garage door open, letting musty camping gear absorb the fresh air of the coming season. I mounted Nimbus, waved goodbye to my friends, and headed southward.

Off the *carretera* at last, I crossed the Baker downstream of town on a swinging bridge over an immense canyon. Traveling through high mountain valleys of uncut *lenga* forest, I broke out in song again, this time for joy, for sunshine, for the forest, and the hundreds of tiny yellow birds that gathered all around me. Old trim lines on the landscape marked the remnants of ice ages that had retreated up valley long ago. Occasionally, views of long, snaking glaciers appeared through small openings in the woods, and I understood vividly, if only for a moment, that our little slice of time is nothing of significance.

Photograph by Fredrik Norrsell.

Crossing the Rio Baker on a swinging bridge.

In well over a month on the trail I had grown into a delightful sense of living in the moment, of being precisely where I was. These days, that peaceful state of mind would periodically vanish, as thoughts of the outside world crept into my consciousness. Part of me wanted to stay forever in every valley I passed through, at the same time, I was anxious to get to Cochrane. Logically, it didn't matter. I had no solid plans beyond arriving in Cochrane and giving Nimbus and, yes, myself a good long rest.

Mornings and evenings I turned Nimbus free. She usually just hung around. During the day, I took her off the lead rope and walked ahead of her. I had taken to walking whenever the terrain was steep or when I was loaded down with a new supply of groceries to save Nimbus's knees. In reality, I walked most of the time. With nowhere else to go and nothing better to do, Nimbus tagged along like a puppy. I finally felt the kind of connection with my horse that I wished we'd had from the beginning. But I knew in my heart I wasn't doing her any favors by taking her on this trip. Her knees were bad and they weren't getting any better because of me.

Descending one last time into the Baker River basin, the trail branched and twisted and threatened to disappear. A man on horseback approached us from behind. Nimbus stopped. Whenever we saw people that meant break time.

A thin, older man sat astride a well-worn saddle on a leggy young *alazán*. He had a *puesto* not too far away. It was unspoken that we were invited to follow him to his simple shelter. He rode ahead, opening each gate for us, but Nimbus and I had been practicing. After we walked through, I nudged Nimbus slowly in beside the gate. Nimbus helped push it closed with her shoulder, and with a long reach, I slipped the wire over the post. Still a bit slow and awkward, we were getting it.

"Are you from this part of the country?" I asked him.

"*No, soy de Chiloé,*" he told me.

Patagonia was primarily colonized by three groups: *huasos* from northern Chile, *gauchos* from Argentina, and *chilotes* from Chiloé. The island of Chiloé, often considered the northern border of Patagonia, has its own culture, rich in mythology and folklore. I recognized the indigenous heritage of the islanders in his strong cheekbones and wide, easy smile.

"How long have you lived around here?" I asked.

"Twenty-five years," he said.

I understood all too well. Even longtime Patagonians were still identified by the region they had come from. That is exactly how it would always be for me, as well. Culture runs deep. If I lived here the rest of my life, I would still be an outsider.

José put the *maté* water on, then proceeded to count for me each of his many blessings: two turkeys with eight baby turkeys, eleven chickens, two cows with young calves so plenty of fresh milk, a good sheep dog with two fat puppies, and, of course, the main necessity of life, a good, strong horse.

José pulled out a piece of mutton from a cool back room and cut into a fresh onion from town. I unpacked the last of my noodles to add to the soup.

Shortly thereafter, a younger man arrived, dismounted, and tied his horse beside Nimbus. He showed no sign of surprise at finding a *gringa* washing dishes in the front yard. The visitor lived up valley, near the end of the Colonia River. This was obviously his normal lunch stop. He was coming from visiting his wife and kids in town. I was four hours from Cochrane.

Distance is time in Patagonia. No one could comprehend when I asked how many kilometers away something was, but hours by horseback was easily understood. I would undoubtedly double his time, but still, I was close!

As I went to leave, I noticed a small spot of blood on Nimbus's right front fetlock. The heads of the shoeing nails on her right rear foot were sticking out just enough that when she walked she nicked her front foot. Her rear shoe was worn thin along the leading edge and quite loose. On inspection, all of her shoes were ground thin. I needed to make them last one more day.

Instead of asking one of the men for help, I grabbed a hammer and a flat board, propped Nimbus's foot up on the board, laid my heavy file on top of the nail, and re-bent the nails to tighten her shoe. I had seen this done dozens of times, but I was totally pretending that this was something I knew how to do. José didn't jump in to help. Either he was less than enthusiastic about approaching the hind feet of a horse he didn't know or my make-believe show of competence was working. I was learning. The confidence and independence I had in my life in Alaska was coming to me here.

The next morning, rain was falling hard. No longer the *gringa* who goes out in the worst of storms because she thinks there is somewhere better to be than here, or that there will ever be a better time than now, I sat snug in my tent, confident that Nimbus and I would not get hurt, lost, or die, and that someday soon I would arrive in Cochrane nothing worse than tired and dirty. The scared girl who had walked out of Sergio and Veronica's gate felt like a stranger. Something deep inside told me to treasure these moments, that this, indeed, is the best life has to offer.

When the rain eased, I saddled up feeling the same excitement to see what was around the bend that I did every morning. But today it was mixed with an uneasy feeling I recognized as approaching change.

Sometimes people refer to their transition after a wilderness trip as returning to "the real world." That phrase confuses me. What part of life is more real than waking with the sun, working your way through an intricate landscape, eating when you are hungry, finding shelter when it rains? Being responsible for your own needs and making the decisions that will keep you and your animals alive seemed at this point far more real to me than endlessly sending messages off into cyberspace. All day I was moody and confused. I had been making this radical transition between wilderness and life in town frequently for decades. Why then was I feeling disturbed? Wasn't arriving in Cochrane supposed to be the consummation of a huge goal?

Town would mean complications in a life that had become exceedingly simple. The problems of the outside world would have, for the first time in more than a month, the opportunity to find me. Most of all, I knew that I would have some big decisions to make about Nimbus.

Again, I arrived on the banks of the Baker River. No bridge spanned this huge and powerful river, but just as Jonathan had promised, a simple ferry system was set up at the crossing. The ability to cross the Baker at this point had been key to opening the incredibly rich Colonia Valley to ranching. Long before the arrival of the automobile in Patagonia, ferries and bridges on major horse trails were considered part of the country's transportation system.

Suddenly, from apparently nowhere, other people on horseback appeared. The ferry operator spotted us, and the *balsa*, a flat-bottom barge slung between taut cables, slowly drifted across the river in our direction. The barge bumped softly onto our shore, lowered a wooden loading ramp, and three horses and riders stepped aboard. A slight change of angle was set by adjusting the length of sturdy chains, and the power of the river alone drove us quietly and efficiently toward the other side.

As I drifted across the Baker River that day on a simple wooden ferry powered by the flow of the current, the fact that the fate of this river would someday determine the future of Patagonia, and to a large degree my own life's path, was the furthest thing from my mind.

Chapter 4

Vagabunda (Wandering)

MY FIRST DAY in Cochrane my friend Samuel helped me rent a pasture for Nimbus. It was the first time my horse and I had been out of each other's company in a long time. By early evening I was missing her.

"I want to check on her. I will be right back," I told Samuel as I took off down the road.

I saw her immediately. She was covered in mud from being wet and rolling in the dirt but that was definitely my horse grazing quietly—on the wrong side of the Cochrane river!

Damn it, this was supposed to be my rest day too. I grabbed a halter and walked toward the river. One step in and the icy water pushed at my thighs. I backed out.

There was a bridge a mile or so up stream. I could cut overland to there. Next door, a young girl was working near a small shed. I hollered over the fence for permission to cross.

"*Si, si no hay problema*," she told me.

I hopped the fence. The second my feet touched the ground, a scraggly, snarling sheep dog appeared out of nowhere and bit me firmly on the calf.

"Ouch!" Pain registered deep in my brain. I bounded back over the fence. Tough blue jeans had kept his teeth from breaking the skin, but I no longer had any desire to walk across other people's parcels to the bridge. I decided to try the river again.

Chest deep in cold water, it became apparent what I needed to do. I put my head down and swam to the other side. Soaking wet and mad at my horse, I tied the lead rope to Nimbus's halter and jumped on her bareback.

"Let's go," I yelled.

She refused to budge.

"Vamós!" I yelled. "Damn it, you just crossed right here!"

Wet, cold, and recently bitten, I lost my sense of humor about the whole thing. My heels came down firmly on her sides.

"*Mueva su poto*!" I shouted at Nimbus to move her ass.

She didn't budge.

Wanting nothing more than to go home, I thought my situation couldn't get much worse when I noticed a man approaching with a gun. Never before had I been met with a gun in Patagonia. Likewise, the tall man with a graying beard, whose long legs were striding toward me, had never seen a soaking wet *gringa* on his land trying to kick a reluctant mare into a river.

We silently sized each other up. In an almost blouse-like shirt with a snappy woolen vest and black top hat, he appeared overdressed for *campo* life, but with the gun pointing downward at his side, he didn't appear inclined to shoot me.

I said nothing.

"I thought I saw a soaking wet blonde woman riding a horse in my field," he said.

I couldn't deny it.

WHEN NIMBUS AND I arrived in town the previous day, the main street had been deserted. The village, arranged in orderly blocks around a central plaza shaded by mature pine trees, appeared to be asleep. What had I been expecting—a marching band? National Geographic had not been informed of my arrival. The fact was no one on earth knew my whereabouts that day, including Samuel, the only person I knew in Cochrane. For the first time in weeks, I felt truly lonely. It is one thing to be alone in the wilderness, another to be by yourself in a strange town.

Fortunately, Cochrane was still a small town where everyone knew everyone. The first person I met pointed me to Sam's place, a small blue house on the edge of town. I tied Nimbus in the street and knocked quietly on the door. Sam answered in a green t-shirt, his long dark hair tied back tightly in a ponytail. The sight of his welcoming grin brought an audible sigh of relief to my lips.

Sitting at Sam's tiny kitchen table, I relaxed into the company of someone I had known for years. While I had made many new friends on the trail, they had not seen me grow and change and succeed and fail and sometimes fail again. Samuel had.

He and I had come to Chile the same year. We had worked together on my first NOLS course, an epic overland traverse of the

Andes. Sam had chosen to make a life here, while I, still unsure of exactly where home was, returned to Alaska year after year.

Like many Chileans, Samuel owned both a remote *campo* and a house in town. He was trying hard to make a go of his small rural tourism business but it wasn't working.

"All the foreigners go to Torres Del Paine National Park, and people from Santiago don't even seem to know the southern end of their country exists, let alone value the cold, wet beauty of this place," he explained.

With no direct road access to the rest of the country, the Aysen region had been forgotten. I understood the blatant incongruity here. Sam and I loved this place exactly because the rush toward a world monoculture, and the extinction of wild places it left in its wake, had overlooked this niche. Yet, if just a few of those people from out there would come here, if they could have a genuine experience, if they could take home only a simple lesson or two, and yes, if they could leave just a small bit of their money behind, life would be easier in Aysen. What neither of us could see from the kitchen window was that Sam was only a few years ahead of his time. Tourism was coming, and fast.

My new home was a corner of Samuel's living room. Nimbus's new home was a grassy parcel fenced on three sides. A deep slow river along the fourth side separated it from the next *campo*.

"Your horse won't swim the river will she?" the owner of the land had asked.

Nimbus had exactly what I had promised her at the end of the trip—rest, fat green grass, and the company of other horses.

"No, why would she do that," I said.

FIVE MINUTES AFTER meeting the man with the gun at the river's edge, I was inside his house, wearing his robe over my wet clothes, sipping *maté* behind the woodstove, and listening to the story of his life.

"I was born near the border of Argentina," Washington told me. "My father was one of the early ranch managers of the Estancia Valle Chacabuco, only thirty kilometers from here."

I was surprised to learn he had grown up in Aysen. His fancy attire had led me to envision a wealthy Santiago neighborhood. He owned almost all the land this side of the river, but apparently made his living selling cheese made from the milk of about twenty cows.

"I spent twenty years living in Sweden," he said, as if living abroad for decades was a normal event in a farmer's life.

"When did you do that?" I asked.

"I left in 1973," he replied.

Of course, the Pinochet Era. His story, a version of which I imagined he shared with many Chileans his age, intrigued me. But before I could ask him more about himself, he switched the conversation to me.

What was I doing in Aysen? Did I live in Chile? And, the inevitable, was I married?

Fortunately, before I could get beyond a simple, "I was not married," and before the incomprehensible, I did not have any children, a woman with long, dark, curly hair walked through the door unannounced. She didn't appear to be his wife, but she moved through the house as if she knew the place well.

"*Hola, me llamo Nancy*," I said, hoping she would return the greeting.

"*Soy Betty*," she said with a warm smile, and with no other questions took over pouring the *maté*.

I soon understood. Betty worked there. She milked the cows and made the cheese. She made me socially comfortable in a way that Washington did not. There was something odd about this man. It was as if he was acting out the life of an aristocrat, but I suspected he had no money. Land rich, money poor is a common theme around here, but there was something else, something in his past I sensed but did not understand. However, his history would have to remain a mystery. Events in Chile between 1973 and 1989 were not conversation for the first cup of *maté*.

With Betty around, I changed the subject to milking cows and making cheese. I didn't want to admit to this competent *campo* woman that I had never milked a cow, let alone made cheese, in my life, but I was curious about the process.

"First, you need to separate the calves from their mothers so they can be milked in the morning," Betty told me, looking at Washington.

"After I move the cows we can cross on the bridge and ride into town together," Washington said.

Washington and I rode into town side by side, him elegantly dressed, with a new black top hat and large silver spurs put on for the occasion, me shabby and still damp, wearing the same clothes I had worn for weeks. After a six kilometer loop across the bridge, through town and out the road, I returned Nimbus to her pasture across the river and trudged back to Sam's place.

Now that I was in Cochrane, I had some tough decisions to make. From here southward lay the trail I had dreamed about for years, the rugged and remote route to Villa O'Higgins. I didn't know it yet, but within a year the last one hundred kilometers of the Carretera Austral would be completed, and there would be a road to O'Higgins for the first time. A strange feeling that if I wanted to ride the old routes in Aysen I needed to hurry was beginning to emerge.

When I tried to extract information about the route south from the locals, I was met by horrified looks and the words, *puro loco* and *imposible.* Even Samuel assured me I couldn't do it.

"That trail is terrible, nearly impossible to follow in places. The route goes over a high mountain pass. There isn't even a path through that part and there will be snow. You will never make it without a local guide."

I was accustomed to ignoring peoples' concerns. Someone had tried to talk me out of a solid fifty percent of the things I had accomplished in my life. But this time I was confused, reluctant to make this kind of decision for another living being. After hearing horror stories of lost trails, snow-covered passes, and big river crossings, I suspected that the 330 kilometers I had just finished was the equivalent of a paved nature tail in Yosemite Valley. The route to O'Higgins would be like climbing my first big wall. I craved the idea of true wilderness, but the thought of traveling through all that territory without a single friendly *poblador* to help me out scared me. Deep inside I couldn't ignore the possibility the locals were right. I couldn't do this.

Running parallel to plenty of self doubt was concern about Nimbus's knees. Even if she could make the trip, it wouldn't be fair to ask her to do another even more arduous journey. In our roughest moments on the trail I had promised her a green pasture, easy work, and the company of other horses once we got to Cochrane. No matter how much I didn't want to look at reality, this would be the end of the trip for Nimbus.

Once again, I found myself stubbornly pushing against the way things were. Trying to force my agenda on Patagonia and the world in general has been a common, if futile, theme in my life. Back in Sam's kitchen, in a desperate effort to make the trip to O'Higgins happen, I broached the subject of hiring a local guide. I didn't want to pay someone to travel with me. All my life I had taken pride in the fact I could look after myself. Nevertheless, I asked.

"Do you know anyone who might be able to go to O'Higgins with me?"

"When?" asked Sam, barely looking up from his soup.

"Soon," I replied.

"In less than two weeks it will be voting day. Voting is mandatory in Chile. Everyone has to be in town on that day."

"Maybe I could go immediately after the vote," I said, disappointed at the long wait.

Sam laughed. "Nancy, everyone from the countryside comes to town at the same time. Voting day will be the biggest party of the year. It will last for a week. No one will be leaving on any expeditions any time soon."

The flow of life in Patagonia was not going to be altered by my personal desires. For the whole last month, even if I was missing a larger direction in life, I had known where I was going—south. Now, I was completely directionless. Christmas was barely a month away. Plus, after Christmas came New Year's and not just New Year's, the whole dang new millennium. I knew people who had been planning exactly where they would be for New Year's Eve 2000 for the past decade. I didn't know where I would be tomorrow.

One evening Samuel and I went to visit Luis and Lucy Soto, a couple I had met years ago in Coyhaique. Their teenage son opened the door and invited us into the kitchen for tea. His hospitality impressed me. At home, my friend's kids, some of whom I have known since they were babies, never even look up from the computer to say hi when I come over. We talked with Mardu, and he played us songs on the guitar while we waited for his parents.

Luis and Lucy returned home to find Samuel and a woman they barely knew in their kitchen. They greeted both of us with a warm welcome and the customary kiss on the cheek. Lucy had short dark hair cut close to her face and enough lines around her eyes from laughing, smiling, and looking into the sun that I guessed she was close to my age. Like many *campo* families, Luis and Lucy maintained two houses. This one, painted with Lucy's artistic flare, had brightly colored triangles ascending to the ceiling in the corner of the living room.

Luis was stocky with short dark hair jutting out from under his black woolen *boina*. Luis's father had settled a rocky, remote piece of land at the base of San Lorenzo, one of the region's highest mountains. At such high altitude it proved a tough place to raise sheep. Occasionally climbers had come by looking for horse support to the mountain and a family guiding business was born.

Most of the Chilean NOLS instructors I knew came from middle class urban families in Santiago. Lucy was the only female Chilean guide I knew who had grown up in the *campos*.

"Why don't you come visit us at our *campo*?" Luis asked.

Something clicked. "That would be wonderful," I said.

"There is a good trail along the side of Lago Cochrane," Luis said, pulling out a map. "It goes by a beautiful lake called Lago Brown and then on up to our house."

"It passes by Señora Verina's house. Do you remember her?" Lucy asked.

"She's from Switzerland," I said.

"She came by NOLS when you and I were working there," Sam added. "You could visit her as well."

A few minutes earlier, I had no plan beyond a cup of tea, now I had a route sketched out before me and friends to visit along the way. All I needed was a horse with good knees, and I had an idea for that.

The next day, I went to visit Washington. When I got there, Betty and her ten-year-old son Omar were milking the cows.

"I have actually never milked a cow," I confessed to Betty.

"Why don't you stick around? Washington will be here shortly," Betty said, setting me up with a three-legged stool and a bucket.

"It's easy," she said.

I sat opposite her and tried to imitate the smooth, strong motion of her hands. It wasn't that easy. Starting at the upper end of the teat, Betty squeezed, index, middle, ring finger, pinky. Milk squirted into the bucket in a steady stream.

I tried—one, two, three, four, nothing.

Here," she said, taking my hand and teaching it a smoother stronger squeeze.

While I produced small dribbles by pulling one teat at a time of the patient beast, Betty took one teat in each hand and alternately squeezed out a full bucket of steaming milk. Omar tried to hide his giggles. Imagine, a grown woman who could not milk a cow.

Another boy, Betty's four-year-old, looked on with shy wonder at the strange blonde lady in the corral.

When Betty finished the last cow, my hands were already tired. I was glad I had not showed up earlier, with my help eleven cows could have taken all day.

We set almost eight gallons of milk in two five-gallon buckets in the creek to cool. It was time for *maté*. As the water heated, I learned that Betty had six children, three boys and three girls.

"Wow, that's a big family," I said, wondering how she could possibly support them milking cows.

"Oh, no not really," she said. "I came from a family of fourteen. My husband and I moved to town fifteen years ago. Cochrane was different then, you passed *saludos* to everyone you saw even if you didn't know them well. Now there are too many people from somewhere else. They have different customs. Sometimes people pass me on the street and don't even say hello. It is rude not to pass *saludos*."

I filed that information away. From now on, I would remember to salute everyone I saw in town, whether I knew them of not.

"I never lock my door. What if my neighbors came by and I wasn't home," she continued. "They wouldn't be able to make themselves coffee and wait for me."

I told her about my life in rural Alaska. "I don't lock my doors either, but, most people in my country do."

A third son arrived from town with a small bottle of *cuajo,* a powder made from the inner lining of the calf stomach.

"Sometimes I make the *cuajo* myself, but buying it in town is faster," she said.

She set aside a gallon of milk for drinking and mixed a cap full of powder into the rest. "That should curdle in about fifteen minutes," she told me.

It was time to wait again. We stood on opposite sides of a *calafate* bush laden with ripe berries and ate until our lips and tongues turned bright purple.

"You are going to have to return many, many more times." Betty laughed.

Next she poured the curdled milk out into big pieces of porous cloth, and we squeezed the curds while the whey, or *la aqua* as she called it, poured out into a big pan. Then we moved the whole operation down to the river where wooden boxes with holes in them were set up in the shade of huge willow trees. It was time to *masa* the curds. We rolled up our sleeves and stuck our hands in the buckets up to the elbow, working the cheese into smaller and smaller chunks. Next, we poured it into the boxes, each one compartmentalized into two kilo blocks.

By late afternoon four two-kilo blocks of fresh farm cheese would be ready to sell in town.

I was humbled by how much time and milk it took to make four blocks of cheese, as well as by how much cheese had I eaten in my life without having any idea how it was made.

Washington was still not home, and the reality was I had nothing to do that day. So while the cheese was curing, Omar and I went for a horseback ride.

Photograph by Fredrik Norrsell.

Galloping across the pampas.

Scrubby ñirre trees came to mid-chest on the horses as we looked out over a landscape of rolling hills and rugged escarpments. Nimbus had a delightful rested energy I hadn't felt in weeks. Bursting into a spontaneous gallop in every meadow, Omar and I chased each other in circles like puppies. Rainbow trout zipped from underfoot as we splashed through the river. I crested a hill, panting nearly as hard as my horse, and the blue waters of the Baker River spread out before me. The beauty of it made me gasp.

Deep inside of me a ten-year-old boy just wanted to run free with his face in the wind. I may have been older than his mother, but today Omar and I were playmates, two kids with their own horses, free on the Patagonia steppe.

The next time I would see Omar he would be fourteen years old, have a girlfriend, and have absolutely no interest in riding horses with his mother's friend.

When I returned, Washington was home, and I made him a deal. I would use one of his horses for my journey to San Lorenzo. In return I would leave Nimbus with him, and he could use her for light work around the *campo*. Leaving my Nimbus behind seemed unthinkable, but it also felt like the right thing to do. Instead of hard days on the trail, she would get the light work of an occasional trip to town, the security of a good pasture, and the companionship of other horses.

Pettie was a short, stocky *colorado*. He had that super-fast Chilean horse walk that Nimbus never quite seemed to master, but he wasn't my horse and he never would be.

On the first cloudy day in over a week, Pettie and I took off down a boring dirt road. I braced myself for a bolt at every flapping piece of roadside debris. Unlike Nimbus, Pettie had no fear of plastic, but he danced sideways at every bridge, refusing to set foot on the hollow sounding platform. Humiliated, I got off and walked him across. Washington would never be seen walking his horse across a bridge. Horses know who you are, sometimes better than you do.

By afternoon the soft gray clouds had parted and the relentless sun shown through. We were going straight east. The country was changing from what looked like Idaho to Colorado. By tomorrow we would be in eastern Wyoming, with rolling hills dotted with tufts of dry brown grass. Nimbus would have thrown a fit at the lack of green pastureland, but Pettie, accustomed to a different set of difficulties in life, didn't seem to notice.

Setting up my first camp on the shores of Lago Cochrane, I joyously let my life slip into a familiar rhythm: Wake, drink coffee, eat breakfast, watch my horse graze, pack, travel, eat, watch my horse graze, sleep.

The next day, just before the end of the dirt road, I met a man herding cows.

"*¿Adónde vas?*" he wanted to know.

"*Al campo Buena Vista,*" I said, choosing the only nearby *campo* I knew by name.

A broad smile spread across his face. "*Ah, a visita la Señora Verina.*"

I nodded. Going to visit someone was understandable. Pointlessly wandering around on a horse was harder to explain.

The man spoke in a heavy *poblador* accent I could hardly understand, but he kept telling me over and over that this was the end of the road.

I was thrilled. The end of the road, and the wild country beyond, was exactly what I craved.

"You will probably lose yourself up there," he said.

More than ready to lose myself into the simple, unplanned life, of wind, and trees, and open skyscapes, it sounded like a terrific idea.

When he realized I was not turning around, he told me, "When you get to the end of the road, go straight up, do not continue along the main valley."

The trail did indeed climb straight up, into wide open country where the vegetation didn't hide the geology. At the top of the hill a view of Lago Cochrane exploded in front of me.

It wasn't going to rain here. I rolled my sleeping bag out under the stars and fell fast asleep. Before I was out of bed in the morning, I could hear a woman's laughter. A group of horseback riders were passing nearby. The parade of people heading into town to vote had begun.

Democracy had returned to Chile just over a decade earlier. Voting was mandatory and taken seriously. You could get an exemption if travel was an undue hardship, but nearly everyone would be at the vote. Many would travel long distances on horseback to do so.

One of the riders was the man I had met the previous day. I could hear him talking about me. "See I told you, there is a *gringa* alone out here with a horse."

I felt like a freak show. Why wasn't I out of my sleeping bag, packed up, and on the trail by now? Another man recognized my horse as belonging to Washington. There were no secrets in these parts. Within hours they would know that my horse was at Washington's, that I had ridden here from Coyhaique, that I was staying with Samuel, and that I was headed to Luis Soto's *campo*.

Outside Señora Verina's gate, I stood frozen. A white picket fence contained a freshly mowed lawn. A gravel path led past a small fountain through a tidy flower garden toward an immaculately built timber-frame house sitting well back on the grounds. I could have been in Switzerland. My upbringing was at war with my experience in Aysen. If this was a Patagonian home, I would simply announce myself at the gate and settle in for *maté,* but in neither Switzerland nor the U.S. does one holler into the yard, introduce herself to someone they hardly know, and invite herself in, especially at lunch time.

I was parked outside the gate, paralyzed by indecision, when a young blonde woman wearing a loose-fitting white blouse, shorts, and a headband, spied me and waved from the yard. There was no backing out now.

The two of us soon discovered that we did not have a language in common, but her smile was an ear-to-ear welcome. An older woman in a neat housedress arrived next. I recognized her as Señora Verina.

She didn't remember meeting me. Why should she? Even shyer then, my Spanish even worse, I had sat in the corner of the living room at NOLS hardly saying a word during her entire visit. She invited me to come in, but with a reserve that was not common in Chile.

I held my questions at bay. Had she built this beautiful house herself? How had she come to live here? Who was the smiling young woman I met at the gate?

Just as I had feared, it was lunch time. Seated at a table set with fine china, I saw my chapped lips and unwashed hair in the mirror. Oh, how embarrassing to sit at this table looking like this, but nothing could be done about it now.

Over lunch my questions began to flow. I stumbled over whether to call her Frannie or Señora Verina. I found myself using the familiar form *tu* and the formal more respectful term *usted* interchangeably to the point no one knew who I was talking to.

"How did you come to live in Patagonia?" I wanted to know.

"Switzerland is much too crowded. My husband and I looked all over the world for a place to live—Europe, Columbia, Canada. Fifteen years ago a Chilean friend in Vancouver said, 'Why not try Chile?' "

Then it was her turn. "What are you doing in Chile? Do you live here now?"

I explained that I was traveling around on horseback, which, even as I said it, sounded like a terribly useless thing to be doing.

"Oh, you are a tourist then," she said with what I interpreted as disdain.

"Yes, I guess so," I said.

"Have you been to Switzerland?" she asked.

"*Si*," I said, and to my own surprise I told her my story. "I was in love with a Swiss man from the Bernise Alps. We spent one whole delightful summer hiking and climbing in the Alps, but it was in the wilderness of Alaska that we chose to build a log house together."

Maybe it was that Señora Verina's house reminded me of our former home—the fine craftsmanship, the attention to detail created by Swiss perfectionism—that I continued speaking. Both our homes had been built almost entirely out of materials from the land. The hand-hewn timbers used for her main beams had been cut from tall, straight *coihue.* Where had they found trees of that quality in these parts?

"Krigi and I had to go nearly twenty miles away to find trees big enough to build with," I told her.

"Yes, it took us years to find these trees," Señora Verina said.

Her massive fireplace made of river rock spoke of back-breaking days spent hauling stone. The few objects brought in from the outside world—windows, a woodstove—had been packed in on horseback. My partner and I had hauled those same few things in on our own backs or sledged them in over snow in winter with the help of our dog. I imagined her, as a younger woman, working hard alongside her husband. I did not ask where he was now.

She, in return, did me the favor of not asking what had happened to the young Swiss man I was no longer traveling with.

Petina, the young woman from the gate, sat quietly throughout the meal, like myself when I had first come to Patagonia, and it was all I could do to listen. I gathered that she was a friend's daughter from Switzerland visiting for the summer. A few words were exchanged in Swiss, and it was decided that Petina would show me the way to the next *campo*.

Once we were alone, Petina became less shy with her Spanish.

"*El aire, el espacio, la naturaleza,*"—The air, the space, nature—she said spreading her arms wide, hands to the sky. "All of this." She twirled around in a circle. "In Europe I was happy maybe one moment every day. Here, I am happy all day, every day."

"Do you ever get lonely?" I asked, thinking of a young girl spending the summer alone on a *campo* with an older friend of the family and of my own, sometimes crushing, moments of loneliness on the trail.

"*Poco, muy poco,*" she said. "The people here are so wonderful. I love it that everything comes from here. The cherries, the vegetables, the meat, the milk, the wood, the bricks, it all comes from right here."

A little farther on, Petina burst into song. In Spanish, English, and German we traded verses. Oh, this is what it would feel like to travel with a companion, I thought. A balloon of loneliness burst inside of me, but my sadness was soon replaced by the feeling of the soft breeze on my skin, the smell of the blooming steppe, and the sweet laughter of a young girl. Appreciation for the moment flooded me with simple gratitude for the opportunity to be here, sharing this particular late springtime day in Patagonia.

We had been traveling for over an hour. "Are we still on Señora Verina's land?" I asked.

"*Si, Si,* a little farther to the next *campo,*" Petina said.

Finally, we came to a gate and shortly we arrived at the neighbors' house. A young man, almost a boy, was shearing sheep in the front yard. Petina jumped off and handed him a note from Señora Verina.

When she returned, she said, "He can't go right now, it is too far, too late in the day."

Then I realized, the note had asked him to accompany me. I was mortified.

"No, no, I'm fine by myself. Could you just point me down the correct trail from here?" I begged him.

"I need to check the sheep anyway. I can go a ways with you after I finish shearing this one," he said.

"*Si, si, pero no hay problema.*" I assured him again he didn't need to escort me.

He returned to the sheep he had left hog-tied on the ground and swiftly and efficiently removed the rest of its wool with sharp hand-shears. He threw a sheep skin over his horse, a dark brown *zaino* with a rusty red nose.

"Quick saddle." He laughed, leaping onto the horse's back. The three of us took off.

The trail ran along the fence line the entire way. He and Petina were riding side by side and laughing. Petina's fluffy, little, white city dog from Switzerland rode on the sheep skin in front of the boy. Maybe I was just an excuse for both of them to get out and enjoy the day. Was there a budding farm-boy romance going on?

At the top of a hill I could see a decidedly guitar-shaped lake—Lago Guittarra. Completely carefree, the two left me and rode off into the distance together. Alone again, the sweet sound of lapping waves on the shore kept the silence from being overwhelming. My travel day had been easy. The evening was peaceful and warm. I slipped into the deep, sweet sleep of wilderness nights.

The next morning as I routinely lifted Pettie's feet I discovered he was missing a shoe. I always carried extra shoes and nails, but somehow the rubber overboot I had carried for over 350 kilometers for just this occasion was missing. I kicked myself for losing this important piece of equipment. Sam's words echoed in my mind: "I would never go on a trip like that unless I could shoe my own horses."

I could try to shoe him myself. I had watched horses being shod dozens of times. I had held hooves and passed tools plenty of times, but no one had ever let me actually pound the nails. A nail too far to the inside, into the meat of the foot, could make a horse lame for weeks, or worse. A horse that jerked its foot at the moment the nails went through the hoof could cause me a nasty puncture wound to the hand.

I could walk him to the nearest *campo*. The locals never traveled with extra shoes and nails, or a rubber overboot. They simply rode their horses barefoot until they could replace the shoe. We were probably only half a day from the next farm, but the *campos* would be nearly empty. Everyone would be in town for the vote.

I started walking. I enjoyed walking, but Pettie was unfamiliar with a rider who didn't ride. He tugged incessantly at the rope, yanking my shoulder until it ached. The first *campo* we came to was unoccupied, not a sheep, not a chicken, not a dog there to greet us. We kept walking. This could possibly be the worst day in ten years to be looking for someone to shoe a horse. Just as it started to rain, I came across another *campo*. Horses, cows, and dogs let me know there was probably someone home.

"*Buenas tardes*," I hollered.

"*Hola*," a voice answered from the porch.

Three young people came out to greet me, a girl and her two teenage brothers.

"Is there anyone here who can shoe a horse?" I broke protocol and stuttered out my request right away.

"My dad is in town," the younger boy said.

"It's okay, it's not important," I lied.

"Is your horse tame?" the older boy wanted to know.

"Oh yes, he's quite tame," I assured him.

The older boy agreed to do it.

I offered to help, but the two boys took Pettie and my shoeing equipment and headed for the barn.

With little energy for fighting tradition, I followed their sister to the house for tea.

Every child in the *campos* grows up in two worlds. They understand both the world of orphaned lambs, and that of iPods and designer jeans. I always made it a point to ask young people I met in the *campos* about their vision for the future.

"I want to be a veterinarian. That way I can come back here and take care of animals," she said.

I was impressed how many young people I met held a strong desire to return to the *campos* to live. How many of them actually would? I did not know.

When the boy returned, I over paid him horrendously. I imagined his father's face when he got home and found out that his son had made two days wages putting one shoe on one horse for a *gringa*. I knew this was perpetrating the myth that *gringos* were made of easy money, but I didn't care.

Photograph by Nancy Pfeiffer.

A young girl and her orphan lamb.

In the morning the glaciated summit of San Lorenzo was half covered by a huge lenticular cloud, a sure sign that the winds were going to build. The sun was intense but there was a glacial chill in the air. I stopped midday to put on the long underwear I hadn't worn in weeks.

I traveled through open grassland on the northern aspects, while the south facing slopes produced *lenga*, *coihue,* and *notro*. A day of dramatic change made me restless and uncertain. Clouds dropped, making my world a gloomy gray, and I wanted to get to Luis's house as soon as possible. Then the sky opened a blue hole to the universe, giving me a brief glimpse of a heavenly snow-covered summit and the desire to travel forever, only to close again and open somewhere else to yet another vision of a possible future.

A line from an old song popped unbidden into my head. "When you're hurried and worried and you can't find your way, remember those peaceful wilderness days." Almost like a chant, I sang that line over and over, reminding myself that my time here was precious, life itself a spectacular event.

A tremendously large, flat area stretched before us. I asked Pettie if he, too, wanted to run. To my surprise he did. After moving at a walk for days, running felt like liberation, a tremendous release of yearning. I hoped this day and this feeling would sink deep within me and stay forever.

We passed a good camping spot late in the day, and another half an hour later. Thickening clouds rolled down the face of San Lorenzo, until only the closest spires shown dark along the skyline. A heavy rain was coming. We weren't going to make it to Luis's. There would be no warm woodstove, no conversation with friends tonight.

The next morning a torrential downpour brought on an exceptionally melancholy mood, but it was more than that. It took me a large part of the morning to figure out exactly what was bothering me.

Everyone around me was running a farm—shearing sheep, milking cows, planting crops. I was wandering around on a horse. My problem surprised me. It was a completely foreign desire; I wanted to be productive. After spending most of my life avoiding it . . . I wanted to work.

I also longed to be with people I had known a long, long time. An idea was hatching. My best friend and her little girl were in the south of Patagonia, a twenty-four hour bus ride away. I wanted to see them.

Late that morning, I saddled up and headed out into the rain and wind, a day I would not have traveled if it weren't for the promise of a warm, friendly place not far away. Pettie could feel the urgency as well. On the open plain just before the house, we broke into a spontaneous gallop.

Mardu met us at the gate. He quickly helped me unsaddled Pettie. A moment later I was inside by the fire. My dripping wet clothes hung on a nail near the door. A puddle formed on the floor underneath. To my surprise, Luis was also out in this weather. He was delivering meat to some Italian climbers higher on the mountain. Mardu played the accordion. I sat on the floor, repairing tack a good part of the afternoon.

When Luis returned from the mountain, he shucked his goat skin *chivas*, heavy woolen poncho, and wool cap to reveal dry cotton overalls. Like everything else I owned, my rain gear was far from new. I had arrived soaked to the skin after only half the time on the trail.

"*Eso no es la ropa de Patagonia.*" Luis laughed, pointing to my brand name outdoor gear which hung still dripping wet near his door. "*Eso es la ropa de Patagonia.*" He laughed and indicated his own clothing.

Someday I, too, would go local; but it would be years until I felt I was a good enough rider to wear a pair of goatskin *chivas* without feeling like an impostor.

Luis was riding to town the next morning to take Mardu to school. I had hoped to stay and rest a bit longer, but the opportunity to ride with Luis and Mardu was too good to be missed.

The next day, clearing weather brightened the fresh fallen snow. It was December 21st, summer solstice in the southern hemisphere, and there was ice on the puddles. No wonder Luis and Lucy hadn't started their garden yet.

The river was running grayish blue and swift from the recent rain, but with Luis in the lead, we splashed easily across. Maybe traveling with a local guide, someone who knew where and when to cross, wasn't such a terrible idea after all. The laughter of a young boy chattering to his father, mixed with the sound of running water, delighted me.

Mardu crosses the Rio Tranquilo on his way to school.

A few kilometers later, at Luis's brother's *campo*, several saddled horses waited in the yard. Moments later, three men on horseback, a packhorse, and three dogs joined our *tropé.* Each new horse urged the others along. Horses live and travel in social groups. Thinking of Nimbus and our long journey together, I wondered if it was cruel to expect an animal to live without others of its kind?

"Your horse will need its left front shoe replaced within two days," one of the men told me.

I felt nothing in Pettie's walk. I heard no clicking sound and saw nothing when I looked down. These people knew horses the way I knew snow, its texture, color, and sound all mean something. Hundreds of subtleties were going on all around me that I could not comprehend.

Farther downstream we crossed the Rio Tranquilo, by far the biggest river I had ever crossed. The deep, cold water pushed against the bellies of the horses and filled my boots. I watched, horrified, as the three dogs got swept violently downstream. A hundred meters below they hauled themselves out over a log jam. Wet and wiggling, they bounded up the banks to greet us.

I was finally living my dream, traveling the country like those who lived here.

All too soon, we arrived at the beginning of a road that had not been in existence three years earlier. A shiny new bus was parked there. People getting off the bus were being met by friends and family who had brought them horses for the last leg of the trip home. Others, like Mardu, were being dropped off to take the bus into town.

Overwhelmed by so much activity after so much time alone, I unsaddled and quietly rested in the shade behind the little shack that served as a bus stop. An elegant older woman got off the bus, snapped spurs onto her city shoes, added another strap to her handbag turning it into a small backpack, and efficiently stepped into a saddle. Who was this lady who so belonged to this place? One day I would find out.

Chapter 5

La Ruta Antigua (The Old Route)

THE PARKING LOT at the rodeo grounds in Cochrane was full of vendors selling exactly the equipment we still needed. After two years in Alaska, I was about to attempt the old horse trail to Villa O'Higgins at last. My good friend Paul and his friend Harry had agreed to join me. Open tailgates displayed handmade bridles and leather halters. Vendors laid out hobbles and spurs on colorful blankets. This rodeo happens once a year. Fortunately for us, today was the day.

A set of long narrow wooden stairs led to the bleachers above the rodeo arena. Two men on well-groomed horses waited on the sidelines. Their horses, both dark red *colorados,* sported roached manes, squared-off tails, deep-seated ornate saddles, and showy handwoven bridles. The men wore matching red, green, and blue striped *huaso* style *ponchos*—shorter and more brilliantly colored than those used to keep the weather off while working on the *campo*. The woolen beret worn on the trail was replaced by a wide brimmed straw hat. Fancy silver spurs adorned knee-high leather boots. Many teams looked to be father-son combinations. There were decades of tradition here I did not understand.

The bleachers around the arena were filled with ranchers from Cochrane and the neighboring *campos.* Surely someone here would have a couple of horses for sale.

Once the gate to the main arena swung open, the game was on. Horses raced to catch and pin a bull calf. Facing the solid wooden fence, horses moved sideways, crossing their front legs like Greek dancers. They pushed the cow along the outside wall until they trapped it, sometimes brutally, against a padded section of the arena. "*Punta buena,*" the announcer called when a clean stop and turn-around were made. "*Punta mala*," he said, when the job was botched. Gorgeous young women in brightly colored skirts with acres of petticoats sat sidesaddle behind the winners as they paraded around the ring.

As the crowd thinned, Harry, Paul, and I stood outside the arena, holding a sign that declared our mission: "*Compra caballos mansos*" (buying tame horses). Paul and Harry seemed unbothered by the stares and snickers of people passing by, but I was embarrassed to be the center of attention. No one else was making a spectacle of themselves.

Having the most Spanish, I had to do the talking, but speaking Spanish all day was still exhausting for me. At the end of the day I was mentally and emotionally beat. I had left Alaska almost a month earlier, with the promise that I would have three horses ready to go by the first of December. We were well beyond that date, and I was in possession of only one horse. The weight of my own unmet expectations hung heavy on my shoulders as I dragged myself uphill to Samuel's cabin. We were still short two horses, but we had the next best thing, a list of people who had horses for sale.

WHEN I HAD arrived in Cochrane alone to begin organizing the trip, Sam had met me on his doorstep with great news. "A guy named Oscar who lives up the Colonia will be bringing three horses into town for you to buy."

After working so hard to find one horse two years ago, I couldn't believe how easily everything was falling into place.

"People call the guy *el gringo pobre.* He is Swiss, but he has lived here long enough to be poor like everyone else." Sam laughed. "He is coming with your horses on November thirtieth."

My mind ran rapid fire into the future. We were supposed to be outfitted and ready to go on December first, which gave me exactly one day's leeway for the multitude of things that can go wrong in Patagonia.

My friend Paul was a university professor as well as my next door neighbor in Alaska. He, like most *gringos* on vacation, had a solid return date. Every day we were late getting out of town would have to be made up on the trail.

In less than a decade HF radios installed at every *campo* on the Colonia would revolutionize communication, but for now, riding two days to talk with someone was the only way to communicate.

"What if I go to Oscar's *campo* on the Colonia and buy the horses there?" I asked.

"Why not just wait till Oscar comes to town?" Sam replied.

Sam had lived here longer than me. He couldn't comprehend my haste, but he agreed that there were a plethora of problems that could arrive at the last moment.

"You will need horses to get up there," Sam reminded me.

"I can borrow Nimbus and another horse from Washington for the trip," I said.

"I would love to go with you, but I can't to go up river right now. Why don't you invite Don Leonitis Ascencio. He would love to get out in the country," Sam recommended.

I was beginning to understand that the prefix *Don* applied to all respected elders. Don Leonitis Ascencio was sixty-two years old. Before the roads came, he had worked as a *tropero*, traveling with huge herds of cattle cross country on horseback, sometimes for months. When the roads arrived, it became both illegal and impractical to move livestock overland. Ranchers needed to come up with the cash for a truck ride for their animals, and Don Leonitis needed a new job. These days he worked in construction.

"He knows where Oscar lives and besides, he's a good friend," Sam said.

Early Saturday morning Don Leonitis Ascencio and I took off. We were traveling with two of Washington's horses, but Nimbus was not one of them.

I had arrived at Washington's *campo* to get Nimbus, and he had informed me that she was "away . . . at the neighbor's."

"Where exactly was she?" I wanted to know.

"*Oh, tan lejos,*" (very far) he replied.

I suspected he had sold my mare, but I had no way to prove it. A hurt and angry feeling welled up inside me. By leaving my horse with him, I assumed that I had secured her an easy, carefree life. Had Washington sold her shortly after I left town? My anger at Washington for not honoring his promise to keep my horse was concealing my own shame. I had abandoned my horse to the care of others, something I would continue to do for years. Apparently, the easy life I had promised Nimbus at the end of our journey didn't exist for Chilean horses. At some level I knew that in Chile, a horse that was eating and not working would not be welcome for long.

With far more questions than answers in my head, Don Leonitis Ascencio and I crossed the Baker River on the same *balsa* I had used two years earlier and headed up the Rio Colonia. Three symmetrical, cone-shaped peaks dominated the end of the valley. Slowly, they came into detail as the miles disappeared behind us and the sun sank low in the sky. As the glaciers at the end of the valley got incrementally closer, I could plainly see their medial and lateral moraines snaking toward the valley floor.

Sam had been right. It was a privilege to travel with Don Leonitis. Eight hours into the day, we had already covered more miles than I had accomplished in several days at the beginning of my first trip. According to Don Leonitis, Oscar's *campo* was still "*tan lejos,*" but he seemed unconcerned, happy to be out riding.

My knees were sore and my butt hurt. Exhausted, I suggested we camp and look for Oscar the next morning. Don Leonitis would not hear of it. We would ride until we found an occupied farm where people would invite us in.

Finally we came to Oscar's *campo*. The place was deserted.

"*No te preocupes,*" Don Leonitis told me not to worry myself. "There will be people at the next *campo*."

The glaciated mountains that we had been riding toward all day faded from pink, to maroon, and into darkness.

When I had resigned myself to riding all night, a well-lit house appeared. The residents of the house came out and helped us unsaddle. Hardly a word was said until we had deposited our gear in the barn and settled into the house for *maté.*

"Oscar, is over on the Rio Nef," one of the men said.

"For how long?" I asked.

"About a week," he replied

I did some quick calculations. There was no way Oscar could make it to Cochrane by the thirtieth. I was bitterly disappointed, but apparently the night was young. Visitors didn't come often, and there was wine to drink and meat to eat.

Eventually the conversation drifted to the reason for our journey. The owner of the *campo* said he might have a horse for sale. But first we would have an *asado.*

We moved to the barn to build a fire for cooking. The flames cast a surreal light on the ceiling. The men eating, the lamb grease dripping from their fingers, and the roosters marching overhead on the trusses blended with a Patagonia downpour thundering on the metal roof of the barn. My mind was as tired as my body, and I understood little of the conversation. But I was strangely happy in this dry place, listening to the men laughing and joking around the fire. I laid my head down on a saddle, curled up with the cat, and fell into a deep sleep in the hay.

The next morning swimming upward though the thick, warm mud of my dreams, I could hear men saddling horses. I dragged myself into consciousness and bolted outside to see my horse saddled and waiting.

Don Leonitis had over twenty years on me. Yesterday, after not being on a horse for years, he had ridden me into the ground. Last night he stayed up laughing and drinking until the first rays of dawn peaked over the horizon, and this morning he had woken up and saddled my horse while I slept. Unaccustomed to being the slow weak one on an expedition, I was mortified.

Four of us rode a mile or so to a corral where Don Leonitis and I were told to wait. The rain was over, and we sat happily for hours in the sweet morning sun.

Eventually, a big, beautiful, dun-colored gelding was driven into the corral. This horse was for sale? He was a *gateaba,* a blonde horse with a dark mane and tail. A dark stripe ran down the center of his back. Faint zebra-like stripes on his lower legs reminded me of the Przewalski, the last remaining species of wild equine in Mongolia.

Don Leonitis pronounced the big *gateaba* good without a second look, but I wanted to ride this horse if I was going to buy him. There wasn't an extra saddle, so I hopped on him bareback and trotted him around the corral. He was huge by Chilean standards. The corners of the corral came up quickly. His trot was like riding a tractor, and I bounced around on my seat much to the amusement of the men. But he was incredibly powerful. I imagined crossing belly deep rivers and trudging through miles of sticky mud with this boy. This horse was exactly the kind of big, strong horse I needed for the trip to O'Higgins. A couple hundred dollars in pesos changed hands, and he was mine!

It was already afternoon. We had to return the same distance we had ridden all day yesterday and last night. Don Leonitis knew what I did not, that the last *balsa* to cross the river today would run at six p.m. He needed to be at his construction job the following morning at eight.

We took off for Cochrane, with Don Leonitis's horse walking so fast I had to trot to keep up. He was towing our new addition behind him on a rope. Suddenly, he stopped abruptly in the trail, unsaddled Washington's horse, and tossed the saddle on our recent purchase.

I threw him a quizzical look.

"I want to ride the better horse," he said.

A couple miles short of the *balsa* Don Leonitis reached into his back pocket. For the first time all trip, deep creases crossed his face. His wallet was missing.

"I got off the horse at that last gate," he said. "Maybe it fell out there."

Don Leonitis looked crestfallen. "It's too far back. If I miss work tomorrow morning I could lose my job," he explained.

A job was not an easy thing to find in Cochrane. Replacing his identification cards could take months and potentially require multiple trips to Coyhaique.

"You head for the *balsa.* I will ride back and find your wallet," I said.

To my amazement he accepted my offer.

Urging Washington's reluctant gelding into a trot in a direction he didn't want to go was a project, but I managed to convince him to do what I wanted. At the gate I swung out of the saddle and plowed my boots through the tall grass. There beside the fence post was the wallet. I grabbed it and tore off for the *balsa* at a full gallop, letting the red horse run full out for home. I felt like a knight rescuing the village, as I dashed down the last hill to the river. Wallet in hand I boarded the ferry right behind Don Leonitis.

A few miles from town, I asked him if he had a name for my new horse.

"Why don't you call him Tamango?"

Cerro Tamango was the mountain that Sam's cabin was perched on. *Tamangos* were also knee-high, calf-skin boots worn by the pioneers for walking in the snow. We would be traveling in snow soon enough. Tamango it was.

When I got back I proudly showed Sam my new horse. He was not nearly as excited about my purchase as I was.

"You cannot buy horses before Oscar gets here," Sam explained to me emphatically. "Oscar will be here on the thirtieth."

I had my doubts, but I was Sam's guest. He had set me and my horse up with a little cabin on a piece of land he owned outside of town. I couldn't go against his wishes. I did my best to let go of my *gringa* impatience. As I did, I fell into the local rhythm of *asados* and *fiestas*. The days slipped by almost unnoticed.

On November thirtieth, Paul and Harry arrived. Oscar did not. It was time to take action. Fortunately the rodeo was in town.

THE DAY AFTER the rodeo, I started following leads. One turned out to be an unbroken two year old. Another lived out past San Lorenzo, which meant we would need to complete nearly a third of our trip in order to get a look at it. An older woman desperately wanted to sell me her horse. She lived thirty kilometers in the wrong direction. Not knowing if her horse might still be our best option, I was indecisive and indirect with her. I hated doing business with people in this manner, but the ticking of time made me feel pressured.

"Maybe we can get there," I told her.

"Young lady, will you come tomorrow or not?" she insisted.

It felt like being reprimanded by my own grandmother. The word *mal creado* popped into my mind. People used the term "badly raised" for those who do not have simple basic manners. I did not want to be one of them.

"No, I do not think we can make it to your farm tomorrow. I am sorry," I told her.

Our best option for a horse turned out to be our next door neighbor, Richardo Fernandez. He would meet me at noon. About three in the afternoon, just as I was giving up, I saw a boy on a bicycle riding up the hill towing a dang nice looking little black horse.

Only five years old, the gelding was a bit edgy and lacked the confidence Tamango had, but he had an energy I liked, and his trot was the smoothest I had ever felt. Oh, I thought, if I lived here and had a *campo* this would be the horse for me. But would this small horse be tough enough for the trail ahead? Was he too young and flighty?

Chilean horses are strong, I told myself, and most of them are no bigger than this one. He would have Tamango to follow and learn from. I wanted this boy!

That night I sat in peace on the front step of the little *puesto* on Sam's land and watched my horses. Tamango stood on a huge rock silhouetted against the evening sky, looking every bit the stallion he still was at heart. The little black horse grazed tranquilly at the base of the hill, living in a moment of green grass and comfort, unconcerned about what lay ahead. The only disturbing thing about the evening was that Harry seemed more concerned with the horse we did not have than the ones we did.

For a long time our new purchase would remain, "the little black horse," but eventually he became "Chucao," after one of my favorite Patagonian forest birds. I liked the sound his full name, *chucao tapaculo*, made when it rolled off my tongue. And the bird's mannerisms matched our little black horse's energy and curiosity.

The next day, we used the divide-and-conquer technique. In the morning, we each took off in a different direction with a list of things to do. The longer we stayed in town the more stuff we needed to buy. It felt like I was puking money.

Late that night we all converged at Sam's *puesto*. Miles from town and exhausted, I found out we had made plans to check out two horses miles apart at the same time the following day. One of us needed to get out of bed and walk back to town to deliver a message, or someone was going to get stood up in the morning. No one did.

Again, I was doing business with people in a way that I didn't feel comfortable with. Paul and Harry would leave the country after this trip. Months later, it would be me who would meet the sweet woman whose husband we had stood up that morning. It would be me who apologized to the pavement, unable to look her in the eye.

Mostly I was frustrated at myself. I remembered how desperately I had wanted to have a partner on my first trip, now everything felt all wrong. Paul was one of my best friends. We had a long history and had been through other trying times together. Harry and I had not.

"We are not on the trail yet. Things will get better once we are out of town," Paul said, trying to sooth my anxiety.

My lesson, which Chile patiently teaches me over and over again, is to accept the way things are. I was too focused on getting us on the trail. There were many things to enjoy here and now. Buying horses was part of the journey. I needed to mellow out.

Fredrico Peede owned one of the largest spreads in the valley. The next morning we arrived in his truck to the front door of a large ranch style house. Branding irons hung proudly over the door. Except for the towering glaciated peaks surrounding us, the place could have been in Montana. Indeed, Fredrico had gotten his start in ranching in Montana. Like many young men, he had worked in the States for several years, earning enough money to start his own homestead. He had done well.

Fredrico excused himself, saddled a pretty dappled white gelding, and took off with one of the hired men to find the horses. I wanted to be invited to ride out with the men, but, of course, Paul and I were left to relax in the sun.

A rusted plow, meant to be drawn by horse or oxen, lay in the grass beside the barn. The bunkhouse, a long line of single rooms, each one with a wooden door, sat empty this time of year. Even Fredrico's wife and children were living in town. I imagined the place was quite different at sheep shearing time.

Eventually, I fell asleep beneath the drooping branches of a weeping willow tree to the whisper of the ever-present Patagonian wind. I woke to the sound of thundering hooves. Dust billowed up as a hundred or more head of horses poured like a continuous wave down the hill into the corral. Duns and blacks, *gateabas* and *tobianos, zainos, alazáns* and *colorados* circled inside the corral in nervous excitement.

Of all these horses, two were for sale. The first was an old broken-down black mare. She was swaybacked and had the most recent of her probably numerous offspring still in tow. I was sorely disappointed.

The second was a *colorado mala cara: Colorado* for his rusty reddish color and *male cara,* or "bad face," for the broad white stripe that ran down his face. Tall and thin, but not skinny, this gelding had lots of spirit.

"He hasn't been ridden in a couple years," Fredrico warned me.

I ran my hands down his strong neck and chest to his front leg and grabbed his fetlock. I picked up his foot. His front feet were flat. He hardly had an indentation between the hard cask of his hoof and the soft, calloused meat of the frog. I didn't have the experience to know how much of a problem his feet would be or how much shoes would help, but I knew his feet weren't great.

Fredrico saddled him up for me, and I got on. I loosened the reins and asked him to go. He took off like a racehorse, ripping across the pasture like he hadn't run in years. I had never moved that fast on a horse in my life. The *colorado* showed no interest in stopping. I was both scared and thrilled.

"*No problema.*" Fredrico assured me he would mellow out within a day or two on the trail.

I wanted to believe him, but I didn't want to buy a horse I couldn't handle.

Next, Paul got on him. Paul never loosened the reins. He kept him at a nice quiet walk, never letting him break into even a trot. The lanky gelding listened well, and I learned an important lesson: If you don't want this horse to go, don't ask him!

I asked the horse's name. The hired hand hesitated a second as if to consider if the question was serious and then said, *"Arlequin,"* which I would miss-pronounce for the rest of his life as "Arraquien." Years later I would learn that his name meant "Joker." Was he named on the spot because of his flat feet, and a joke that was meant to be on me? Or had these men actually known his personality from a herd of a hundred?

That afternoon I rode back to town, not only with Fredrico's horse but with his saddle and bridle, as well.

"You can pay me in town tomorrow," he said, trusting and unconcerned.

That night, three fine strong horses grazed in front of the *puesto.* Surprisingly confident about what we were about to do, I was content to the core. By now everyone in town knew we were preparing to take the old trail to O'Higgins. Unlike two years earlier, not one person had approached me on the street to tell me I was crazy. Traveling with two male companions seemed to be doing the trick. Never mind that I was clearly the expedition leader.

On a chilly December morning, we lined up outside Sam's house wearing nearly everything we owned. Sam took the obligatory leaving-town photo, and we were on our way. Harry rode Arraquien. I rode Chucao. Tamango, being towed along with our gear, was the *pilchero* of the day. Paul was walking as he would most of the expedition.

As the sun grew stronger, it warmed our bodies, and we fell into a rhythm. Ten kilometers into the trip we were congratulating ourselves on actually getting out of town, when a man carrying a fence post rounded the corner. Arraquien startled at the strange apparition of a man, with a giant, oscillating log on his shoulder, and leapt into the bushes, dragging Tamango with him. Tamango panicked and bucked. Arraquien joined him in his hysteria. At the end of our first rodeo, Harry was lying in the road, Tamango was running free, Arraquien stood forlornly with his saddle hanging from his belly, and the man with the fence post had stopped dead in his tracks with his mouth wide open. Oh, the story he will have for his wife tonight, I thought.

Harry jumped up, fortunately unhurt. We caught Tamango and calmed him down, and tried to right the saddle on Arraquien. The *mandil,* the thick felt pad that fit under the saddle, was nowhere to be found. The man with the fence post stood watching the show, with the post still on his shoulder, as we scrambled around looking in the bushes beside the road.

"Could the pad have come off before the rodeo?" I asked tentatively, looking down the long straight section of road behind us. Surely, that was impossible. Harry would have noticed if he was riding a horse without a pad.

Then again, I could remember galloping wildly across the steppe and looking down to find my saddle pad had slipped nearly off my horse's butt behind me.

"Maybe you didn't put it on this morning?" Harry told me.

I did not saddle that horse without a pad, that much I knew. The pad was behind us.

I took off down the road at a trot on Chucao. Still spunky at the beginning of the trip, he had a smooth easy trot, which was a joy to ride. I felt I shouldn't have favorites among the horses, but already I did.

A rental car coming the other way slowed down. The father of a vacationing family from Valdivia leaned out the window and asked with a smirk, "Are you looking for something?"

I could see Arraquien's *mandil* in the back seat.

"We picked up your pad six kilometers ago," they said in disbelief.

To my complete mortification, they insisted on pictures of Chucao and me with the lost pad. No doubt, the story of the stupid *gringa* who lost her stuff on the road lives on in family journals in Valdivia.

We passed the place where two years earlier the bus had stopped at the end of the road. That road now snaked off into the distance. At exactly where I had watched three dogs get swept downstream as our horses crossed the river belly-deep, a new swinging bridge spanned the Rio Tranquilo. From there the road headed toward San Lorenzo. Whether he wanted it or not, there would soon be a road to Luis Soto's *campo*.

An indistinct looking path took off to the south. Could this be the route to O'Higgins? It fit the description people had given us, but it looked intimidatingly inconsequential.

We headed up the steep, narrow trail. At the next valley, we dropped down as steeply as we had climbed. The Rio Pedregroso flowed in front of us. We were on our way to O'Higgins at last.

We found a slow, wide spot to cross the Pedregroso and pulled off our first river crossing without a hitch. After our rodeo, our first day had been blessedly uneventful. Living with three horses, I soon learned to appreciate any day without major drama.

The next day, we got to where the Calluqueo Glacier was clearly shown on the map. The glacier had retreated miles up the valley, leaving a rocky scar and a tremendous milky blue lake at its base. A distinct trim line marked the level where once grinding, pulverizing ice had filled the valley. Far above the destruction, a mature *Lenga* forest thrived. The occasional tree, undercut by erosion, toppled back into the ice age below.

Our maps were only twenty-five years old. Most of the world's glaciers are receding but the Ventisquero Calluqueo was diminishing at a phenomenal rate.

Mount San Lorenzo, the peak that the Calluqueo Glacier tumbles from, sits directly in the gap between the Northern and Southern Ice Fields, the solitary vestige of glaciated terrain left from the once massive ice sheet.

A narrow path etched its way along the steep morainal scree between the forest above and the glacier lake below. Not even moss had time to grow between the rocks along the trail. Accustomed to a mountain landscape with rocky slopes at the top and timberline below, looking up from non-vegetated terrain at mature forest well above our heads gave me a bizarre topsy-turvy feeling. At the top of the valley, we eked past the toe of the prehistoric ice.

Photograph by Fredrik Norrsell.

The Ventisquero Calluqueo recedes in the distance.

Blessed with a period of good weather, we started to fall into a rhythm of long breaks midday. The horses grazed peacefully with their saddles off. The three of us sprawled out in the sun below San Lorenzo, reading, writing, and napping. That mix of tranquility and wonder that I cherished from my first trip began to filter back in. I was slowing down, noticing more of the world around me. My senses, tapped down from living in the constant drum of civilization, were opening again to the smell of *calafate* in bloom, and the familiar, delightful sound of the *chucao tapaculo* trilling through the forest.

After lunch we entered yet another magical *lenga* forest. Far from the devastation caused by the unending need to stock the wood piles of Coyhaique, the forest this far south was ancient, uncut, and unburned. During the last glacier maximum, small isolated populations of *lenga* had survived in areas along the coast, where large mountains upstream had protected them from glaciation. The entire forest we rode through had been repopulated from those few survivors.

Being virtually the first travelers of the year, the trail was barely distinguishable. The horses constantly stepped over fallen logs. When the deadfall was too broad to step or jump over, we had to pick our way through the woods and re-find the trail. For decades, this winding mountain trail had been the only overland access to the town of O'Higgins and the government had paid *pobladores* who lived along the route to maintain it. Two years earlier a highway was built in the next valley, over thirty kilometers away, and money for trail maintenance had stopped. Each winter trees kept falling. How long would this trail remain open?

Bong, bong . . . bong, bong, bong, a powerful pounding broke the stillness. *Carpintero gigante*, a nearly twenty inch version of Woody the Woodpecker clung perpendicular to a dead *coihue*. His shiny blue-black body was accented by a fully crested ruby head. Another more distant drumming let me know his mate was nearby. Much harder to spot, she would be black, as well, but with only a tiny bit of red around her beak. I could not find her in the thick forest.

Just before evening, a man on foot appeared on the trail. We had not seen anyone for days and there didn't appear to be any farms nearby. The man informed us that he had seen hoofprints on the pass.

"Someone crossed about six days ago with a *tropé* of several horses," he said.

That was terrific news. Chilean maps of remote areas bordering Argentina are restricted by the government. Before our trip I had managed to cobble together a strange conglomeration of Argentinean and Chilean maps of various scales. Our Argentinean maps showed only a tiny slice of the Chilean side, leaving a big blank spot right where we wanted to go. It was early in the season to be traveling this route. There would be snow in the pass. Without tracks to follow, the way would surely be lost.

That evening we camped by a shallow, warm lake. Towing the *pilchero* while riding Chucao all day had left me mentally and physically beat. Dragging an extra horse through difficult terrain, I was once again on a steep learning curve. I needed to feed rope out when the *pilchero* was slowing down for a tricky spot and take it back in before it got tangled in his feet. At the same time, I had to keep the reins of my own horse active but not tight. Several times that day, I had gotten the rope stuck under Chucao's tail. This particular indignity threw Chucao into old-fashioned rodeo style bucking fits. Thrashing wildly, he tried to rid himself of me, anything else on his back, and that horrible thing that was now tightly clinched under his tail. If I managed to successfully hold the reins, free the rope from his tail, and hold onto the saddle with my thighs, I felt like a wild west bronc buster. If not, I either ended up in the dirt or I let go of the lead rope and had to chase a loose horse all over the countryside.

Harry had a bad hip and couldn't walk much. Paul, although he had been a Wyoming cowboy for a short period in a previous life, chose not to ride much because riding hurt his knee. I traveled by both walking and riding and the *pilchero* carried the gear. It all worked out, but we were dealing day and night with six distinct individuals.

I was ready for a break. December tenth was officially still spring, but the temperature was warm. The guys cooked dinner while I slipped around the corner and eased myself into the lake. The water was cool but delightful. The warm sun and soft breeze made my skin tingle. Drying myself on the muddy bank, in no hurry to put my clothes on, I let the moment elongate. Loneliness no longer haunted me and traveling with two male companions had at last sprung me free of the "*estás sola*"? stigma I had suffered on my first trip, but occasionally I noticed a flip side. I found myself less immersed in the place. I had other people to talk to, other subjects to occupy my mind. Beside this lake, with only the soft croaking of frogs and the sweet smell of new *lenga* leaves, I luxuriated, at peace with solitude.

The next day we packed up early and started climbing under a deep blue sky toward the highest pass of the trip. The winds were blessedly calm, the sun warm and welcoming. Crossing on any other kind of day would have been impossible.

The day went fairly well, until the trail, that had been surprisingly easy to follow, disappeared on the edge of a deep canyon. A small shrine stood at the end of the path. The *Santuario de San Sebastián* was a small house-shaped box containing a tiny altar decorated with plastic flowers and half burned candles. It was a miniature version of monuments found all along the Chilean road system in places where a traveler's luck needed to be blessed. This one was surrounded by a circle of bleached horse skulls. A small wooden cross behind the *santuario* made me suspect that horses weren't the only ones who had perished here.

I got off my horse gingerly and peered skeptically over the edge of the canyon.

"Don't tell me this is the trail," I said aloud.

Tracks descended a steep rocky scree field, crossed a narrow but turbulent torrent at the bottom of the ravine, and ascended an equally steep pile of rocks on the opposite side of the river.

"I think that is the trail," Paul said.

We scouted around on foot but could not find another way. In the end, we resigned ourselves to what we knew all along. The trail did indeed go down that terrifying precipice and into that surging gray river.

I would later learn that this spot was known as *la picota*, a place to literally pick your way though. Beside the shrine, a pickax with a wooden handle lay ready for use. If the constant flow of scree had closed the route since the last passerby, the next traveler used the tool to rebuild the trail. Years later, that axe handle would break, closing *la picota* forever, or at least until someone contributed a new handle.

Before we took off, I lit a candle in the little shrine for Arraquien, Tamango, and Chucao. I have never been a religious person, but this seemed like an appropriate moment to pray.

The horses were hesitant. I trusted them. These weren't spoiled pets. They were Patagonian trail horses, and if they didn't want to go, they probably had a reason at least worth considering. I decided to descend on foot, leading Arraquien. I knew that wasn't how the *gauchos* would do it, but I wasn't feeling exactly *gaucho* at the moment. Arraquien sat far back on his haunches, his hooves skidding in the loose sandy soil, I jumped to his uphill side to protect myself. Fully concentrating on getting my own horse to the bottom, I tried hard not to think about that pile of horse skulls.

When Arraquien and I got to the bottom, sweet relief flooded my body, only to be followed by complete horror as I saw Harry ahead of me trying to kick Chucao into the river.

I wanted to scout it first. I wanted to try a bigger horse. I wanted to rest, to get over the adrenaline still pulsing through my veins. Fear was driving my emotions. In my mind's eye, I saw Harry and Chucao washed downstream.

"Stop it now!" I screamed.

"Why!" Harry hollered. "People here would just ride across."

"Yes, but some of them die," I snapped.

Chapter 6

Al Interior (The Land Within)

THE MILKY GRAY glacier runoff made it impossible to tell which parts of the river were deepest. I probed the river with a long stick, looking for holes. Leaning on a sturdy stock to help steady myself, I entered the edge of the river to feel the power of the flow. Using a technique I had often employed at NOLS, I faced upstream, moving first my right foot, then my left sideways into the current.

Harry probably thought me completely daft. My behavior did not surprise me. I had done ludicrous things before in defense of my animals. The consequences of losing my footing and taking a wicked, cold, nasty swim would not be fatal. However, a *pilchero* that slipped with his load might possibly drown. Slow and cautious was how I had learned to cross Patagonian rivers. I intended to approach this one the same way.

Meanwhile, faint mares' tails, the first sign of a possible weather change, whipped across the western sky, reminding me of the need to keep moving. We still had the snow-covered pass ahead of us.

Finally, I was satisfied we had a safe route across the river. We led the horses up the steep rocky slope on the other side, where I noticed another small shrine nailed to a tree. I left a few pesos in thanks for our safe crossing. No trust had been lost between us and the horses, but Harry and I were furious with each other. Our differing opinions as to how to treat the horses remained painfully irreconcilable.

We were well above the timberline. Snow patches started to link together until unbroken snowfields stretched before us. We traveled on foot, carefully leading our animals. Again, we were not being *gaucho*, but if a horse were to put a foot in a hole or behind a log and stumble, it could break a leg. Having a horse in pain and suffering because of my own inattention or stupidity was my greatest nightmare.

However, the late spring snow was still firm and surprisingly supportable. Best of all, we had the tracks of four horses, only a few days old ahead of us. No other sign of a trail was visible. Somewhere high on the pass we slipped across the unmarked border into Argentina as people had done since before there were borders.

In 1881, a treaty between Chile and Argentina fixed the boundary as being "between the highest summits" and "along the water divide." The discrepancy this language induced has proven problematic. In Patagonia the exact border is still uncertain in places.

In this wild country, far from any official border crossing, locals frequently made short trips across the imaginary line between their two countries. A few hours later, with no one to know or care, we stepped back into Chile.

Dry Argentinian peaks to the east turned pink with the setting sun.

"Condor," Paul hollered.

A mature male with a white collar around his neck rose in lazy circles over the summit. Wingtips arched characteristically upward, it was definitely an Andean Condor, the largest raptor in the world. Paul had been waiting all trip to get a glimpse of this rare monstrous bird. Still, from this distance, it was hard to believe it had a wingspan of over ten feet. The Andean condor had been working its way to the wrong end of the endangered species list since 1973. We stared, transfixed, lost in the moment, the hardships of the day fading with the sunset.

We could see forest below. Our long day was nearly over.

We found a green spot big enough for the night. After unsaddling, I ran my hands over Tamango's coat to check for sores and give him a little rub down. He had been a fantastic *pilchero* on a tough day. Suddenly, my good sweet boy turned and bit me hard on the leg. Tough blue jeans prevented the skin from being broken, but I was badly bruised. For weeks I would carry a blueish purple reminder to tie his head up when messing with him and to change that packsaddle so it doesn't sore him up!

A place called *puesto de tablas* was the only man-made object marked along our entire route. Where there was a *puesto* there would be grass. The following day would be another tough one, but I was determined to make it there by nightfall.

The next day, I was admiring the forest around me on a rare section of easy trail when Arraquien snorted, bounced aside, and stared. He had nearly stepped on a strange elongated creature with short stubby legs. An armadillo, or *pichi,* as it is known in Argentina, stood defiantly in the trail. Long, dark reddish hairs grew from its armor, like unwanted whiskers. Could this tiny creature really be related to the two-thousand pound armadillo of prehistoric Patagonia? His short bowlegged limbs, with long claws for digging, did not seem capable of taking him far from his desert home. But here he was deep in the forest. Maybe, I thought, this one was like me, wandering simply to see what was out there.

We arrived at the *puesto de tablas* just at dusk. Smoke curled from the rooftop. Don Rial, a wiry older man in a faded denim jacket and black *boina*—the only inhabitant of this country and the man whose horse's footprints we had been following for days—greeted us at the gate.

"*Saque la montura,*" he said with the invitation to unsaddle. In typical *poblador* fashion it was understood we would be staying awhile.

Photograph by Fredrik Norrsell.

Drinking *maté* and listening to the stories of Don Rial.

Saddles deposited in a shed, we were ushered in for *maté.* The *puesto* was, exactly as noted on the map, a simple cabin made of *tablas,* graying four-inch hand-hewn boards. In order to keep livestock out of the immediate living area, the place was surrounded by a small wooden fence. A few chickens and a dog roamed the yard. Outside the gate, we tied one horse and left the others free to eat.

At this altitude, grass was still poor this time of year. Don Rial didn't give a second thought to grazing three extra animals for the night, but I was aware we were asking a lot.

This man, with his simple dwelling, sparse cooking utensils, and dirt floor was in charge of the entire valley we had just travel though, the *campo* we had slept on the previous night, as well as the country we would travel through the entire next day. Fortunately for us, he had just returned from his semi-annual trip to town with three *pilcheros* loaded with *maté*, flour, and sugar for the summer. At the end of the summer he would push his fattened cows back up over the pass to market in Cochrane.

We made a pot of soup from ingredients in our saddle bags and meat Don Rial hacked from a lamb hung to cure in the back room. The sky darkened and the light faded away inside the *puesto* as we sipped *maté* and talked.

I longed to understand everything about how this country had shaped his life, but my Spanish failed me miserably. Nevertheless, long after Paul and Harry had gone to bed, I stayed up listening to his stories by the light of the open fire.

Don Rial had three children. One was in living in Cochrane. The other two were studying in Santiago. I tried to imagine where their lives and studies would take them. I doubted it would be back to this beautiful, desolate country. What would become of this tremendous expanse of land with the passing of Don Rial?

Right before bed I hobbled two horses and tied Chucao. I liked to change who got tied at night so each had a chance to eat. In the middle of the night, I untangled Chucao who had wrapped himself up tightly in his rope. Sleeping with one ear open, as camping with horses had taught me to do, I heard hobbled horses nearby most of the night. Come morning, I could hear nothing except Paul and Harry making breakfast.

"Are there horses?" I asked hopefully.

"No," they replied in unison.

None of us were too concerned about the horses until I discovered Don Rial's four horses grazing nearby, unaccompanied by Tamango and Arraquien. Then I knew. Our boys had taken off. The thought of my horses jumping logs and negotiating the muddy trail behind us in hobbles disturbed me deeply.

Paul and Harry were confident the horses were still nearby. I was equally sure they had returned to the last gate.

Four miles back, two horses stood looking forlornly at a closed gate, their hobbles thankfully missing. I slipped the halter over Arraquien's ears, and he resolutely followed me down the trail. Tamango stubbornly stood his ground at the gate.

"Oh, Tamango," I said, taking off Arraquien's halter. I slipped it over Tamango's nose and whispered sweetly in his ear, "Tamango, you pig-headed jerk, let's go."

By the time I arrived at Don Rial's it was lunch time. One could not leave before the midday meal.

Some time well into the afternoon we took off for Lago Christy. We were headed *al interior,* into the heart of wild country, the land farthest from all roads. Two inches of soil covered a recently glaciated landscape. A series of bald granite steps made up the trail. Each time we lost the route, we dismounted and crawled on hands and knees, examining the bare rock at eye level, looking for the scratch marks of shod horses that had gone before us.

That evening, we camped beside a crystal clear lake. Snow-covered peaks rose steeply from the shoreline. Dense, verdant rain forest vegetation lay to the west, the dry mountains and huge stacked lenticular clouds of Argentina to the east.

This country felt wild, untouched, raw—exactly what my soul had been craving. Like others need food, shelter, and money, I need silence, open space, and the raw, clean, sometimes volatile elements of nature mixing randomly, the way they do in Patagonia. If landscape creates culture, if a tough, wet climate creates patience, if natural disasters create perseverance, and surviving in a harsh, windblown landscape creates good neighbors, it didn't surprise me that rural Patagonians seemed so solidly sane compared to the rest of the world.

The next day we passed the *Salto de Rio Perez,* a tremendous waterfall coming out of Lago Christy, and continued on through miles of blooming red *norto* trees. In the clear water of the Rio Perez, a showy black-and-white-stripped duck played in the waves. He caught an eddy, surfed the foam at its apex, efficiently ferried across the river and, with the finesse of an expert kayaker, caught another eddy and continued upstream. Impressive to watch, the *pato cortacorrientes,* or current-cutting duck, falls from its bankside nesting holes and begins running rapids.

The milky blue glacier water of the Rio Ventisquero was converging with the rapid clear water of the Rio Perez, leaving us traveling down a narrow peninsula. It was time to camp. At exactly the same moment, three people and three horses noticed an inviting patch of deep green grass the other side of the Perez, and without saying a word, crossed the river. We were headed for camp, food, and rest, but upon arriving at our haven, things went suddenly wrong.

Our pasture was not grassland but a *mallín,* a wet muddy swamp. Harry, Chucao, and Tamango had time to turn around, but Arraquien and I had plowed too far in before we realized the danger. My poor boy was thrashing, bucking for all he was worth, getting mired deeper and deeper into the muck. Normally I respond to emergencies in a cool, levelheaded manner. This time I freaked.

My high-pitched scream startled all of us. Panic pulsed through Arraquien and I, as if we were one animal. My voice rose to a screech. With Arraquien up to his belly in muck, I jumped in nearly to my own waist. I managed to undo his cinch and dump his saddle and saddlebags in the mud.

"*Arraquien! Mueva su poto.*" I yelled at him to move his ass. Shaking with fear, I slapped him violently on the rear. His only chance was to fight and fight hard.

Paul tugged on his lead rope from a drier patch of ground. I pounded on Arraquien's butt as hard as I could. We couldn't let him give up. I had heard of horses that had quit and died in this kind of situation.

This trip was proving to be every bit as treacherous as the locals had warned me about two years earlier. I was more than thankful for the help of my two friends. The people of Cochrane had been right. Alone on Nimbus, this would have been a crazy, foolish endeavor, maybe one we would not have come home from.

This was no time to descend into that ever deepening spiral that always ended in, "Why do I get myself in situations like this?" This was the moment to fight—hard.

Finally, Arraquien broke free of the muck and plowed headlong into the forest, where we all stood, wet, shaking, mud covered, and sweating. I wanted to cry. I wanted to quit for the day. I almost wanted to go home. But, there was nothing to do but put saddles back on and keep looking for a better camp.

Hours later we found it—horse heaven. Huge, widely spaced, nine-hundred-year-old *coihue* trees lifted their twisted trunks a hundred-and-fifty feet into the sky. The richest pasture we had seen in weeks grew in the diffused light beneath their curling branches. With profound pleasure I watched my boys bury their noses up to their halters in thick young clover. Dinner for us was three rainbow trout Harry had pulled from the river. That night, for the first time in days, our entire *tropé* was happy and well fed.

The night was remarkably clear and warm, a combination that rarely goes together in high latitudes. As I drifted into much-needed sleep, the Southern Cross peeked in my tent door. I tried to see an ostrich in its four bright stars, as the Tehuelche had when they named the constellation *ñandu* after the sixty pound flightless bird of the *pampas*. I saw a kite. Why hadn't I noticed the Southern Cross before? Had it been lost in the clouds, hidden by trees, or overlooked by the muddled, unobservant brain I had brought with me from town.

A lot of 599-foot hills can be missing from a map with 300-foot contour lines. Expecting a straightforward, wide open river valley, we found ourselves trapped in a confusing maze of small hills. The trail was marked as crossing the river at a canyon. This didn't make sense either. The water would be slower and shallower at a wide spot. I suspected that, once again, the map was wrong, but we rounded the corner to see a neatly constructed red-and-white *pasarela* spanning the canyon.

On the other side of the bridge, near a small paddock filled with angora goats, we lost the trail for what seemed like the hundredth time. There was a small *puesto* nearby, but no one was there to ask for directions. A swinging wooden gate, built so a person can open and close it on horseback, led out of the corral. The other possible exits were gates made of horizontal poles or barbed wire, both of which required dismounting to open and close. Extrapolating that the trail with the superior gate would be the main route, I pushed my conclusion on my companions.

We took off on a wide, well-brushed trail. Soon something seemed odd. The Rio Mayer had been flowing downstream on our left, we had just crossed it, and now it was flowing downstream on our right. That made sense and no one else felt anything disconcerting, so we kept going.

Our trail divided and divided again. Each time we chose the path most traveled. Years earlier, traveling with NOLS students, I had learned the first rule of travel in Patagonia. "If two paths divide in the woods, don't even think of being poetic, take the one most traveled by."

Nevertheless, we were soon ducking under branches, a sure sign that we were on a cow trail. A *poblador* on horseback would simply take out the huge knife, always tucked in the waistband of his pants, and slash the offending branch. Eventually, we came to a fence without a gate. We sat down, defeated, lost again.

Confused, I scrambled over the fence and climbed a small hill to get a view. On the other side of the rise I saw something too strange to believe, a red-and-white freshly painted swinging bridge. Where the hell were we? Could there really be two bridges? My confusion reminded me of reading the intensely vivid stories of Chilean author Isabel Allende. Had the Patagonia landscape created this distinct style of writing where places and things are never as they appear? Or, could magical realism actually have created Patagonia?

Lost in abstract thoughts, I sat silently on the hill, staring at the bridge. When my mind finally cleared itself of preconceived convictions, I understood. We had somehow come full circle. I was looking at the bridge we had just crossed. It took another several minutes to convince Paul and Harry. Two hours later, only a hundred meters past the bridge, we found a faint trail taking off unannounced, not to a paddock of angora goats, but to the town of O'Higgins.

All too soon, we were starting to lose the wilderness feel of the trip. There was something different about the first occupied dwelling we had seen since Don Rial's. Instead of hand-hewn wooden shingles, this house had a metal roof, a sure sign that this homestead was accessed from the O'Higgins side, and, at least during certain seasons of the year, an ox cart road. At the house, we stopped outside a swinging gate to ask directions. The first female I had seen since Cochrane walked briskly toward us, smiling and wiping her hands on a pink-and-white flowered apron.

Pointing toward a thin space between two trees just past the corral, she assured us the trail was good from there on. It began at the corral, then went downhill until crossing a stream, and then took off to the right.

"Is it easy to find?" I asked, unsure if I had gotten it right.

"*No problema,*" she said, laughing at the idea of getting lost.

"Have you lived here a long time?" I asked. I imagined that she had, of course, lived here her entire life, but I desperately wanted to continue talking to the only woman I had seen in weeks.

"This is where I was born, so this is where I live," she told me as if it could be no other way.

I had lived five places before I was ten years old. For me the place I was born was little more than a name on a map. Her concept of home, like her concept of time, was as foreign to me as mine was to her.

"Do you see many people passing through?" I asked, still wanting to talk.

"Oh, yes, I have seen other people, *sin pegamento,*" she said.

Sin pegamento, "without glue"? I didn't understand.

Then I got it. She had met others like myself. People who, for some unfathomable reason, did not have the glue to stick them in place.

Long before I was ready for the trip to end, we stepped out of the forest onto a freshly bulldozed mud track, another reminder that every year new roads were being built in previously roadless valleys. The opportunity to live this life that I loved would not last forever, even here.

A road construction crew was drinking *maté* and eating meat alongside the road.

"*Maté, amigos,*" the men shouted into the wind, inviting us to join them.

The thought of a little *maté*, some lamb, and a bit of conversation was appealing, but glancing at Paul and Harry I knew the answer.

"*No, gracias,*" I said.

We had miles to make. The once-a-week bus from O'Higgins was leaving in a couple days, and Paul and Harry needed to be on it. *Maté* in the forest would have to wait.

The next morning while we cooked breakfast only six kilometers outside of town, a bus passed us going north.

"There goes the weekly bus from O'Higgins," Paul joked.

"No, that can't be," I said. "The bus is definitely tomorrow, Right?"

"That's what they told me in Cochrane," Paul said.

The town of O'Higgins was a neat grid of orderly streets lined with small wooden houses leading to a newly landscaped plaza. Not wanting to become the focal point of the village, we parked the horses on the edge of town. Almost instantly, a man pulled over in an old truck to ask if we had anything to sell. Our expedition, rather than feeling like a huge accomplishment, looked and felt like a yard sale.

The bus that had passed us was indeed the only bus out of O'Higgins that week. Harry and Paul suddenly needed to hitchhike out of town on a road that saw about three cars a week. I was faced with being suddenly, if not surprisingly, at the end of the trail with more horses than I could easily move by myself. Harry wanted a convenient place in town for the night. I wanted a reasonable place to keep three horses for what could turn into quite a while.

The answer to all our dilemmas came in the form of a local official named Ramón. He knew someone driving north the next day and had a pasture to rent just outside of town. The next day Paul and Harry were on their way north, and I was in O'Higgins with three horses. Now what?

Once I was comfortably installed in Ramón's pasture, my energy lagged. I wanted nothing more than to lie around, read, and watch my horses eat. Was it much needed relaxation after a long trip or a lack of *ganas,* the enthusiasm for another solo? Handling one *pilchero* had been tough on sections of that trail. The thought of dragging three horses back over the pass by myself exhausted me.

One day, with nothing else to do, I took off with Chucao to explore the shores of Lago O'Higgins. In the morning, I passed a couple of men moving a large herd of goats.

Within a few hours the trail grew narrow and slippery. The jungle became denser and the trail more overgrown as we worked our way west. The lake narrowed. The ice field loomed closer. Somewhere, well ahead of me was the Rio Pascua, the outlet of Lago O'Higgins, a river so wild and remote it had never been run in its entirety. Only sixty-two kilometers long, the Rio Pascua drains nearly 15,000 square kilometers of wild country. Fewer than a hundred people had ever visited its banks. I wasn't going to be one of them, not today and not with a horse.

On my way back I heard the familiar call, "*Maté, amiga?*" coming from the forest. The men I had seen earlier were resting in the shade with their goats. I joined them, first for *maté*, then for a big chunk of roasted goat, and later a long nap.

How many places in the world was it the accepted custom for a woman traveling alone to stop, eat, drink, and fall happily asleep beside the trail alongside two men and a hundred goats?

The people of southern Patagonia had told me many times, "Don't worry, there are no bad people here." They could say that with confidence because everyone knew everyone in the valley. That was, until the road arrived.

Deep inside I knew I was living in a special time and place. I hoped somehow it would survive the coming years. But, change was already brewing. Unbeknownst to both me and the people of O'Higgins, someone thousands of miles away was making big plans for the Rio Pascua.

Chapter 7

La Vuelta (The Return)

OFFICIALLY, I HAD given up on the idea of getting to the southern tip of Patagonia a long time ago. Getting to somewhere in particular wasn't what my journey was about anymore. Still, I was having a hard time letting go of the idea of continuing south even though I had been told it was impossible. Sometimes in Chile the answer isn't "yes" until you have asked the right person.

The answer at the *Servicio Agricola y Ganadero* (the Department of Agriculture) was absolutely not. No one could take Chilean horses over the border into Argentina.

"Sell your horses here for *charqui* and buy new ones on the other side of the border," the woman at the desk recommended. With more horses in O'Higgins than people to work with them, excess animals were often sold for making dried meat or *charqui*.

I had no intention of selling my horses, especially for meat. Crossing the border illegally for a short time in a remote region was different than being a *gringa* conspicuously bound for the southern end of the continent. I had to face reality; the only direction I could go was north.

I looked into hiring a truck to take one horse north, but the cost of making a special trip for one horse was completely outside my reach. I dug deep, looking for answers to the question, what to do next.

Right before my trip with Harry and Paul, I had met a young NOLS instructor named Lindsey. "Oh, I would love to do that!" she had exclaimed when she found out I was headed to O'Higgins by horse.

How many times did I need to learn that when people said, "Oh, I would love to do that," they mean, "I would love to do that, if only circumstances were different. If I had more money, if the kids were older, if I was younger, et cetera."

Yet, occasionally there are those who live life to its fullest, taking advantage of every opportunity that comes their way. Lindsey seemed like one of those unique people. For one, she was living in Patagonia, an idea I had considered for years but never acted upon. I suspected she would be a good traveling companion. Why not give her a call?

Giving her a call meant multiple trips into town on horseback and resulted in hours of waiting in front of the town's only public telephone. I left numerous messages for Lindsey with mutual friends. Spending lonely frustrating hours on the steps of the telephone office, I longed for the fast paced efficiency of home.

One day, a happy, round-faced woman hollered over her white picket fence, "*Pasé a la casa, toma maté.*" I accepted, thrilled to have someone to talk to.

A healthy rotund two year old crawled on and off her lap while we talked. I could tell by the way the boy launched friendly, confident smiles my way that his life was full of love and approval. Sonya didn't seem much older than me, yet Gonzalo was not her son but her grandson. She and her husband had a *campo* twenty kilometers north of town. A little over a year ago the *carretera* had arrived at her doorstep.

"But it doesn't matter much to us. We still come to town on horseback," she explained.

Before I knew it I had agreed to spend Christmas with her family on the *campo*. As a single person far from my own family, the opportunity to spend the holiday in the country with new friends seemed like an incredible gift.

What had I been thinking? Christmas was only a little over a week away. I still had too many horses, no partner, and a huge list of things to do before heading north. All of that was irrelevant. I had said I would be there and no doubt they would be waiting for me.

I ARRIVED AT Sonya's *campo* mid-morning Christmas day.

Why hadn't I arrived the night before? Sonya wanted to know.

A bad cold had recently become laryngitis. Even if I had a voice, how could I begin to explain the crazy line up of events that week?

BACK IN O'HIGGINS, I had finally gotten ahold of Lindsey.

"My parents are visiting," she told me.

My heart sank. I had been foolish to think anyone, even Lindsey, could drop everything and take off across Chile on a horse.

"Can I come down in a week?" she asked.

"Absolutely," I answered.

A few days later, still camping in Ramón's pasture, I noticed I was one saddle short. My gear had been piled beside the road for over a week. Ramón and his wife had probably moved it into their barn so it wouldn't get wet. I walked over to their house. No, they had not moved my saddle. We couldn't imagine what had happened.

Eventually, we had to agree, it must have been stolen. Ramón apologized profusely. I felt awful as well. Most places in the world, to leave your saddle beside the road for a week would be considered stupid.

Word traveled fast. On my way into town a guy in a red truck rolled his window down. "Did someone really steal a saddle from you?" he asked.

"Yes, it's true," I had to admit.

"Oh, that is bad, very very bad," he said. "Now with the road anyone can come here. Everything is changing, it's awful."

Everyone seemed so apologetic. I didn't want to dwell on my misfortune. "Do you know anyone with a saddle for sale?" I asked the man.

"I know a family who just moved to town from the *campos*. They probably have a saddle they don't need." he said. "Look for a house being re-built right near the plaza."

Only a block from the plaza stood the skeleton of a gutted house, a blue tarp covered the kitchen area, and there around the woodstove lived the family in full view of passersby. What would it be like to live literally without walls? A glance from the road was all it took to get myself invited in. An older woman, obviously the wife and mother of the family, was thrilled to hear of my mission. Yes, her husband had a saddle. He would probably sell it, but I would need to talk to him.

I could read the hope on her face. If he would sell his saddle to this *gringa*, there would be money and food in the house again for a while.

"He will be back soon," she told me, passing the *maté* my way.

We talked about their building project.

"Oh, yes, it will definitely be done before winter," she assured me.

I hoped so for her sake. Five or six kids came and went. A beautiful young girl about twelve sat down beside me. The girl's long dark hair pulled back and tied with a neat pink ribbon that matched her shirt made me self-conscious about my own hair, unbrushed and unruly, blowing constantly into my eyes. Her dark eyes fixed on mine, but she was too shy to talk. What kind of life was lining up for her future? What did she want to know about mine?

Eventually, she asked in a soft, sweet voice, "Where are your children?"

I was tempted to lie. Traveling alone in other foreign countries, I sometimes lied about my husband at work and my children in school. It made things easier. But I never lied in Patagonia. Here if people didn't know you, they knew someone who did. Plus, a casual acquaintance might become a good friend.

"I don't have any children," I said.

Her dark eyes became even quieter as she tried to grasp the concept. She didn't have any other questions.

The father came home with the smell of alcohol on his breath. He wanted to talk about North American politics and flirt with me in front of his wife. I wanted to buy a saddle and get out of there as soon as possible. One of the young boys came to my rescue by bringing a well-worn saddle from a shed beside the house.

"How much?" I asked, knowing I would pay whatever he wanted.

"*Veinte-cinco mil,*" the man told me.

Fifty bucks wouldn't go far, and the family probably wouldn't see much of it, I thought as I put the bills in the man's outstretched hand. I wanted to hand the money to his wife, but there was no acceptable opening to do that.

The next morning, I was sick with a sore throat, and Arraquien was limping. Everyone had an opinion about what was wrong with my horse. His shoes were too tight. He had tendonitis. He hadn't been used enough. He had been used too much. He was too old. Some people thought it was his right front foot. I thought it was his left.

Arraquien had been used hard and then left standing in a pasture. My gut feeling was that he was stiff—as I'm sure I would be under the same circumstances. Still, I was hesitant to trust myself. Even with almost 700 kilometers behind me, I still believed that everyone in Chile, particularly those of the male gender, genetically knew more about horses than me. With a leap of faith in both Arraquien and myself, I decided to take off for Cochrane with a limping horse. Lindsey's bus was three hours late, but at least it arrived on the scheduled day, and we headed north.

Our plan was to take the *carretera*—which was basically devoid of automobile traffic this far south—to just past Sonya's and then go upstream along the Rio Bravo and join the same route I had come south on.

A couple of hours into our day, the tug on the *pilchero* rope slackened, and Arraquien's ears came forward. He was moving well. My sore throat on the other hand had turned into full-fledged laryngitis. On Christmas Eve, exhausted and ill, we had camped only a few kilometers short of Sonya's.

When we arrived, the fattest lamb of the year was splayed out over a fire in the barn. A metal spike stuck into the ground at an angle held the four appendages apart and suspended the entire sheep over the fire while it slowly roasted.

"*NO IMPORTA*, YOU are here now," Sonya said, reading my tired smile.

Even on Christmas there were chores to do. We took a walk on the *campo,* brought a cow in to be milked, collected some lettuce for dinner, and ran the chickens out of the orchard. Gonzalo toddled around with a furry four-month-old sheepdog on a string. We laughed as he stumbled around the orchard, unclear of who exactly had whom on a leash.

Lindsey and I helped prepare the salad, using lettuce from the greenhouse and the standard Chilean salad dressing of lemon and salt. Potatoes grown the summer before were thrown near the edges of the fire to bake.

When the lamb was cooked, we cut chunks off with our knives and ate it with our fingers. Letting the grease drip down our chins, we tossed the bones to the dogs. With a little red wine I became unbelievably sleepy. I hadn't spoken much all day. Talking was difficult and painful. I went to bed early, sweetly content with my Christmas day.

Long into the night, I heard Lindsey and the family playing *truco,* the traditional card game of the *campos.*

"*Envido,*" Lindsey called out.

She was winning points. Rumors exist of whole *campos* being lost in *truco* games of days gone by. Tonight, Lindsey and the family were keeping score with match sticks. I envied her easy banter with our new friends and fell asleep assured I that I had found a good traveling companion.

"*Levántate*, Nancy,"—Get yourself up—I heard Sonya call.

It was well past ten and most of the morning chores were finished. I had asked Sonya to wake us in the morning, but the day was blustery and raining lightly, so she had let us sleep. Lindsey and I debated staying another day, but our theory was that if we didn't travel on at least *medio feo* days, we wouldn't get far in this country.

To my surprise the horses took off at a spontaneous trot. It was fun clipping along the deserted *carretera,* but as usual I was ready to get off the road. We climbed steadily. As we gained altitude, the weather became truly *feo.* We were looking for a trail that led up the Rio Bravo. We topped a hill that looked down at the river and wind pelted painful hailstones in our faces.

Something was wrong, the vegetation beside the road was getting thicker and the drop into the Bravo more precipitous. Huddled behind the horses, their butts to the wind, Lindsey and I let them take the brunt of the storm while we attempted to open the map. Sonya had described the trail as leaving from a small house. It had been I who had assumed that the house was on the right side of the road. Several kilometers back with our faces buried in our hoods we had passed a small house on our left.

We trudged back the way we had come. At least the wind was now at our backs. Giving up on finding the trail, we just wanted to camp.

We encountered nowhere suitable until we were back at the tiny house. The place looked abandoned, but that didn't mean no one lived there. It just meant no one lived there right now. I felt horrible about moving into their tiny piece of grass with three horses, but that is exactly what we did. I felt even worse to be glad that there was no one home to ask permission. My throat was getting worse, and I spoke, even to Lindsey, only when absolutely necessary. It was crazy to be out in this kind of weather. We camped right behind the house, the only windbreak available. I prayed that if the family came home that night they would be more understanding about finding two people and three horses camped behind their house than I imagined people in my country would be. How would I react to finding strangers camped in my yard? With grace and hospitality, I hoped.

The next morning we found a small muddy path exactly across the road from the house. Could this really be the trail? Humbled again by what it took to live in this country, we headed down the slippery path, saddlebags dragging through the wet vegetation on both sides of the trail. We lost our way only once that day and arrived late at *La Chirola,* the *campo* of my *gringo* friends, Andy and Molly.

The place was horse heaven. Flat valley bottom land that had not been recently grazed sported knee-high grass. A three-room house made of hand-hewn planks, a covered front porch perfect for cooking, and a note from Andy and Molly welcomed us.

We had missed them by two weeks. They had returned to their lives in Wyoming. Still, it felt wonderful to move into a place where we were, for once, expected guests.

Looking up at tumbling glaciers from the porch, I immediately slipped into my favorite fantasy, imagining myself living on a remote *campo* in Southern Patagonia. Did my fantasy include that the house desperately needed a new roof, the orchard was long overgrown, and a woodstove would have to be brought along that narrow, muddy trail on the back of another long-suffering *pilchero?*

Molly and Andy had all the typical problems of absentee landowners. There were animals grazing their land that were not theirs, and one of the neighbors had let a fire rage out of control scarring much of their land. That wound was fresh and painful for Molly and Andy. Their note let us know that they were looking to hire a *cuidador.* Did we know anyone who would watch their place? What would it be like to insert myself here, to watch the sun slide over the mountains each day, letting the seasons change around me?

My dream world came crashing to an end when I realized that three-hundred-and-sixty-some days a year I would be alone—alone in paradise—but alone all the same. Single women did not run *campos* in the middle of nowhere by themselves.

Even if I couldn't stay forever, lying in the orchard, watching my animals graze, I felt a sweet pulse of happiness rushing though my body. I sipped chamomile tea in the sun, and my throat began to relax.

Leaving *La Chirola* was not easy, and we didn't accomplish it until late afternoon the next day. From there the trail climbed steeply. The map showed it running along the valley bottom, but it was hard to have faith in a map on which an entire glacier was also missing. The trail seemed to have direction, and we seldom had to duck under branches, two things that helped distinguish it from a cow trail, so we stayed on it. Eventually it neatly completed the loop back to the trail Paul, Harry, and I had taken south. Another twenty kilometers or so and we would be at Don Rial's.

Smoke was curling from his *puesto* when we rounded the corner. We decided to drop our camp a little ways away so our animals didn't eat all the grass near his house.

Photograph by Fredrik Norrsell.

Don Rial sharpening an ax.

Don Rial met us at the gate, asking why we hadn't put our saddles in his shed.

"*No quiero molestar te,*" Lindsey explained.

"You don't bother me. You entertain me," he answered honestly.

Don Rial placed a steaming bowl of soup before us and explained, "When you visit my house I maintain you, when I visit your house you maintain me."

My *gringa* brain could not get over the fact that he would never visit me in Alaska, but who you returned the favor to, of course, did not matter.

My voice was improving but Lindsey spoke better Spanish than I did. I enjoyed, for once, not bearing the responsibility of communication. At times I lazily let the conversation drift by me.

The next day Don Rial showed up at our camp just as we were finishing packing. He needed to look for some cows at the far end of his *campo* and wanted to ride north with us. His horse fully saddled, he leaned against a tree, smoking a cigarette while we saddled three horses and loaded Chucao as *pilchero*.

Our *pilchero* system was a cobbled together mixture of Western, Chilean, and my own invention. An old backpack without the stays was loaded as evenly at both ends as possible and tossed over the wood and metal tree of a Chilean saddle and tied down with a Wyoming style diamond hitch.

Keenly aware of Don Rial's expert eyes watching every move, Lindsey and I worked as a well-honed team, she on one side of the horse passing ropes and cinches, me on the other tightening the load. I had experienced *gauchos* plenty of times stepping in unbidden to rearrange my *pilchero* load. I was sure Don Rial would do the same once we were finished.

As I prepared to grab Chucao's lead rope and swing my leg up over Tamango's saddle, Don Rial snuffed his cigarette butt out on a tree stump, said, "*Bien campesina*," and mounted his horse. I turned away beaming. We had just been judged competent country women by one of the best. His simple acknowledgment stood in my mind as one of the highest compliments I had ever known.

Traveling with Don Rial, we moved quickly. When he left us, there was a *puesto* only a couple of hours ahead. He assured us that we could make it over the pass from there in one day.

The *puesto* was perfect, a shelter for a fire and plenty of good grass. It was Lindsey's birthday and a celebration was in order. We took a much needed and invigorating dip in the lake. To the east a spectacular cloudscape of overgrown thunderclouds sent anvil tails sweeping downwind, turning first pink, then deep magenta. I suggested that we follow my own birthday tradition and go for a gallop.

Not wanting to bother with saddles, we took off bareback. It was Lindsey's first time. One of the things I admired about her was her way of embracing the unknown. How much richer would all of our lives be with her attitude? Start every year, maybe every day, with something new!

Chucao and Arraquien seemed to enjoy the romp as much as we did. After a month on the trail, my horses thundered across the wide open *pampas* with an energy I never imagined. A rollicking game of chase ensued. Chucao was coming into himself. Finally confident enough to play with the big boys, he spun quickly on his hindquarters, and we charged off chasing Lindsey and Arraquien.

At the *puesto* we set them free to graze. We were relaxed these days about tying horses. My boys hadn't tried to desert me in weeks. We were becoming a real *tropé*.

Looking up, I saw Chucao and Arraquien side by side heading north and walking with intent. Could they possible know which way was home from here? Apparently so, I thought, as they picked up the pace. They wouldn't cross the river without me, would they? Now was no time to find out. Barefoot and in shorts I jumped on Tamango bareback. Chucao and Arraquien were trotting now and glancing back at me as they left. Yep, those two would definitely cross the river. Would they go all the way back to Cochrane without us? Not if I could stop them.

I gave Tamango a good solid squeeze. We took off at a gallop. We circled wide. I didn't want to appear to be in direct pursuit. Both of them could outrun Tamango on the short haul. I needed to cut them off at the river.

We got to the river first. The two escapees peeled back toward the open valley. A scene from an old Western movie flashed through my mind as we wheeled around, got ahead of them again, and cut off progress in that direction, as well.

I had no idea Tamango could move like that. Somewhere in his past he had learned this game well. My big steady plodder turned first on his hindquarters and then on his front as we worked the two runaways into a corner by the rocks.

"Okay, my sweet boys, game over," I said.

Just a regular part of living with horses, I no longer took these games personally. Lindsey laughed out loud at my Wild West show, and we promptly tied up our horses.

The next day was over-the-pass day, and I wasn't looking forward to it. I longed for an uneventful day with nothing to report in my journal. Something told me I was not going to get it.

We woke early and got moving, but the weather was moving as well. Rain clouds were building over the passes to the west. I had been dreading revisiting the *picota* since crossing it the first time. What if the descent into the canyon was slippery? What would we do if the water was even higher this time?

So far none of the obstacles we encountered on the return trip had been as tough as I remembered. I prayed that trend would hold true for *la picota.*

It started to sprinkle right as we got to the canyon. Damn it! I tried to control my fear. Just breathe deep and keep going, I told myself.

I stopped again at the little wooden shrine nailed to a tree and left a few pesos. The river at the bottom looked gray and ugly, way worse than it had been the last time. I wanted to check the crossing on foot before dragging the horses all the way down there. Lindsey readily agreed, and we tied the horses mid-slope to the few tiny bushes available.

Using a big stick to form an upstream-facing tripod, I stepped in the icy river. Each time I got a couple steps in, the current threatened to take me for an icy swim, and I stepped back to shore. I asked Lindsey to belay me with Tamango's lead rope. The horses stood huddled a hundred feet up, watching, unmoving. Were they as scared as we were?

The third time, I got in nearly to my waist and my feet were swept out from under me. The rope I held tightly in my hand caught me. Saved from being swept downstream, I rode the pendulum back to the bank, cold, wet, and scared, but with a decision made.

We had no idea what to do next, but this time my partner and I were in complete agreement about what not to do. We were not going to cross that river. Chucao and Arraquien had already cast their vote by pulling free of their tenuous tie downs and heading back to the top of the hill. Tamango felt differently. The stubborn boy refused to re-climb the hill. "Home is that way, you stupid wimps," he appeared to be telling us.

"You stubborn pig, just defer to my judgment this once will you?" I said as I dragged a thousand pounds of balking horse back to the top of the hill. Lindsey and I huddled in the rain.

"Don Rial mentioned something about another trail somewhere to the left," Lindsey said.

"Really?" I asked, searching my brain for how I could have missed such an important piece of information. Just last month, Paul and Harry and I had spent a good chunk of time looking for another trail. Was my Spanish really that bad? Or, had I been so sure I had already looked for every possible option that I had mentally jettisoned vital information?

I volunteered to scout for another crossing, while Lindsey horse-sat at the top of the precipice. I left without much hope of finding anything, but it was a way to keep warm while thinking.

Spotting a cairn on the left, I figured I had found something. "I will be back in a few minutes," I hollered. Each step the route got more and more improbable, and left Lindsey sitting longer in the cold. The last section resembled fourth-class rock climbing. Could I take a willing horse down this? Maybe. An unwilling one, impossible. A steep four-foot drop into the river answered my final question, no horse in its right mind would be willing to make that move. I headed back to Lindsey.

"I want to check something a mile or so behind us on our left," she told me.

"A trail in that direction would have to climb up over that cliff," I said, looking up at a five-hundred-foot wall entirely lining the valley. But, I didn't have a better idea. With no grass, and nowhere to tie horses, camping here would be impossible.

I sat quietly in the drizzle and tried to imagine the end of this day, in fact the end of this year. It was December thirty-first. Every time the thought of a seriously injured horse entered my mind, I kicked it out. Forever seemed to go by. Cold slipped deep into my muscles and water trickled down the back of my neck. I scrunched my shoulders together, and a familiar pre-hypothermia shiver began. At last, I heard a yell from well up valley.

"Lindsey!" I hollered.

No reply.

Had that sound been happy? Had she sounded hurt? I couldn't tell. I got up and got moving in her direction.

Moments later Lindsey came jogging down the trail.

"There is a trail up there," she said, smiling. "A real trail, cut by human hands."

"Wow, amazing," I said, trying to hide my embarrassment at not believing it could be true.

Diagonal cuts in the brush made by a machete let us know this was no cow trail. This was deliverance! Steep, narrow, and over grown, the trail was also no sidewalk. But without mortal danger it felt like heaven.

Tamango slipped once climbing a steep rocky face, and Lindsey nearly got pinched between two boulders, but progress was being made. I could feel Chucao's hind legs trembling. Was he tired, cold, scared, or a combination of all three?

Finally, we descended the last drop. The same river that had been ferociously gushing through the canyon up stream was wide, braided, and easy to cross. Waves of anxiety that had been pent up for weeks left me with nothing except deep love for my good, hungry, brave, patient horses and a desire to get them to good grass.

Fat grass was not far away, and Lindsey and I managed to fall fast asleep well before midnight on New Year's Eve.

In the morning I went to check on my boys. Arraquien was laying down enjoying a spot of sun. He made no attempt to move when I approached so I curled up next to him and lay my head on his silky belly. Breathing deep, I sucked in the sweet horsy smell of him as I watched the morning light unfurl.

Things that had been so difficult on the outward-bound leg of the trip went so easily now. We were a team. We knew each other's idiosyncrasies, our strong points, and our foibles. Tough sections of trail went nearly unnoticed.

All too soon, Lindsey and I were on a gravel road passing through a pine plantation that I had now traveled through multiple times. Already I longed for wide open spaces and the mental attention that route finding requires. I loved the constant rocking rhythm of horse travel, and I knew I wasn't done yet.

Cachaña (Austral Parakeet)

Chunco (Austral Pigmy Owl)

Guanacos

Bandurria (Buff-necked Ibis)

Chucao Tapaculo

Andean Condor

Huemul (South Andean Deer)

Chilco (Fuchsia)

Calafate berry

Huet-Huet

Chaura berry

Pato cortacorrientes (Torrent Duck)

Photographs by Fredrik Norrsell

Chapter 8

Estancia Valle Chacabuco (The Regions Largest Sheep Ranch)

SAMUEL'S *PUESTO* HAD a strange time warp feeling. As if I had never left, I could clearly see Harry, Paul, and I spreading out our odd conglomeration of mismatched maps under the lone cherry tree, trying to piece together a route to O'Higgins. Yet, branches that had been in full bloom in November, now hung heavy with ripe cherries. These rosy yellow cherries, called Heart of the Dove, were proof that time had not stood still. As if there could never be enough, I crammed two or three at a time into my mouth. It was my first taste of fresh fruit in months.

While the past was amazingly vivid, the future was fuzzy and unknown. Lindsey had returned to Coyhaique, and Sam was out of town. I wanted to continue riding, to go north, to travel the wide open grasslands between here and Chile Chico. I needed a plan. I needed horseshoes, food, maps; mostly I needed the *ganas* to keep going alone. That would come with a couple days' rest, I assured myself. With nothing better to do, I climbed high in the cherry tree and stayed there until the sun sank low over the hills and my belly ached from so much goodness.

Friends, neighbors, and the man at the bank all invited me to endless *asados* and *maté* sessions. My list of social obligations grew large enough to stop all progress in a northerly direction. Still, in that lovely Chilean way, everything—talking with Don Leonitis Ascencio about horseshoes, Tamango getting restless and jumping the fence, trying to get ahold of someone in Chile Chico about putting horses on the ferry—was all part of the process. The seamlessness between work and play that comes naturally with farm life was new to me. Whether literally or figuratively, I come from generations of punching a time clock.

I looked, asked, and called around for a truck to take one of my horses north. It was a bit un-*gaucho*, but I didn't want or need the challenge of dragging along an extra horse.

Eventually I found someone who could take my horse to Coyhaique, but the price would be affordable only if I waited until he had a full truck load of animals.

"When would that be?" I asked.

"Soon, maybe one week," he responded.

"Absolutely less than three weeks?" I asked, knowing full well how things worked.

"Absolutely," he replied.

The important thing was that Chucao would arrive at my friends' farm in Coyhaique before I did. I decided to leave my smallest, youngest, and least experienced horse. I would miss him.

A couple of days later, I rode out of town with Arraquien, Tamango, and the truck driver's word that he would bring Chucao first chance he got. Not far outside Cochrane, Arraquien began to limp. What was this, some kind of joke? Hadn't this exact thing happened before? By the time we got to the Reserva Tamango, where I planned to camp, it didn't appear to be a joke.

"Tu caballo tiene una problema," were the words the ranger used to greet me.

I knew my horse had a problem, but I was embarrassed to hear it from him. This was a man whose opinion I respected. I had met him briefly a couple years earlier. These days he worked at Reserva Tamango, studying the endangered *huemul.* With nothing I could do about Arraquien's problem at the moment, I set up camp with the resolution I would take him back to Cochrane if he was still limping the next day.

That evening the rangers invited me to dinner in their cabin. A hundred-and-twenty *huemules*—about ten percent of the world's population—lived in the Tamango and Chacabuco area. And these two men knew each of them as individuals.

"They all have a name or at least a number. The females are the most important for keeping the population going. We watch them the closest."

If one-hundred-and-twenty animals were ten percent of the world's population, there weren't many *huemules* left, I thought.

"Pumas occasionally kill *huemules*, but it's habitat loss, hunters, and domestic dogs that have brought the *huemul* to the brink of extinction," a young female volunteer from North America told me.

I was curious about her, but we continued to talk about the *huemul* in Spanish. To do otherwise would have been rude.

Slowly, due to nature reserves like Tamango, the deer were beginning to show signs of recovery in Aysen. The *huemul* stands opposite the Andean condor on the national shield of Chile. The survival of both these species is a matter of national pride.

After dinner, as we rambled through the woods, commenting on every woodpecker hole and animal track, I rediscovered the joy of sharing something I didn't know I had been missing, a mutual love for *la natualeza*. Wandering in the woods with naturalists, who took delight in each living thing, was different than walking in the fields with farmers, who saw the land primarily for what it could produce. It was midnight before I left their easy companionship and went to my tent.

In the morning, I woke early. Not wanting to bother anyone, I made coffee and breakfast in my tent. When I showed up at the cabin all packed up to go, my new friends had breakfast waiting for me.

"Sorry, I didn't want to bother you," I said.

"The people, they do not like it when the people are separate," my ranger friend told me.

How many times did I need to learn how to accept Chilean hospitality? What was it about my cultural upbringing that led me to believe that I was always a bother? Did people where I come from desire to be always separate?

I longed to wander off in search of *huemules* with my newfound friends, but it was late in the summer and the deer would be well above timberline on the northern aspects. It would be a full day's hike to find them. Arraquien was still moving stiffly. I would have to take him back to Cochrane. What if the truck took Chucao to Coyhaique in the next day or two? I worried. Obviously, Patagonia's sense of endless time had not yet sunk in.

I returned to town with an impatience and frustration that didn't fit the place, my neighbors, or even myself very well. By noon I had left Arraquien behind and was back on the trail headed north with Chucao in tow.

Arraquien, of all my horses, would suffer the most from being left alone. Chucao constantly lagged and tugged on the lead rope. Thoughts of dragging a reluctant *pilchero* all the way to Coyhaique put me in a deep funk. I ambled along cursing my fate. As I passed the now empty ranger's cabin, I wished for the twentieth time that I was out counting *huemules*.

Even traveling on a good trail through mature *lenga* forest couldn't break my mood. The gap between the way things were and how I wanted them to be haunted me throughout the day. Any Patagonian would have given two seconds' thought to the fact that they had to leave their best horse behind and then, grateful that they had another horse, simply accepted things as they were. After months on the trail, I was a still an apprentice.

In barely perceptible ways the country began to change. Glimpses of vistas reminding me of the Big Sky Country of Montana appeared through holes in the forest. A skyscape of stacked lenticular clouds hung as if levitated over the mountains far to the east. A fancy white orchid, its petals laced with green veins, shot up beside the trail on a tall stalk with large grass-like leaves. The *pico de loro* (beak of the parrot) was an indigenous flower of the *pampas*, the wide open landscape about to embrace me.

As the country broke open, so did my mood. I imagined myself racing though this open hilly country at a full gallop, blonde hair whipping behind me, saddlebags flying. Instead, I settled for a good fast walk and an occasional trot. The horses seemed to feel the exhilaration of space as well. It was the fastest we had traveled in days.

All trails eventually funneled together and deposited me in the backyard of the headquarters of Estancia Valle Chacabuco, the third largest sheep ranch in Chile. Tidy white houses with green trim and well-maintained lawns lined a new gravel road. The place felt orderly, rigid, and controlled, a bit too much like the British countryside for Patagonia. In contrast to the friendly family farms I usually passed through, I felt awkward here. There was no one around to either stop me or welcome me. Marching my ungainly parade through the neatly kept grounds felt like an intrusion. I had no other option; my only exit was in front of me.

Between 1930 and 1970, the eastern half of Patagonia had gone from being the home of *guanacos*—a wild cousin of the llama—to pasture for sixteen million sheep. Now a hundred dusty sheep waited in a corral outside a long wooden sheering barn. Between overgrazing and the relentless Patagonia winds, the sheep waiting to be shorn were so covered in the topsoil of the region that they appeared brown.

I could hear men shouting over an electric buzzing sound. Inside the barn at least a dozen men were working. *Agarradores* grabbed sheep and tied their feet together. *Esquiladores* did the shearing. *Playeros* cleaned the wool from the floor, and *velloneros* tightly packed the wool into huge bags. Outside, the grounds were deserted.

It wasn't apparent by the spotless buildings or tidy green lawns, but times were changing in Patagonia. Established in the early 1900s, this ranch had, in its heyday, grazed over 85,000 sheep on 500,000 acres, but falling wool prices and the desertification brought on by overgrazing were taking a toll. By the mid-1990s wool prices had hit a record low of thirty cents a pound. On the day I passed through, Estancia Valle Chacabuco grazed only 25,000 sheep.

Unbeknownst to me, an even bigger change was looming just below the horizon. Two unique circumstances were converging—the surge of money behind a boom in the manufacturing of outdoor clothing and equipment in the United States and a wave of philanthropy, the desire to give back to the places that inspire us. Unable to see into the future, I never imagined the trim lawns and shearing barns of Estancia Valle Chacabuco as headquarters for the regions' largest national park. This land had been on the Chilean Park Services' national priority list for more than thirty years, but it would take outside money to make it happen.

Within the next four years, this 174,000-acre Estancia would be purchased by Conservacion Patagonica, a private land trust set up for the conservation of biodiversity. Someday, behind the willow trees along the creek, will stand a modern visitor center powered by the sun.

Over the next decade, Conservacion Patagonica's president Kris Tompkins, formerly of the Patagonia clothing company, along with her husband, Douglas Tompkins, founder of North Face and Esprit and his partner organization Conservation Land Trust, would work to protect over three million acres of prime habitat in Chile and Argentina.

Passing through the Estancia unnoticed, I turned east, down what would turn out to be a long, fence-lined dirt road. Over the next decade the new landowners would remove over four hundred miles of the fence line that now separated me, if only by a wire, from that open space I so craved.

Not far beyond the Estancia headquarters, a band of *guanacos* surprised me. A male, a dozen females, and their young stood highlighted on the crest of a hill. I could not tell the male from the others by size or shape, but it was obvious who was in charge. When he noticed my presence he sprinted to the highest rock, stopped in plain view, and yammered at me. His loud trilling voice was otherworldly, but his message was clear. I was an invader. He posed for my camera, backlit by a stack of purple lenticular clouds.

This tactic of stopping where he could get a good view of his enemy served his species well for avoiding pumas, but it made him an easy target for men with guns. Fifty million *guanacos* once inhabited the arid areas of Chile and Argentina as far north as the west coast of Peru. As early as the 1800s, the trade in baby *guanaco* hides was decimating the population. Only one in ten *chulengos* (young *guanacos*) managed to evade hunters who pursued them on horseback, throwing heavy stone balls linked together with rope between their running hooves. Like the Techuelche themselves, only a small percentage of the original *guanaco* population survived the 1800s.

By evening, I found it hard to believe that *guanacos* were considered vulnerable. I had seen hundreds of them. Elegant and endangered black-necked swans swam in Laguna Cisnes (Swan Lagoon). Flocks of pink flamingos rested along the shores of other shallow lakes. A couple of condors, a fox, and a skunk added up to constitute by far the biggest wildlife day I had ever had in Patagonia. After a hundred years of heavy use by humans, this area still included at least a representative sample of all of its original inhabitants. I was starting to realize that in a land of special landscapes, this one was extremely precious.

That night a swamp separated me from the river and made getting drinking water a chore. The reality of traveling alone with two horses was sinking in. It would be me who saddled and unsaddled every horse, set up every camp, cooked every meal, washed every dish, and in this land of poor grass, moved the horses several times every night. On top of that, Chucao needed a new pair of front shoes, and I hadn't seen a house since the Estancia.

A few kilometers ahead was the only structure marked on my map, a place called Casa Piedra. The beautiful old stone house sat back in the *alamos* just the other side of the Rio Chacabuco. A saddled horse was tied in the yard, a sure sign of people nearby, but I saw no one. The river between us was running deep, swift, and brown. I contemplated crossing. The water was so laden with muddy silt I couldn't tell how deep it was. Imagining it to be well over belly deep on Chucao, I decided against it and moved on.

Little did I know that the Casa Piedra would reappear in my future. Nearly ten years later, I would sleep in the stone house, track radio-collared pumas, and help remove pine plantations as a volunteer for Conservacion Patagonica.

Late the next day, I saw a gate, a corral, and from deep in the brush off the road, smoke rising from a stack. What luck, two men were in the yard shoeing a horse. I rode in and, breaking tradition, asked immediately if they could shoe my horse.

They urged me to unsaddle and take a rest.

I was quickly ushered into their small plywood house to drink coffee by the woodstove. One of the men looked familiar. He wore a blue ball cap with yellow letters that said, "Maipo," the name of a canyon near Santiago. I had recently seen that hat, but where? My mind frantically ticked backward.

"Up river, when I bought this horse?" I asked him.

He broke into a wide grin. "Yes, I am Luis. I know you and your horse as well."

He had been at the *asado* that night with Don Ascencio in the Colonia Valley.

It was assumed that I would stay for dinner. It impressed me that every man in the countryside knew how to make bread, a skill that I had managed to get well into my forties without learning. Single men usually made *sopaipillas*, a simple, delicious deep fried bread made with baking soda. If home-baked yeast bread was in the house, it usually meant a woman was in residence. However, Luis pulled fresh yeast-raised bread and roasted lamb from the oven.

The sun had slipped below the horizon, but on this mid-summer evening it would be hours before soft blue twilight melted into darkness around ten o'clock. It was obvious I was going nowhere. There were stories to tell.

Over dinner I picked up critical information about the next day's travel. The trail did not go anywhere near where it was shown on the map. I would need to cross the river much earlier than expected and look for a fence with a gate. From there I would head up the Valle La Leona (Valley of the Lion).

"Are there still pumas in the valley?" I asked Luis.

"*Oh, si,*" he said.

The other man got up and proudly produced a fresh puma skin and skull from the back room. The golden blonde coat was soft and inviting to touch, but the hardened skull held a haunting expression deep in its hollow eye sockets.

"I killed it this September," he said.

"How many pumas have you seen in your life?" I asked, trying to cover up my horror at seeing a wild animal that I had never seen alive presented in the form of skin and skull.

"I don't know for sure, but I killed them all," he assured me.

"How many sheep do they kill a year?" I asked, trying to understand his motives.

"*Oh, various,*" he replied, his eyes wide open.

I thought pumas were protected in Chile, but I wasn't sure. I doubted it would matter.

"Aren't you afraid to camp near pumas?" Luis asked.

"Have you ever actually heard of anyone killed by a puma?" I asked in return.

Neither of the men could name anyone, but like the wolf in the western United States the cougar still held a reputation as a vicious killer. *Leoneros* were men employed by the Estancia with the specific job description of tracking and killing pumas. In the early days of sheep ranching, a man could get twenty days' pay for slaughtering a puma.

I assumed that nothing except a new generation could change things here. I was wrong. Within a few years this would be Conservacion Patagonica land. Former puma hunters would make use of their tracking skills as rangers protecting the animals they once hunted. Years later, I would hear a former *leonero* exclaim, "Paid to kill pumas, paid to protect pumas, paid all the same."

The next day, I found the trail easily, a wide, smooth path ascending above a deep gorge. Big mountains and a bigger sky dominated the landscape. To the east, one last stunning mountain, Mount Lucas Bridges, towered skyward before the Argentinean *pampas* stretched out flat all the way to the Atlantic Ocean.

One morning, sixty some years earlier, Lucas Bridges, one of the first *estancia* managers and the man charged with opening the rich Baker Valley to ranching, headed for the top of this mountain. He lit a fire on top to prove he made it. But that is not his story.

Lucas Bridges was the third European child born in Tierra Del Fuego. However, history doesn't start there.

In 1830, Captain Robert Fitzroy returned to England from Tierra del Fuego with four Patagonian natives. His plan was to "Civilize and Christianize" these children of Patagonia and through them spread the gospel in the land of fire.

Two years later, the second voyage of *The Beagle* set sail with Captain Fitzroy, the three Patagonians who had survived their time in England, and the young naturalist Charles Darwin. The plan was to return the young converts to Patagonia along with a missionary keeper and evangelize the natives. Only a few weeks later, the first missionary in Patagonia was found hiding from his potential converts, and the young Patagonians had been left to return to their former lives as best they could.

It seemed the natives were not taking kindly to being saved. Thirty years later, when Reverend George Pakinham Despard—the third missionary to attempt to settle this windy place—departed in despair, one person was left standing on the shore. Reverend Despard's then nineteen-year-old adopted son Thomas Bridges, the first permanent settler in Patagonia and the man who would become Lucas Bridges' father, had decided to stay.

Lucas Bridges, like his father Thomas, learned to speak the native languages. The last twenty-five years of his fascinating life were spent as operations manager of this tremendous piece of land at the head of the Baker River.

The *estancia*'s initial contract with the Chilean Government specified that "land access through Chile must be provided for materials and goods." The result was the Sendero de Lucas Bridges, a famous trail which bridged glacial rivers and etched its way across two thirds of a kilometer of vertical cliff, linking the navigable part of the Baker River to the rich Colonia Valley. Pack trains of a hundred animals, each loaded with fifty-kilo bundles of wool marched over this treacherous trail only a few times before the route was abandoned in favor of an easier, more profitable route through Argentina.

Photograph by Fredrik Norrsell.

The most rugged and dangerous part of the Sendero de Lucas Bridges, a 645 meter cut through a vertical cliff connects the rich upper Baker River Valley to navigable waters below.

The Chacabuco Valley had never been forested or burned. Grassland was the natural state of the open steppe. At the far end of this gigantic valley, near the Tamango Reserve, I had marched out of the *lenga* forest into the open sky. Soon, I would be back in the safety and comfort of mature *lenga* forest.

What I didn't understand at the time was that this land would be purchased with the intent of linking the Tamango Reserve to the south and Jeinemeni Reserve to the north in order to create a 722,000-acre national park. With a new national park the size of Yosemite, a bridge for two, now separate, populations of *huemul* was also in the making.

The next afternoon was hot and calm. Thankfully we traveled in the shade of mighty *lenga* trees. Just over the pass we got our first introduction to what was to become the bane of our existence. *Tabanos,* a gigantic version of the horsefly, swarmed around us, taking huge chunks of flesh from any unprotected spot.

Tired of dragging Chucao, I decided to ride him and use Tamango as *pilchero*. Tamango knew the drill and simply followed along without the rope. I was congratulating myself for figuring this system out when we came across a dried-up lake. Tamango suddenly dropped to his knees. A dust bath was just what he needed to rid himself, if only temporarily, of those horrid, biting *tabanos*. He lowered himself to the dirt, and before I could turn around and gallop back yelling and waving, he was fully over onto his back, rolling on our gear.

As I hammered smashed cooking pots back into a usable shape, I remembered a man I had seen at a trailhead. He had gently lifted two cardboard boxes from his *pilchero*, and unwrapped a hundred eggs, each carefully nestled in a piece of newspaper, not one of them broken.

Just in time, Lago Jeinemeni, clean, blue, and sparkling in the hot afternoon sun, came into view. Saddles stripped, the three of us waded into the cool, sweet water.

Coming out of the mountains and dropping into the desert, I saw the first people I had seen in days. Two English tourists sat beside the road, the woman waving so frantically, I thought she was hurt.

"Lorry!" she hollered.

In the distance, a truck was approaching. I wondered if she was going to throw herself in front of the truck in her desperation to get out of there.

"Don't worry," I said. "They will stop."

And they did. Torrie the "lorry" driver offered them a ride on top of his load of firewood.

"There is a nice place to camp with water and grass just ahead," he told me. "Some workers are building a *puesto,* just stop by."

I was delighted to hear it. I was afraid I had passed the last green grass and water for a long, long way.

The *puesto* José and Francisco were building was made of adobe. Trees are rare here. Dirt is abundant. Adobe is cool in summer and warm in winter, and it doesn't rain enough in a hundred years to erode the bricks.

The men were scavenging bricks from an old, tumbled-down *puesto* nearby. "When these run out we will begin to make more," José explained.

When I asked him how they moved the bricks, he replied, "*A mano, poco a poco.*"

Little by little they were bringing them over by hand and mixing a cement of mud, cow dung, and grass to hold it all together. Francisco pointed to the fence around the outhouse. "That is so the cows don't eat the outhouse in winter." I tried to imagine this land in winter, a land so sparse that adobe looked like good fodder.

This was serious desert country, a scary, intimidating kind of hot that I was not accustomed to. As an Alaskan I had spent most of my life learning to keep myself warm. The wind sucked moisture from my body. One day, I huddled in the shade of a *calafate* bush, afraid to move until nearly sunset.

In the last chapter of *Voyage of the Beagle*, Darwin describes the plains of Patagonia using only negative statements. "Without habitations, without water, without trees, without mountains," But, he goes on to ask, "Why then . . . have these arid wastes taken so firm a hold on my memory?"

At night and preferably mid-day, as well, I needed to find an oasis. One afternoon tall *alamo* trees surrounded an area of green grass, wild mint, and rhubarb growing beside a spring. I threw off saddles, feeling I had arrived in heaven.

Seconds later, hell, in the form of millions of minute biting terrorists called *pulcos,* arrived. For the next hour or so I kept moving in circles, swatting myself as I bounced from one tiny patch of shade to another, while my horses ate.

Suddenly, Tamango looked up from grazing and walked away. He was full, or the bugs were now worse than his hunger. So, he left. Not down the road from where we had come, but up toward the mountains, looking for a breeze. Without a water bottle I headed after him, unsure of how long I would last. I pleaded with him not to take me on a long hike. Fortunately, he stopped, looked over his shoulder, and waited for me. He just wanted to let me know it was time to leave this bug-infested place.

Walking a dusty dirt road through what looked like Wyoming but felt like Texas, was like living inside a blow dryer. We camped in an abandoned road construction camp. Old underwear, broken bottles, girlie magazines, and a filthy fire pit were my companions that night, but there was grass. Around about midnight the temperature cooled and the bugs became bearable.

A few miles farther on I encountered a small shrine at a rocky intersection. Inside a wooden box, a dainty figurine of a dark-skinned young woman with long black hair and a red peasant's skirt lay on her back nursing a baby. Stacked around her were hundreds of plastic 7UP bottles and glass jars filled with water. Hot and always thirsty, I took a deep drink. It appeared that the saints were indeed looking out for me.

I later learned the legend of Difunta Correa, a young woman who died of thirst in the early 1840s while following her husband's battalion across the desert. When she was found, the baby boy at her breast was still alive, having survived off his mothers' milk. *Santuarios de Difunta Correa* appear frequently in this dry country—beacons of hope and symbols of survival in a hostile land.

While I rested beside a hundred bottles of water, Torrie came by in his rickety red truck and stopped to add another bottle of fresh water to the collection.

"There is a boat leaving for Puerto Ibáñez in an hour," he told me.

We took off at the fastest pace I could convince Chucao to go. I arrived at the ferry terminal window, fully loaded and sweating buckets, only to be greeted by the sour-faced woman inside.

"Horses, no," she said.

I tried to explain about my phone call last week . . . and that they had said . . . and they promised . . . and . . . but . . . My arguments were of no use.

The answer was no! They took animals, but only in trucks.

Standing there in the sun, thinking about a few more weeks of riding on the road to get around the lake and all the blind corners and steep drop-offs that lay ahead, I saw a truck pull in. Could it be empty?

"*¿Tienes carga?*" I asked the driver,

No, he was returning empty.

He decided to help me. We would load the horses first, then talk about a price.

With no loading ramp handy he backed up to a huge pile of gravel. I was supposed to walk my horses up the loose pile and into the back of his hot, orange plastic-covered truck. It worked fine for Tamango. Pulling and panicking, Chucao refused to go. For the umpteenth time that trip I wished for my Arraquien.

Time was audible. The ferry would leave whether or not we were on it. I pulled him, sweet talked him, swatted him on the butt; the answer was no!

The driver said he knew a better place and took off at high speed. I could hear Tamango stomping alone inside. I traveled as fast as I could behind him with Chucao in tow. When we got to a slightly more solid pile of dirt, the driver wrapped the rope around a stanchion on the truck and started winching Chucao inside. When he got him close enough that his next step would be into the truck, Chucao reared like the wild black stallion still inside of him. Front hooves high in the air, the halter snapped and my boy was running free in the streets of Chile Chico.

Honoring me with his trust after all I had done to him, Chucao waited for me and patiently allowed me to slip a rope over his withers. I tied a knot in his halter that I knew would not hold a tenth of the force he had just put on it.

With the same fever I had begged him to take us, I now begged the driver to let Tamango out of the truck and leave us behind. But I was no longer in charge of the situation. The driver had seen a chance to make some money that the company did not know about, and he was putting these animals in his truck.

My poor horse had a rope around his neck and another under his front lip. The guy was winching him into the truck with his lead rope wrapped twice around the stanchions. A man off the street was recruited to help out by hitting him on the butt with a branch.

Chucao lunged into the truck with Tamango, and the driver took off for the ferry at a tire-squealing pace. I rode in back with my animals, afraid for their lives if they fell, afraid for my own if hooves started flying.

Big macho Tamango appeared completely *tranquilo,* but his body gave him away. He was sweating profusely and his rear legs were trembling.

I could feel it. We were stopped. Then I felt the gentle movement of a boat. We were aboard. Under the tarp it was about 110 degrees. I talked the driver into opening up the trap and letting the lake breeze in. I stepped out of the truck into a completely different scene. A gentle wind was blowing across a turquoise lake, and passengers were out of their cars, taking in the fine summer day. I stood outside, letting my sweat dry and my panic subside.

Upon arriving in Puerto Ibáñez at the other end of the lake, it became obvious that the driver was planning on taking us all the way to Coyhaique. The road from Ibáñez was under construction. With no desire to ride through more road construction and my horses finally inside the truck I decided, for once, to go with the flow. Besides, there was a good unloading ramp at my friends Carolina and Patricio's farm outside Coyhaique. I definitely didn't want a repeat of the show I had just experienced.

Even driving what I thought was way too fast, it was dark when we arrived in Coyhaique. We arrived at Carolina and Patricio's farm at midnight, and the horses calmly stepped out of the truck, put their heads down, and quietly began to graze. An important lesson was mine: horses live in the moment. The trauma of putting them in the truck would upset me for days.

The driver stood by while I emptied my wallet and deposited everything I had down to the random pesos in my pockets into his palm. It came to within a few hundred pesos of his price. That would have to do. I would be okay here without money. I had friends.

The next morning I woke up confused. Clean flowered sheets and sunshine streaming through a window? Where was I? Everything had changed so suddenly. Then it came to me. I was in Carolina's guest bedroom. Tired and dirty, with my face aching from too much sun and wind, I knew I had been on a trip and it was over. I wasn't ready to be back.

Carolina and I had met when she was a young NOLS instructor-in-training. Now she was the director of Spanish Programs and a new mother. She and her husband Patricio were wonderful friends and hosts. They assured me I could stay as long as I liked, and Patricio reiterated Carolina's promise that they would be happy to take care of my horses as long as I wanted to leave them there. Still I felt awkward. That familiar feeling of believing I was always a bother wouldn't leave me alone.

The worst thing was my Arraquien had not arrived.

A familiar process began—hitch into town, call the truck driver, miss him, wait three hours for the phone store to open after *siesta*, miss him again, leave a message, hitch back out to the *campo*, try again the next day. My mood plummeted.

Eventually, I reached him.

"I will have a trip to Coyhaique soon, very soon," he promised me.

There was no way I could leave Patagonia without Arraquien safely in his new home.

Living on the farm helped save me from my own foul mood. Whenever I visited the little cabin out back where Patricio and Carolina's *cuidador* José lived, four-year-old Ali Miguel and his brother Moses ran to greet me. The boys adopted me. Or did I adopt them? We did everything together—catching horses, climbing the cherry tree, looking for lost sheep. Tough *campo* kids, they understood many things I did not, like where the hens hid their eggs, and how to hang from the highest branches so you could get the last of the cherries. I adored them because they adored me. They made me feel wanted, something I was sorely in need of.

One day I rode Chucao to the upper *campo* with Patricio. On the way home, Patricio, confident he would win, challenged me to a race. I gave Chucao a squeeze, and he shot forward with all the sprinting power he had. I rose from my seat and clung to his neck the way I had seen jockeys do. We bolted through the flooded spot at the end of the pasture, muddy water flying into our faces. After 475 kilometers and three months on the trail, we poured through the pasture lengths ahead of Patricio and his finest horse. I was so proud of my little Chucao. He had done a lot of growing up on our journey. Maybe I had too.

Cerro Castillo was having a traditional festival and a few people I knew were going. Exactly as advertised, it was a demonstration of skills useful in *campo* life: sheep shearing, calf roping, cow milking. A full-size log was supported by two structures much like goalposts. With one man above and the other below, teams competed at cutting two-inch planks from the log with a huge crosscut saw. In another demo, rounds of logs were efficiently sliced with a machete into shingles.

Both distanced and protected by my own walls, I was moody the entire weekend. It bothered me that many of the people of Coyhaique were witnessing their own heritage for the first time, as if their parents' lives were a display in a museum.

I needed assurance that this life still existed, when an elderly woman from the audience stepped forward and quickly, efficiently demonstrated how to tie a load onto a *pilchero.* Still, it was painfully obvious that the people showing off their skills that day were getting old. Part of my own life was also becoming history.

The promised, "next week," the truck driver had spoken of had come and gone. With only a few days left until my flight to Alaska, I had no plan, no Arraquien, and no money. Should I get on a plane to Alaska or a bus to Cochrane? What would I do in Cochrane, ride Arraquien to Coyhaique? I had trusted the driver when I paid him. I needed to trust him now, but getting on a plane for Alaska without my horse safely in his new home was something I sorely did not want to do.

In the end that is exactly what I did.

Two weeks later I got an email from Patricio and Carolina entitled, "Horse in Home." My Arraquien was safe.

Chapter 9

Cambios (Changes)

"*TIA NANCY! TIA Nancy!*" Moses and Ali Miguel saw me and came running across the yard, arms open. My tired heart melted as I swept them both into a huge hug. The delightful Chilean custom of children addressing anyone their parents age as *tia* or *tio*, "auntie" or "uncle" made me feel like family.

A year had slipped by. I arrived exhausted from working a mountaineering trip at the southern end of the continent. Ali Miguel grabbed me by the hand. "Come see my baby lamb."

A fluffy lamb was romping outside the cabin door. Neither Ali's mother nor Don José seemed to be around.

"How old is your little lamb?" I asked.

"I don't know but he is getting sooooo big."

"What will you do with him when he grows up?"

"We will eat him," Ali responded, as if it was the most natural thing on earth. How could a grown-up not know that?

With chickens to feed and puppies to play with, the heavy "to do" list that I had carried around for the last several months began to evaporate.

Still, my horse trips were beginning to feel like a race against time. Where today there was a trail, tomorrow would be a road. Next year or the year after someone would put a lock on a gate and my ability to travel freely across Patagonia would come to a halt.

Arraquien was no longer the leggy young gelding I had bought in Cochrane. He had filled out and looked noticeably older than when I'd left him a year ago. I walked up to him. He slipped his soft muzzle under my hand. He knew me better than I knew him. I ran my hands down his legs and picked up a front foot. His feet looked terrible. A trim and some new shoes were desperately needed.

"Who do you think you are just leaving your horse and going back to another life?" I chastised myself. "You should be ashamed to own a horse with feet like that."

Tamango and Chucao were in the nearby paddock. They looked healthy, and their feet looked surprisingly good, but neither of them seemed to know me. I had long ago accepted that my love affair with Tamango would be a one way deal, but I still hoped Chucao would someday warm to my embraces.

Patricio came out from the barn. "Can you help me move the cows?"

"Sure," I said, anxious for an opportunity to play cowgirl.

"José is in the hospital. A tractor rolled over on him while he was working alone on the upper *campo*," Patricio told me. "He has several broken ribs. His dog laid on his chest for hours splinting his ribs until help arrived. He could have died."

The harsh reality of lying nearly dead for hours under a tractor, waiting for someone to stumble upon you, didn't fit the idyllic country life I was so busy imagining.

I threw a saddle on Chucao. The cinch barely reached around his fat belly. After an idle winter, he was huffing and puffing before Patricio and I got up the first small hill. My boys needed to go on a trip as much as I did.

Patricio and I managed to get behind the cows and push them toward an open gate. Most went uphill, the rest turned downhill, none went through the gate. Patricio owned the farm and had a degree in agriculture, but it was Don José who did the work. The bovine equivalent of teenagers, these two-year-olds weren't interested in listening to us. I tried riding patiently up behind them. I galloped wildly toward them, whooping and hollering. Dogs chased cows, more often than not, in the wrong direction.

What seemed like hours later we had successfully moved twenty-four cows into an adjacent pasture. Congratulating ourselves on a job José could have done in five minutes, we rode downhill, laughing.

I wanted to put some miles on my three fat boys before I did a real trip, but with so many horses to ride it was hard to give them any real exercise by myself. A few days later, my friend Corey from NOLS came out to ride with me.

On a bright windless day, Corey and I rode Tamango and Chucao to the top of the *campo* and opened the gate into the Reserva de Cohaique. Corey hadn't ridden much but he was game for anything.

He had a delightful Chilean girlfriend and a command of the Spanish language that seemed to have magically appeared overnight.

Inside the *reserva* we galloped on wide forest trails. We climbed to the highest point we could get to with the horses. Chucao bushwhacked confidently through *chaura*-berry bushes so thick I couldn't see the ground beneath his belly. We found an open meadow and took a break. How long since I had just laid back and watched the clouds float by? How badly I had needed this.

My mountaineering trip in southern Patagonia earlier that month had taken its toll. Relentless wind and rain, difficult logistics and, above all, challenging relations with the people I worked with had left me drained. I desperately needed to get off *gringo* time. I craved simply watching my horses graze.

A couple of evenings earlier, my friend Pancho had told me about an old trail that began near his house. "That trail was the original route into the Simpson Valley from the coast, but now with a tunnel and a paved road to Puerto Aysen in the next valley, no one uses it anymore."

That sounded like just the project I was looking for. The idea intrigued me into ignoring the fact that the trail would take me west of the divide, into the dense rain-soaked forest I had so far avoided.

"Want to go on a longer trip?" I asked Corey under the drifting clouds.

"Ya, why not?" he told me. But, he had only a few days off. Then NOLS would get busy for the rest of the summer.

In minutes, a trip was planned. I would move the horses to the other side of Coyhaique, and Corey would meet me at a friend's house in a few days. He would travel with me as far as he could and then hitch back on the new road.

At least I would be free from the shocked greeting, *"¿Estás sola?"* for a while. Hearing those words made me want to rummage around under *nalca* leaves, searching for the partner I had apparently misplaced. Gone were the days when I adamantly wanted to change the world's attitude toward women traveling alone. Now I just wanted to be left in peace.

The morning I left, Carolina accompanied me for the first few miles. When we first met nearly ten years earlier, Carolina had talked excitedly about joining me on a horse trip. As a new mother with a full-time job, a chance to ride with a friend for even one lovely, late spring day was a rare treat. For her, month-long wilderness expeditions were over, maybe forever.

She didn't seem to mind.

Buses, cars, and *colectivos* crowded the streets of Coyhaique these days. Horses tied in the vacant lot just outside town, awaiting the return of their owners shopping the main street on foot, were becoming a rarity. By slipping out the back gate of Carolina's farm, we avoided Coyhaique. The forest trails were wide enough to ride side by side. Our laughter and the twittering sound of the tiny *rayadito* was all we heard as we looked down on the honking, bustling town below. At the far end of the reserve Carolina turned toward home. Chucao, Tamango, and I were on our own.

Poor Arraquien got left behind again. His feet still looked terrible and without Corey along for the entire trip, I didn't need, or want, three horses to manage by myself. Still, I would miss him. Arraquien held us together as a family.

I soon passed a young man on a pure white *yequa*. His mare pranced nervously while we chatted.

"Where are you going with a *pilchero*?" he asked.

I weighed my options. I could tell this stranger I was headed for a trail going west into the jungle, a trail no one had probably used for years? Like the old man at Mira Flores, this guy might proclaim me crazy, forbid me to camp anywhere there were sheep. Or, I could lie. Four years earlier, unable to admit to anyone I was headed to Cochrane, 300 kilometers away, I had simply given the name of a nearby lake. With a thousand kilometers under my belt, one person's opinion no longer held the power to turn me around.

"*A Valle Rio Blanco,*" I told him.

"I am training this horse for the rodeo," he told me. "Can I accompany you as far as the rodeo grounds?"

The rodeo grounds were half a kilometer away. Fortunately, this young man from Coyhaique had no idea where Rio Blanco was.

By evening, clouds that had been threatening all day thickened and lowered, and it began to rain. A heavy Patagonian all-night downpour was building. It was fully dark when I arrived at Pancho's house.

Pancho settled me in with a warm cup of tea. "I am so glad you are going to see the Rio Blanco Valley right now," he said. "In a few years that valley could be under water."

Rumors had been circulating for years, but I wanted to hear the details.

"Noranda, a Canadian mining company, has plans to dam three rivers in the area, the Cuervo, Blanco, and the Condor, to produce power for a huge aluminum smelter near Puerto Aysen."

The data was daunting: six dams, three hydropower plants, an industrial waste facility, 79 kilometers of power lines, 94 kilometers of new roads, and expanded port facilities. I tried to imagine all this in an area of nearly impenetrable wilderness.

Aluminum ore would be shipped from Australia, Brazil, or Jamaica to Aysen. From the small town of Puerto Aysen 440,000 tons of aluminum bars a year would be shipped to the far reaches of the world where they would be re-melted and turned into beer cans, leaving behind 60,000 tons of solid waste a year.

I was having a hard time wrapping my head around the idea that a beer can could travel through several continents before being tossed into the trash. Then again, hadn't I purchased Chilean grapes, a delicious taste of sunshine in the middle of the Alaskan winter, at the grocery store in Palmer?

"Producing aluminum is tremendously energy consumptive," Pancho said. "Chile's water rights are owned almost entirely by foreign companies. When some people look at Patagonia's free-flowing rivers, they see what the industrial world craves most—cheap energy."

When Carolina and I were young NOLS instructors, the indigenous Mapuchi and the worldwide whitewater rafting community had been up in arms. Endesa, an international energy company, was trying to dam the Bio-Bío River.

Back then, what might someday happen on a river 500 kilometers north of here barely registered in my gray matter, along with a hundred other wars and injustices in the world. That the world economy could affect my life, or the rural Patagonians I knew, people who consumed mainly what they produced on their farms, seemed ludicrous.

We are all connected in ways I never imagined.

Cory arrived the next day, and we took off down a dirt road that ran much farther into the western wilderness than was shown on the map. The dry, open steppe of eastern Patagonia was already far behind us. The prickly leaves and tiny apple-like berry of the *chaura* bush were being replaced by rambling branches of *parilla,* its grape-like leaves hiding drooping clusters of white flowers soon to be fruit. Already the evergreen *coihue*, outnumbered its deciduous cousin, *lenga*. Flora not found two kilometers to the east grew rabidly: Prickly leafed *mañio*, the crazy compound leaves of *tineo*, and the aromatic *arrayán* with its large, peeling flakes of cinnamon-colored bark. *Quila*, which until recently grew in aesthetic, isolated clumps, now fanatically overtook the landscape. The impenetrable wall of vegetation that lined both sides of the road, both intrigued and terrified me. I understood all too well that when the road ended the adventure would begin.

The road ended at a gorgeous *campo* sitting on what looked like the last piece of flat land in existence. Above the small opening the owners had hacked in the forest, a trail ran straight up. The summer snow line was still well down into the trees. There was no house nearby.

"The trail couldn't possibly go up that hill," I said.

Just then a six-year-old boy stepped out of the forest.

"Is your mother around?" I asked.

Wide-eyed, he stared at us in disbelief and vanished into the woods. Not too long afterward a woman appeared.

"That's the way," she said, pointing at the impossibly steep hillside. "My husband is up there working, but nobody uses the trail beyond here."

The path climbed straight up on wet, slippery clay. Chucao lunged upward on the verge of panic. Within half an hour we lost the trail again. The map showed it swinging distinctly west, paralleling the lake. Every trail in that direction was a dead end.

I could hear men working in the woods. Our reception was one of disbelief, followed by disapproval. Once again, I was glad not to be traveling solo.

"¿Adónde vas?" the woman's husband questioned, even though Corey had just told him where we were going.

Thinly built with dusty blond hair, Corey looked as gringo as I did, but his Spanish was impeccable. The man slowly warmed up to us. Not only did this man know the local trails, he also understood how to read a map, a rare thing where people simply hold a map of an area in their heads.

"The trail doesn't go anywhere near where it is shown here," he said. He then drew us an accurate route, including a dead-end trail that led to a swamp.

"The trail you want goes straight up, then through a gate, past a corral, by a little *casita*, around a lake and to a house near the other side," he said. I tried desperately to remember everything. Corey wasn't saying much, but I was hoping he was taking it all in.

"I will be working farther up trail after lunch if you get lost," the man said.

We shook hands, all of us assuming we would be seeing each other again shortly.

The trail was hellacious. Even with good directions we lost and re-found the route at every possible junction, including fully exploring the trail to the swamp we were warned against. The lay of the land matched the man's description perfectly. We bushwhacked well above the lake for two days, sleeping on a steep hillside in an eight-by-eight spot hacked out of the *quila*. Blessedly, blue skies dried the slippery trail. I tried not to imagine what this trail would be like in heavy rain.

Clear streams tumbled from every crevice. Chile's national flower, the brilliant red *copihue*, dripped from the bright green moss-covered canyon walls. Copious quantities of luxurious vegetation against the backdrop of rugged snowcapped peaks, this was the Patagonia of textbooks and tourist brochures.

Nalca leaves big enough to offer shelter from a storm grew from spiny stalks as big around as my arm. This land was prehistoric. A third of these plants had shared the mega-continent Gondwana.

With an annual precipitation of 157 inches, it rains practically every day in this country. Our good luck was doomed to change. The clouds lowered, thickened and the rain began. The classic signs of a slow-moving warm front foretold a weather pattern that was here to stay. With nowhere to picket horses or to camp in this maze of deadfall and vegetation, we trudged onward.

Just before nightfall, I could see cleared land in the bottom of the valley, the first *campo* on the other side. Francisco and his wife Thadi met us at their gate.

"*Pasé,*" Thadi said. In one word communicating that we would unsaddle, eat dinner, and spend the night.

Their farm reflected generations of hard work. A cherry orchard, flowers just changing to fruit, lined the path to the house. Rhubarb grew in huge clumps in front of a small greenhouse. We passed a well-maintained garden that Thadi said, "never gets enough sun."

Against strong protest from Corey and me, our hosts insisted that we bring our whole dripping mess inside the house. Although it had once cost me plenty, my raincoat was old and these days it leaked like it was made of cotton. Tired of ending each day soaked to the skin, I had long ago cut holes in a garbage bag for my arms and head and donned it inside my coat for extra protection from foul weather. Embarrassed, I tried to slip my garbage bag off unnoticed in the entryway of their small house.

Over *maté* I learned that Thadi and Francisco had lived on their land for fourteen years.

"The first nine years or so we walked in from the *balsa*," Thadi said. "Now the road comes much closer. It's easy now."

Thadi was busy sewing a man's dress jacket complete with pleats and cuffs. This kind of sewing was something my mother knew how to do and my grandmother before her, but of which I am incapable. I wondered if we, as humans, are forgetting as much as we are learning every day.

Over rice with fresh cow's milk, we talked about all the things that Thadi knows how to do that her daughter does not. "Sewing, knitting, making cheese, butter, marmalade, all these things my daughter just buys in town."

I also bought all those things in town.

"Do you ever come in from Coyhaique?" I asked Francisco.

"Oh no, no one uses that route anymore," he said. "A guy came through, maybe seven years ago. But nobody since then, not until you."

The next day, to no great surprise, it was still pouring. Before we left, Thadi insisted I take a brand new yellow plastic rain poncho. It was made of cheap thin plastic. In a land where every plant was protected by thorns, it wouldn't survive the first bush. What's more, I suspected that the bright yellow plastic rustling in the wind would send Chucao into bucking fits. However, there was no arguing with Chilean hospitality. I left with a poncho over my rain gear. The first breeze sent Chucao bolting in terror from the flapping yellow thing on his back and my new poncho went under my coat where the plastic bag had once lived.

Corey and I assumed that the worst was over. We had made it through the trail no one used anymore and reached a *campo* people approached from the west. How bad could the rest of the trail be?

Bad.

On those last few slippery, muddy, steep kilometers my respect for Thadi and Francisco grew to tremendous proportions. This trail was how they got home.

At one point, Chucao stumbled into a mud wallow. His hind legs came out from under him, his front legs buckled and the whole side of his face went into the mud. He lunged out the other side, packsaddle covered in mud, ears laid back, pissed. This was a bad hole. There was no way around it and, at the end of the journey, there would be no way home but to retrace our steps. I began to worry incessantly about an event weeks into the future. Completely unrealistically, I started praying for dry weather.

On this side of the range, the road didn't come up valley nearly as far as shown on the map. We were well past Lago Portales when we saw a gravel road winding out of the wilderness. Gravel was awful for the horses' feet and boring to travel on. This time I was ready to exchange terror for boredom.

We arrived in civilization to find ourselves on the wrong side of a barbed-wire fence. A man around my own age trotted across the pasture toward us. "Uh oh," I thought, my *gringo* mind assuming he was there to tell us we were trespassing.

Hand extended, he reached across the fence to greet us. I fumbled over whether to say *buenas días* or *buenas tardes* as I hadn't known what time it was for days.

"Did you come from Coyhaique?" he asked.

"*Si,*" I said, none too proud of our crazy adventure.

"*Buena, muy, muy buena,*" he said, a huge smile racing across his face. "Nobody uses that trail anymore."

"*Pasé, tomamos maté.*" He invited us in, nodding toward his house not far away.

I looked at Corey, knowing he was in more of a rush than me, but also knowing there was no way we could turn down this man's offer.

"*Bueno,*" Corey said.

Andrés led us to a gate in the fence. He unsaddled our horses outside his house with the smooth motions of someone well accustomed to the work.

We were ushered inside and seated in the warmest seats behind the woodstove.

"*Saque su zapatos.*" Andrés instructed us to take our soaking wet shoes off.

Uncomfortably aware of the nasty, disgusting state of my socks, I removed my shoes.

Andrés handed me a towel to dry my feet, a pair of clean dry socks, and a pair of house slippers. The luxury of warm, dry feet and of being cared for felt like springtime after a long Alaskan winter. The finest hotels couldn't make their guests feel this welcome.

Andrés's wife Eulandia was spinning yarn with a drop spindle. She pinched off a piece of clean, soft sheep's wool and deftly twisted it into the existing yarn. Then she gave the spindle a twist and let it drop toward the floor. A fine long piece of yarn emerged. She wrapped the new length around the ball of yarn on the floor and began again.

It looked easy. It wasn't. Years ago in Peru, I had tried to learn to spin and weave. Thinking it would bond me with local women, I brought my projects out in public only to solicit cries of, "Oh, my dear, you will never get a man, you are a terrible weaver," and, "What in the world was wrong with your mother? Look at you, you can't even spin."

Eventually, I gave up.

With *maté* water heating on the woodstove, Andrés began his story.

"I was born north of here, on the east side of the mountains, near Ñiregauo. It's drier there, so much better than this," he said, looking out the window. "I worked a lot with horses. When I was sixteen I traveled from La Tapera to Lago Verde by horse." His eyes lit up with the memory, and I understood why he had come trotting up the hill to greet us. We represented something he loved.

I longed to make the trip from La Tapera to Lago Verde. I was still waiting for that magical combination of time and a competent partner to attempt such a difficult journey.

Andrés pulled a finely crafted *pilchero* saddle from the back room. The tree was the same as that of a riding saddle but with tightly crossed wooden x's for attaching the *chequas*, baskets woven from rawhide used for carrying gear. "You put your *pilcha* in here," he told me, shoving his hand into the empty space between the hoops.

The word *pilcha* meant "old clothes." For the first time, I put it together. The word *pilchero* literally meant the carrier of your old clothes.

The cinches were gorgeous—long, wide, and made of finely woven wool in soft tan and brown colors.

"Eulandia made these," he said, nodding at his wife.

"They are beautiful," I said, stroking them, acutely aware that my hands were filthy and my knuckles bruised from when Chucao unexpectedly jerked the lead rope. I knew better than to carry coils. Looping extra rope back and forth over an open palm so a sudden jerk won't crush your hand was a basic mountaineering practice. I was lucky my fingers weren't broken.

Embarrassed by my *gringa* get-up, I wanted to buy his *pilchero* saddle. Nothing like it could be bought in a store. But it would be wrong to ask. He would never charge me what it was worth and he might never make another one.

We drank *maté* and talked for hours. The timeless flow of *campo* life was about to collide with the reality of those who work in town. Andrés and Eulandia assumed we were staying the night. Corey had work the next morning at eight in Coyhaique.

"When does the ferry close?" I asked.

"*A las seis,*" Andrés said. The last boat across the river would leave in two hours. Corey needed to be on it.

"We need to go," Corey said. He hadn't said much all afternoon while I had babbled on. Maybe he had been in Chile long enough he didn't feel the need to fill every silence the way *gringos* did.

"I will come back by when I return from up valley," I assured them.

"*Por seguro, seguro*," Eulandia made me promise as we left.

The horses had also assumed their travel day was over. They weren't bothered by our schedule. At this pace, we wouldn't make the ferry. The first car we had seen since Coyhaique crested the hill and Corey thrust out his thumb. The amazed faces of the last family we had met on the Coyhaique side peered out the window.

"*Que buena sopresa*," the man said, genuinely amazed to find us here and not dead along the trail. The door opened and Corey was gone.

To my surprise, when I arrived at the *balsa*, Corey, the family from the other side of the pass and the driver of the boat were all waiting for me.

"If it continues to rain the river will be too strong and the ferry will be closed until the water goes down, so we waited for you," the boat operator said.

It did not escape me that if this rain never stopped—and it didn't seem as though it ever would—I could be trapped on the far side of this river for a long time.

Once across, Corey headed toward the highway, and I headed *al interior*, back into the land beyond roads. The rain let up to allow views of towering vertical cliffs falling straight to the valley floor. The deep quiet nature of the Rio Blanco at this point did not hint at the tremendous rapids upstream or of the hundreds of megawatts hidden within its flow. Thick vegetation clung to cliffs. The low evening light filtered through thin clouds into freshly rinsed air. Rays of diluted sunshine streamed through the clouds. The scene was part primeval forest, part religious postcard. We were five miles from the coast.

A woman was moving cattle in my direction.

"There is a beautiful place to camp just up the way. It is my mother's farm," she said, as if she had read my mind. As soon as camp was set up, I went over to visit the woman's mother, bringing chocolate. I was glad I brought a gift. Anna Louis's three granddaughters sat quietly beside the woodstove.

"Do you know about the aluminum plant?" Anna Louis asked me.

"*Si, un poco*," I said.

"The dam would go right there. You can see the spot," she said, pointing out her window.

Sure enough, that narrow spot in the valley would be the logical place to put a dam.

I couldn't imagine a 380-foot dam rising from the valley floor in front of Anna Louis's, let alone the roads and power lines it would bring. This forest, quiet for millenniums, filled with the constant sound of reverse beacons and backhoes? Now I understood why Peter Hartman, president of the group Aysen Reserva de Vida, had called the project "a Tyrannosaurus Rex in paradise."

"Some families up valley have already sold out to the aluminum company," she told me. "Forty-four families will have to move. We are not selling, but we will be flooded just the same."

Her eyes dropped to study the tablecloth. One of the toughest social by-products of major industrialization is pitting neighbor against neighbor. In 1991, a proposed highway to the roadless community of Cordova Alaska put the locals who lived there for peace and quiet in conflict with those that saw a road as money to be made. People took their opinions out on each other in editorial pages, coffee houses, and businesses all over town.

"It is not good, but these companies they have too much power. They have threatened many times before, but they will do it this time for sure," Anna Louis said.

Anna Louis had lived for decades under the threat of dams. In the late 1980s, the family of Francisco Walker negotiated with Pinoche and acquired the rights to the nearby Cuervo River. While dodging regulations to develop or lose those rights he was able to keep the Cuervo, and in 1990 he acquired water rights to the Blanco as well.

"I would love to improve my farm, put in a big greenhouse, but I worry," Anna Louis said. "You never know when they are coming."

I understood exactly what she was talking about. Coal mining in the part of Alaska where I live began in 1916, in what was then wilderness. The coal was sold to the Alaska Railroad and the Navy during World War II. Then mining went dormant.

In 1991, I was ready to settle down and buy land. The Palmer newspaper ran the headline, "Wishbone Hill Coal Mine Project Cancelled." Naively, I bought property a few miles from a proposed mine site. Years went by, and I built a tiny cabin and put in a garden.

In Aysen, the Walker's made a deal with the Canadian company Noranda, one of the world's largest mining companies. In 1995, Noranda came out with an environmental impact statement that stated there would be "no major impact" involved in flooding 9,600 acres of temperate rain forest.

In 1997 the Usibeli mining company bought the mining permit for a 7,400-acre parcel near my home. In the meantime hundreds of families had moved into the area and built homes. Usibeli's plan was to strip mine the neighborhood and sell coal to Korea. I had the foundation dug for my house.

My best friends moved away. With a three year old to consider, they were not willing to invest their life savings in a place downwind of a coal mine.

In Aysen, prices declined for aluminum and the project affecting Anna Louis was suspended. In the year 2000, Noranda was back with a surprise, another environmental impact statement and renewed interest in the project. Anna Louis seemed tired. I, too, was worn out by it all. We would continue the fight tomorrow.

"*Buenas noches y buenas suerte,*" I said, hoping that, if not luck, the rise and fall of a turbulent economy would come to her rescue.

I woke to yet another uninspiring downpour. The sheep skins I used for both saddle and bed cushion were soaked and the fleshy underside was beginning to rot.

I wanted to see as much of the valley as I could, but if we got a weather window, I wanted to use it to get back across the Lago Portales trail. That mud hole experience with Chucao was still haunting me.

Even though my body said stay, sleep, drink *maté*, I headed up valley. I used Tamango as *pilchero.* My big macho boy didn't like walking behind, but Chucao was growing up, becoming more confident, wanting to take the lead. I milked their rivalry for all it was worth.

The trail soon deteriorated into the same slippery muddy mess I was more than familiar with. I lost and re-found it several times, making for slow progress. Disinclined to drag my boys through the mud just to turn around in a day or so, I found a sweet green spot to leave the horses. I took off up valley on foot, with *ganas* to see as much as I could before nightfall.

I peered at the tremendous rock walls upstream. As darkness approached, the clouds parted just enough for me to take a few photos. Was I looking at all I, or anyone, might ever see of this valley?

I didn't know half the story. Five hundred kilometers north of here, Endesa was building the second of five proposed dams on the Bio-Bío River. Multinational companies worldwide were lining up for Patagonia's resources and nearly every river in the region was in danger.

In the morning, winds from the north and the feel of colder, drier air on my skin alerted me that a cold front had arrived. A break in the weather was coming. This was my chance to get back through that mud hole.

The day was delightful and dynamic. While eating lunch on the black sand beach at Lago Riesco, blustery wind and rain changed to intense sunshine. Intent on making it all the way to Andrés and Eulandia's house by nightfall, I kept the horses moving.

Andrés met me in his yard.

"If you ever sell this horse, look me up," he said, grabbing Chucao's lead line.

I promised I would, knowing his horses would receive more than just decent food and fair work. His horses would receive love and respect.

"Why don't you have horses of your own?" I asked.

"My horses are in Ñiregauo. I am only caretaking this farm," he told me. "I own a *campo* in Ñiregauo but I couldn't make money there so we had to take this job. This *campo* belongs to some *extranjeros*."

"Oh really, what country do they come from?" I asked. The word *extranjero* meant foreigner to me.

"They are from Santiago," he said.

Of course, anyone not from here was a foreigner.

Over a dinner of potatoes and carrots from their garden and rice from my saddlebags, I found out Andrés and Eulandia had a thirteen-year-old daughter living with Eulandia's sister in Ñiregauo. After a while I asked about the dams and the aluminum plant.

"Oh, if that happened we would just go home," Andrés said.

I could only imagine how much these two must have wished to leave this wet country and return to their daughter and their horses.

I gratefully accepted their offer to sleep on soft, dry sheep skins by the fire under a roof that was not dripping. I slipped into dreams, asking myself: What does it take to call a place home? What makes some places hold a special spot in our hearts? I had travelled to the opposite end of the earth and found a place a lot like Alaska, a frontier with big mountains, glaciers, and a unique group of people shaped by a harsh and beautiful landscape. Would I stay? Could this place ever be home?

The next morning, Andrés helped me saddle horses, his trained hands tightening the cinches perfectly, checking each move. In the middle of saddling Chucao he went into the house and returned with the beautiful cinch Eulandia had made.

"This one is better," he said, as he started to un-cinch Chucao.

Chucao had a standard rope cinch that you could buy in any hardware store, but there was no way I was going to let them give me that cinch. It had taken Eulandia a week to make it.

"*No, no puedes*," I begged.

"We want to," he insisted.

Andrés wanted to give the soft, woolen cinch to Chucao as much as he wanted to give it to me. In the end I took the cinch.

The week before I had left Palmer for my first horse expedition in Chile, a friend whose parents had colonized the Mat-Su Valley took me into the family barn. There, still hanging on the walls, were bridles, breast collars, and britchins used by his family's draft horses in the 1930s.

"Take anything you think you can use," my friend said.

Unaware that the horses in Chile were notoriously small, I had chosen a large, heavy, hand-tooled bridle. I gave it to Andrés. It looked like the bridles seen in old Western movies. He loved it.

Andrés and Eulandia accompanied me to the end of their *campo*. Andrés rode Tamango and towed Chucao. I trotted along behind. He was in his element—natural, at ease, smiling. With hugs and *besos*, I promised that I would send them a message on radio Santa Maria when we all arrived safely in Coyhaique.

Once I was in the saddle myself, Tamango tugged on the reins wanting to go faster. Chucao tugged on the lead rope trying to go slower. I was in the middle getting yanked from both ends. By the time we got to the mud hole I had worried about for over a week, I was already in a foul mood.

I kicked Tamango. "Let's go," I said, just wanting to get it over with.

He lurched reluctantly forward. Near the far side his front feet sank, then his back legs sank deeper. I jumped off into waist-deep muck. Tamango lunged forward with all the power I knew was within him. Pulling himself out the other side, my big strong boy was trembling. I was sweating and trying hard not to cry.

"I'm so sorry, Tamango," I said, burying my face in his mane.

I couldn't stay with him long. Chucao was alone on the other side and screaming. I waded back. Chucao was lighter. I prayed that would make a difference, but it didn't matter. Chucao wasn't budging. No how. No way. I tried pulling and pushing but he could read my own hesitancy. Horses die in places like this. If I killed my horse I wasn't sure how I could live.

Maybe there was a way around the mud wallow. Why the hell didn't I have a huge machete stuck in my belt like everyone else who travels here, I thought as I crawled on my belly through the *quila*. Nose to the ground, I came face to face with a *chucao tapaculo*. Its upturned tail flicked nervously at me. We stared at each other in disbelief. Why was I surprised? A *chucao tapaculo* on the forest floor was normal. A wet, muddy, terrified *gringa* was not.

There was no getting a horse through this jungle. I could hear the distressed whinnies of my horses getting louder. They hated being separated, and I worried that one or the other would break free and charge across. With my luck it would be Tamango and we would all be back on the wrong side.

I went through the list of possibilities. I couldn't take the road, a quarter-mile tunnel separated me from Coyhaique. We would more surely be killed there than here. I wished Andrés were here. He would know what to do.

Then I remembered my first few days in Chile. I had rented the first car I had ever rented in my life in Puerto Mont and taken it out to a remote forest reserve for a few days of backpacking. Three hours before the ferry was to leave for Coyhaique and my new job in Aysen, both front wheels of my rental car plunged through a rotten bridge. I hadn't seen anyone in three days. My first thought was, "I need a tow truck." My second thought was, "I'm not going to get one!" Chile had just given me my first lesson in self-sufficiency. I could do what I did then; build a bridge!

For years I had traveled on the corrugated log trails built by pioneers. I had stood on the backs of the hard workers who had opened the way for me. It was time for me to contribute to Patagonia's trail system. I hauled logs like a woman possessed, laid them sideways, and filled the cracks with brush and mud.

As I worked I noticed something solid underfoot, a place where the muck was not as deep. I was standing on the remains of an older log bridge now buried under a half meter of muck.

When the bridge was finished, I tried Chucao again. He tugged on the lead rope, but this time it was a superficial, "You have to make me," not the absolute, "I am not going, not now, not ever" that he had given me before.

Both of us equally scared, we stepped into the mud hole.

Barely more than muddy to the knees we made it across. Tamango let out a long sweet whinny. Any show of emotion was not his style. It touched my heart.

A week later I sent a message over the radio Santa Maria. "*Para Andrés y Eulandia en Valle Rio Blanco: La gringa Nancy con los dos caballos llegué bien a Coyhaique.*"

Chapter 10

*Otoño en el Campo (*Fall on the *Campo)*

THE ENTIRE FLIGHT down I worried that I was making a huge mistake. Two years had somehow slipped by. It was fall going on winter in Patagonia. With a long, dark Alaska winter behind me, why was I headed back into cold and darkness?

My life had changed in predictable North American ways. My former bosses at the Alaska Avalanche School, where I had worked for years, had moved on. I was the logical person to take on the directorship—in fact the only person willing to take the job. As an instructor it had been easy to waltz home mid-winter and teach the rest of the season. As director I was committed. From October until April, I had a job. Against all best intentions, I was climbing the corporate ladder. Springtime in Patagonia had been ripped from my life.

My friends Paty and Scott, a Chilean-American couple living in Alaska, had offered their *campo* for me to live on. Other than a strong desire to be in Patagonia, I didn't have much of a vision. I didn't even know exactly where their *campo* was. I figured I'd stay until the snow flew, it got too dark and cold to ride horses, or I came up with another plan.

I landed in Balmaceda on the only windless day I had ever experienced in that town. The sun was high in the sky and still gave off a warming glow. A dusting of fresh snow glistened on the peaks, but the valley bottoms were still covered in lush, green grass. The *ñirre* leaves were a deep auburn that put fall in New England to shame. Happiness flooded my veins as it always did when I arrived in Patagonia.

My friend Raúl gunned the engine. His four-wheel-drive jeep pushed through mud puddles halfway up the doors. Once again, my rich resource of friends were making life easy for me. Paty and Scott's was a lot farther off the main road than I expected, and the two-lane track to their house much worse than I ever imagined. When we arrived, it was raining hard and nearly dark. From what I could see, which wasn't much, the house was a cute Alaska-style cabin made from half round logs.

A strange feeling slipped in. I didn't remember the cabin, but this valley, I had been here. Only a few days into my first horse trip, I had taken a short cut. This road had been a trail. Nimbus and I had met our first *gaucho* at the gate a bit farther on.

The cabin wasn't new. Had I passed right by it? Where was Nimbus now? In fact, where was the girl I had been back then? So green, so scared. What would she have thought if someone had told her she would someday return to live in this valley?

"You should camp in your tent tonight. The place hasn't been aired out in over a year," Raúl told me as he quickly dropped me off.

The baffled look on my face gave away my ignorance.

"You know about Hanta virus, don't you?" he asked.

Hanta is carried by rats and mice. The virus becomes airborne and gets into people's lungs. Abandoned buildings are prime habitat. I had seen billboards advising farmers about the disease, but never thought the warnings would apply to me.

Raúl must have read the look of horror that crossed my face. "Don't worry, you can air the place out in the morning. Hanta virus is killed by fresh air and sunshine, but you should still wash everything down with bleach before you move in."

"Sure, no problem," I said with a confidence I did not feel.

"If you feel sick, like you have the flu, you should get yourself checked out by a doctor. Hanta can be fatal if you don't treat it," Raúl reminded me as he drove away.

Tucked in my tiny nylon shelter, listening to the rain hit the walls in sheets, I tried to keep my spirits from plummeting. For weeks I would be concerned about every small headache or unsettled stomach. The scared girl I had once been was trying to push her way back in. I shoved her away. How many times in our lives do we get an opportunity to try out a life we think we want?

The next morning everything looked entirely different. The previous night's cold rain had put a fresh, crisp snow line halfway down the mountains. Cerro Sombrero, freshly painted white, rose fifteen hundred feet above the *campo*. The Estero El Arco tumbled and splashed in front of the cabin. Was this charming little creek named for the brilliant rainbows that always seemed to hang in the western sky, or for the big rainbow trout that rested in its quiet pools? Drinking water gurgled out of a natural spring nearby. Best of all, behind my little cabin was a big pasture with knee-high grass untouched all summer. I was finally going to live with my horses.

I took inventory of my new home. The fence needed a few minor repairs. If I cleaned out the dilapidated pole barn, my horses would have a place to stand on nights like the last one. Cautiously, I opened the cabin door.

Paty in her womanly wisdom had set out rags, a broom, and a fresh bottle of Clorox. There was no furniture in either room, but I figured I could pound something together from the boards left in the pole barn. My biggest problem was that the cast iron cook stove—the center of life in every kitchen in Patagonia—was missing.

What truly disturbed me was that the woodstove had been stolen, not by someone who was destitute and cold, but someone with a truck. Whoever took my stove had driven in here in the kind of four-by-four truck few could afford.

I could buy a stove and leave it here as a present for Paty and Scott. On this bright, sunny morning anything was possible.

If I was going to fix up a *campo*, I needed tools: a hammer and nails, a shovel, an ax, a length of wire for the fence. In my shed in Alaska, I had all of these things. I had arrived in Patagonia with a mountain of outdoor equipment, but my entire tool collection consisted of a Swiss Army knife. What had I been thinking?

My neighbors had accumulated over generations the basic equipment needed to run a farm. Buying things I already owned felt ridiculous and wasteful, but possessions at the other end of the world did me no good. Also in my shed back home were two kayaks and a half dozen pairs of skis. If I were to move here, I would need to ship everything I owned to the other end of the Earth or buy it all again. The ecological consequences, not to mention the financial reality, of either option was daunting. Wasn't simplifying my life what I was looking for?

A few days later, fog still hung cold and damp in the valley as I tromped out the dirt road toward town. The first hard freeze of the season crunched underfoot. Villa Frey, the tiny town Veronica grew up in, had a store, a phone, and twice-a-week bus service to Coyhaique.

Already craving social interaction, I started my day in town with *maté* with Veronica. Outside Chile I have never had the kind of female friendships that centered around the kitchen, yet just sitting, even silently, in Veronica's kitchen felt good. Two kittens born too late in the year to grow up in the barn played on the floor behind the woodstove. Yet, something was missing.

During the Alaskan winter I had just left, even on the shortest days, my girlfriends and I got out for a quick, exhilarating ski on the mountain behind town, nearly every day. Those moments, of breathing hard and laughing in the snow with friends, saved my winter sanity. There would be no women in the *campos* to ski with this winter.

That evening I returned to the *campo* with my newly purchased tools, a kerosene heater, and five gallons of fuel tied to my back. The kerosene heater was a cheap, stinky, temporary fix for a cold house that would only get colder. What the place needed was a three-hundred-dollar woodstove, a hundred dollars' worth of stovepipe, the tools, and expertise to install it properly and a truck to haul it all out there.

In Alaska, I had built my own cabin, but I had done it with the help of a multitude of friends, power tools, and a logging truck. Here, I had settled for a cheap to buy, but expensive to run, oil stove. It didn't make me feel strong or wholesome or anything else I had imagined I would feel living on a *campo*.

In a few days the fences were mended, and I was ready to bring my horses. I walked out to the road again. The puddles had diminished significantly and the edges were now coated with a thin veneer of ice.

Carolina and Patricio were living in town, waiting to move back out to their *campo* until their new baby, little Cristobal, was a bit older. José was living alone on the farm. Tamango was saddled and standing under a huge willow tree when I arrived. He looked terrific, but, being Tamango, he couldn't have cared less about me. Arraquien looked fat and healthy. He lifted his heavy head and laid it in my hand. He remembered me, and he loved me. For this he could have flat feet, a tough-boy attitude, and a spoiled-child temperament, he would always be my horse. Chucao's black coat was shiny and soft to my touch. I put my face to his withers and breathed in the sweet horsey smell of him. I was seeing the horses in the fall after a summer of fat green grass instead of in the spring after weathering a winter of blizzards without a barn. Not my strongest, too young to be truly mountain savvy, too small to be my best river crosser, Chucao was built tight, compact, quick to turn, the horse I always swore I would have if I lived on a *campo*. Arraquien and Tamango were my tough Patagonian tractors. Chucao was my Ferrari.

I threw a saddle on him, and we went for a welcome-home ride to the top of the *campo*. He moved like a horse who wanted to run. I let the crisp fall day and the movements of a willing horse sink into my work-weary soul.

Early the next day, I saddled Arraquien and threw a halter on Chucao. We were going home. Tamango would have to stay for now. José needed Tamango around the ranch more than I needed three horses standing in my pasture.

Before the sun hit the valley floor my *tropé* and I headed up to the top of the *campo*. My plan was to exit through the gate I had used for years, pass through the nature reserve, bypass Coyhaique as I had done before, and arrive at Pancho's before dark.

When I got to the gate in the upper most corner of the *campo*, it was wired and nailed shut. Whoever had rigged this was serious about keeping it closed. If Patricio had done it, he wouldn't mind if I undid it, passed through, and then re-wired it. If the rangers had closed it, I could simply ask for forgiveness and drop the name of Orlando, a long-time friend, who was now the head ranger.

A wimpy pocket knife was again my only tool. I twisted and pulled and banged nails with rocks. Twenty minutes into the process the gate was no closer to opening. Dejected, I returned to José's cabin.

Maté in José's tiny kitchen brought things into perspective. Why would it matter if I went home today or tomorrow? Still, the difference between the way things were and the way I wanted them to be was causing me great distress.

"Why don't you just go the other way around town?" he asked.

I had no idea there was another way around Coyhiaque's busy, car-packed streets.

José carefully described a series of roads on the eastern edge of Coyhiaque.

A left here, a right at this corner, by a few government houses, I could touch just the outer edge of Coyhaique. If I was going to go I needed to get moving.

"*Gracias*," I said, the traditional response that lets your host know you are finished with the *maté* session.

When I first came to Chile this particular custom had truly baffled me. My parents had taught me to say "thank you" every time anyone offered me anything. When the *maté* came my way I said, "*gracias.*" The gourd and its contents were immediately withdrawn, leaving me confused and *maté*-less.

Not far into José's proposed route I realized getting through town was definitely going to suck. Even on the back roads cars stacked up behind us, their occupants staring out the windows mouths wide open in disbelief. Behind us, a taxi driver laid on the horn. Chucao danced sideways into the middle of the narrow road. Hadn't this guy seen horses in town before? Then again, if he moved here in the last five years he probably hadn't.

"*Mama, caballo, Mama, caballo.*" A little girl ran out of one of the government box houses that lined the street. She appeared to be about four years old. No doubt she had never seen a horse in town before. Maybe she only knew horses from picture books. I wanted to let her pet my horses, feel their sweet soft breath on her cheek, but the last thing I wanted was a rodeo in her front yard. I needed to keep the momentum going forward, the horses' nervous energy positively directed. Still, I felt sorry for the girl when her mother called her back indoors.

I crossed one last main street and was able to turn south. Soon, I was blissfully back on country roads. It was now raining a familiar Patagonia downpour, the kind that has no intention of letting up any time soon. The days were getting shorter fast. By the appearance of the sky, it would be dark long before I got to Pancho's. I pushed my already cranky beasts into a good trot.

It was fully dark when we got to Pancho's house.

"*Hola*," I hollered from the metal gate a hundred yards from the house. A dark, hooded figure on a black horse, I surely resembled the grim reaper.

Pancho came out anyway.

"*Hola, Nancy, Pasé,*" he said, grabbing Arraquien's lead rope. "Last time you were here, it was a night just like this. Remember?"

ALMOST TEN YEARS later Pancho and I would be sitting in his kitchen listening to a torrential downpour on the roof, his two children playing on the floor, and he would remind me, "Whenever it rains like someone opened a trapdoor in the sky, I know I will see you soon."

IN THIS REGION where most houses are uninsulated, a thick smoke hangs in the air above Coyhaique on winter days and truck loads of wood, often still green, caravan into town from the countryside. In contrast, Pancho and Cuchi's warm, friendly, straw bale house sported a solar panel and a homemade wind-turbine in their front yard.

"Straw is cheap, readily available, and well insulating, a natural building material for the region," Pancho said. "People stop on the road to check out our house all the time. Maybe it will catch on."

But, what Pancho really wanted to talk about was his latest creation, an organization called *Esquela de Guías.* All the guiding jobs in Patagonia's budding tourism industry were going to outsiders. "Why should all these jobs be going to foreigners? Wouldn't tourists prefer someone who was born and raised in the area? Couldn't rural Patagonia use a little income?"

As a guide in Patagonia for years, I was one of those foreigners making my living from the world's last wild places, yet I thoroughly agreed with him. In the two years since we had visited, he had created a school teaching local Patagonians to be wilderness guides.

Every summer plane loads of visitors flew through Alaska's native villages on their way to the great Alaskan wilderness, most with guides, most leaving not a penny behind in the local community. Over the two years I had been away I, too, had created a guide-training program, this one for rural Alaskans. It was uncanny, but it wasn't a coincidence.

Patagonia and Alaska—two distinctly different rural communities at opposite ends of the earth, both with a rich human and natural history and no real source of income—were my heart's twin homes.

Pancho and I stayed awake until the early morning hours, discussing how to best preserve the life we enjoyed, not trying to avoid inevitable change, but to move forward with grace.

Another long day of riding brought me home, and I settled into the multitude of daily chores needed to keep myself alive: food to cook, water to haul, laundry to do by hand. All over the world women were doing exactly this. It all seemed so temporary. All these chores would need to be done again tomorrow. Was the difference that these women were laboring for their families? I doubted that for me the drudgery would be any different if I had a slew of kids to take care of. I longed to put in a garden, tend it carefully, and watch it grow, but it was May, nearly winter in the southern hemisphere.

On clear days, I took the horses for long rides in the woods. The mountains behind the cabin were laced with old, ox-cart roads. Sometimes the trails ended abruptly in an opening where logs had been pulled from the woods by oxen. Sometimes they ran for miles across still green forest floor, through the brilliant rust-colored *lenga* forest. It would take me weeks to figure out where they all went. I had always considered getting to know the lay of the land around your house a worthwhile use of time.

Some days I would gallop Chucao in circles in the pasture, running, dodging, changing leads. Just for the fun of it, I'd pretend we had a herd of cows to move. I tried to get each horse out every other day. That meant I needed to ride every day. I told myself the horses needed the exercise.

One afternoon I was pounding a makeshift table together outside the cabin when a visitor, a teenage boy, who lived up valley, stopped by. I wanted to invite him in, but I had no *maté* and no stove to heat it on, no chair to offer him. What kind of neighbor was I? I feared that this was exactly what he had come to find out.

We chatted awhile, but the young man remained on his horse. I wanted to go riding with him, but horseback riding was something you did when you needed to go somewhere. No one except me rode wildly in circles. The visitor, all too soon, went on his way.

The weather was as good now as it would be until spring. Maybe I could slip in one last horse trip before winter. The morning I left was cool, but not cold. The previous night's frost hadn't even frozen the puddles. Maybe we were in for an Indian summer. I had barely gotten off the road system into wild country, when I met a man carrying a fence post.

"Where are you going?" the man asked.

"Lago Atravasado," I replied.

"You can't get there from here," he said.

"*¿Porqué no?*" I asked.

"It's closed," he said, walking off with his fence post over his shoulder.

A hundred yards farther a locked gate stopped me in my tracks. The man's matter of fact, "*esta cerrada,*" echoed in my ears. Did it not matter to him that you could no longer travel through this valley on a horse?

Was this guys "Oh well" attitude just another manifestation the of Patagonian people's amazing ability to accept what is? Or was it the beginning of the end of a lifestyle I loved? I couldn't wrap my head around it being both.

Foreigners and people from Santiago had moved in, bringing their habits with them. When roads arrived so had strangers in automobiles. The woodstove in my cabin had been stolen. Patagonia was changing. It disturbed me deeply.

I gave up and tried an alternate route. Cow trails wound between small tightly packed hills. Small pocket lakes filled every hollow. My disappointment about not getting to Lago Atravasado simmered, but the intricate landscape pulled me in. My horses were happy. They didn't care where we were going. There was fat grass, the moon was rising, and the night was exceptionally warm for this time of year.

A few days later, a scruffy looking sheep dog mix, probably Border Collie or Australian Shepard, appeared out of nowhere. Dogs often followed my ungainly parade for a quick mini-adventure, but they usually went home after a few kilometers. This one didn't.

"*Fuera!*" I yelled at him in the tone I had heard others use.

But, I had a soft spot for Australian Shepherds. My best friend for fourteen years of my life, and all of hers, had been an Australian Shepherd.

The little brown-and-black dog sported a frayed rope around his neck. Did he belong to someone nearby? There were no farmhouses in sight. Part of me wanted him, my days were lonely on the *campo.* Maybe the more animals I had the better.

"Come on, be realistic, the last thing you need is a dog," I told myself. I would be going back to Alaska at some point. Leaving my horses was hard enough. What would I do with a dog?

I threw rocks at him, careful not to actually hit him. Nothing worked. He was coming on our parade.

At lunch break, I held a chunk of meat in his direction. I had just thrown rocks at him. Now I was offering him food. He approached, then ran away, tail tucked between his legs. I needed his friendship, but didn't want an attachment. Which one of us was more schizophrenic?

Just outside Villa Frey he disappeared. Maybe he went into town searching for the inevitable open garbage container. Maybe he had been here before and knew someone. Either way, I told myself, it was good that he wasn't following me. I already missed him.

Back home, I tried not to think about the little dog. Lots of dogs wander the streets in Chile. The next day dawned clear and blessedly calm. Cerro Sombrero was beckoning. The neighbor's gate was open. I rode through.

When I first moved into my little cabin, I had stopped at the their house. A barefoot boy stood in the yard, staring at me. His mother peered at me from behind the front door. A man came out of a tool shed.

Praying that they were friendly, I asked for permission to cross their land.

"*Si, por supuesto*," he said. He seemed confused about why I had come out of my way to stop at the house and ask. There had been no invitation to come in for *maté* or stop by again later.

Arraquien huffed up the steep incline toward the base of the mountain where we entered the *lenga* forest. Auburn leaves were still on the trees and green plants covered the forest floor. The Christmas-red flowers and green leaves of the *copihue* wept from the walls of every crevice. Occasionally, a three-petaled, pure-white trillium still bloomed, an innocent but sexy bride peeking out through the foliage of the forest floor.

A couple of hundred feet overhead, patches of new snow covered the greenery. A thousand feet up permanent snowfields glistened, white with fresh powder. Summer, fall, and winter existed simultaneously. I tied Arraquien in the last patch of open forest before the mountain steepened up. Drawn by a powerful urge, I headed uphill on foot. Immersed in what I know to be heaven, I was puffing upward through my favorite forest on earth covered in six inches of new fallen snow, when I noticed that a set of cloven hooves had wandered the forest floor, green tracks in a white landscape.

In eight years of traveling the remote backcounty of Southern Chile I had seen exactly one *huemul*, but I recognized these prints. I did not expect to actually see these elusive animals. Just knowing that these gentle forest creatures were living nearby made me happy.

Suddenly, I got the feeling I was being watched. The soft, brown eyes of a doe were calmly observing my every move. Branches became antlers as a buck stuck his head out from behind a tree, curious as to what type of creature had entered his forest. To my amazement, the doe came striding toward me. The Inuit believe that in the distant past animals and people spoke the same language. I stood motionless, wishing I understood, both honored and thrilled to share their forest. We stared at each other for minutes, or was it hours, until the two wandered quietly into another part of the forest.

A decade of protection from hunters and the establishment of nature reserves seemed to be making a difference. I had just seen my second and third *huemul*. Within the next few years *huemules* would become a common sight along a nearby section of the Caraterra Austral. The symbol of wild Patagonia was coming back.

I clambered upward through a long patch of thick forest. One moment I was standing, nose to branch, in thick undergrowth, the next I stepped out onto an open gently sloping snowfield forming a long, perfect ramp to the ridge. After growing up hiking through the scattered, wind-beaten, krumholtz of the Colorado high country, I'm always amazed at the abruptness of timberline in Patagonia, the way the alpine world materializes without warning.

Topping out on the summit ridge, the North side of Cerro Castillo towered in the distance. On the shady, southern face of Cerro Sombrero, I was surprised to see long running, half-bridged crevasses arching across the entire slope below my feet. The map said nothing of a glacier on this mountain. *La Patagonia*, she is always full of surprises.

One short scree scramble, and I was on top of the Sombrero. A long ridge stretched out toward yet another summit, and then another, but this one would have to do for now. I had a horse tied in the woods.

A full-on giggling glissade down the thirty degree snow ramp brought me swiftly to the edge of the woods. Slowing down, becoming more observant, I walked quietly through the *huemul's* territory just in case I was to be blessed with seeing them again. They had vanished.

Upping my observational level helped me find the exact spot I had left Arraquien.

I found him impatiently pawing the ground. I saddled quickly, and we headed down. The sun set more north than west these days and always sooner than I expected.

The gate was still open as we trotted through the neighbor's farm. My mind was still on the lovely day in the mountains and the *huemules* when something hanging from a big pine tree beside the trail caught my eye. Furry, brown, and black, I had to look right into its eyes to be sure. The empty, dead eyes of the little dog stared back! He was hanging by his homemade rope collar, as if he had been put there for me to see. I felt sick to my stomach. A flood of could-have-beens and should-have-dones came pouring in and the tears came pouring out. Why hadn't I turned around to look for a farm as soon as I noticed he was following us that first day? Why hadn't I followed him into Villa Frey? Why hadn't I wanted him? A friend was something we had both sorely needed. It was all too late. The little guy was dead. I felt like throwing up.

I wanted to be as far from where I was as I could get. I let up on the reins, encouraging Chucao to run full out for home. Hanging on but not really caring if I fell off, I clung to his neck, my tears falling into his mane. I wanted to be thousands of miles away. I wanted to live next to people who did not kill stray dogs.

At the cabin I threw what food I had in the house in my saddle bags, along with a pot, a sleeping bag, and a tent. In half an hour, I was gone. We traveled south toward Lago Elizalde. Darkness caught us near the same place I had slept so many years ago with Nimbus. This time my camp was a sad, dark hovel, a place run to in desperation.

The next day, I turned toward the Rio Mogote Valley. The map showed seriously mountainous country up there. I was sure to get dead-ended at some point, but I didn't care. I wanted the solace of rugged country. I wanted to be turned around by cliffs and glaciated mountains, not by a locked gate.

Despite all my promises not to push the horses too hard, it was cold, late, and much to my dismay we were still on the road system when we were forced by darkness to camp. In the morning we passed a little *campo* near the end of the road with a small wooden sign that said, "camping." Too bad we hadn't stumbled upon this place the night before.

Once again, uncertainty began where the road ended. The map showed the trail staying on my side of the river, but it promptly disappeared into the Rio Mogote. Would I be crossing and re-crossing this frigid river all the way up the valley?

To my amazement an ox-cart trail ran the entire length of the valley on the other side. Dug into the hillside with steeply cut banks, the old trail proceeded up valley at a gentle grade. Miles of huge logs laid down like corrugated cardboard protected the trail from erosion.

At two p.m., which was solar noon, last night's frost hung heavy on the bushes, and I was still waiting for the sun to come up over the northern wall. Then it hit me: In this deep, east-west facing valley, the sun wasn't going to come up again until spring. Tonight's frost was going to accumulate on top of last night's and on and on until snow came to bury the valley. It was also highly probable that no one would enter this valley again until next summer. If an accident were to befall me, I would be on my own.

An old saw mill and a decrepit pile of boards explained the ox-cart road. People had been hauling logs out of this country, possibly for decades, but the land didn't have the devastated look of a clear-cut. Old trees mixed with younger trees and a full canopy covered a diverse forest floor. Where were the stumps? Either this was an extremely old cut or this valley held an exceptionally rich ecosystem, one that recovered more quickly than most.

Too many hours of darkness hung over my camp, like a sad memory. With nothing to read and nothing to do, I crawled into my sleeping bag in all my clothes and piled horse blankets on top. The evening turned into exactly what I feared it would, a long, cold, restless night.

During the day, finding the trail and keeping the horses moving occupied my mind, but at night the questions rolled in. What was I doing here? I wasn't raising sheep or even growing a garden. I would either have to go home to my friends' *campo* or go home to Alaska at some point. I couldn't stay here and freeze.

The next day I was determined to climb up into the sun, whether or not I could take the horses with me. Bush-whacking upward on foot, I felt my own exhaustion. Raising my legs up and over downed trees felt like lifting lead. Was this how my horses felt, as well? Still, I craved an open view of the huge glaciated peaks surrounding me and a moment, however brief, of sunshine in my life. Climbing was the only way I was going to get it. In the entire valley there appeared to be only one way a person could gain the ridge without a partner and a rope. The mountaineer in me was frustrated by that lack in the same way the younger mountaineer in me had been frustrated walking miles of muddy horse trails without a horse. I set my sights on a small, open, sunny spot well above the river. I pushed hard, scrambling hand over hand up wet scree. I had to get there before the sun abandoned even that spot.

I arrived in time, stripped off my wet shoes and socks, and plastered myself against the warmish rock, breathing in the last, sweet fifteen minutes of sunshine the day had to offer.

Thankfully, clouds came in and that night was warmer. Still, by morning I had been flat on my back in a tiny space for twelve hours when I convinced myself to get up. There was no use waiting for sunrise.

Back on the trail, I felt tired all the time. Was it mental? I didn't feel stressed or scared out here, but I didn't have the joy I normally felt waking up in the mountains. I was ready to leave this cold, dark, beautiful valley.

The farm with the "camping" sign was my next destination. Even from the outside, it looked inviting. Everything the residents needed was close at hand—an orchard, chickens, a big vegetable garden.

"We hardly ever have to go to town," Hortencia told me. "The grand kids come out here. We have an extra house for the family when they come. It is way too cold to camp. You can stay there."

I objected, told them I was happy to camp, but they wouldn't hear of it.

"Oh no, camping is for summer. It is winter now," her husband Luis said.

I took note, fall was now also officially over. As I settled in with this family, their welcome warmed parts of me that had been cold for weeks. Over *maté* I learned that Luis had lived in Villa O'Higgins.

"Do you know the old trail to O'Higgins?" I asked.

"Of course, I traveled it many times," he said.

He didn't seem shocked that a *gringa* had ridden to O'Higgins, or that I was now wandering around the Rio Mogote in almost winter. Neither of them mentioned the obvious fact that I was traveling alone. At last, people who didn't think I was nuts, or at least didn't let on.

Later that evening I got the story of Hortencia's family. She was one of ten kids raised not far from here. Thirty years ago she married Luis and moved to this *campo*.

"I raised three children here. That was long before the road came in. When the children needed shots we would all ride into Coyhaique. We put a small one in front of each of us and the oldest would ride behind."

Three people on one horse all the way to Coyhaique? To me, that sounded uncomfortable, but to her, these were happy memories.

When her oldest was six they sent him to boarding school in Valle Simpson.

"That lasted one year. The other kids, they made fun of him and stole things from him, so I moved into town. I had two in school by then. We rented a place to stay in Valle Simpson. I worked two jobs and took in laundry to pay for it."

Next she had followed her kids to Coyhaique while they finished high school.

"We only got to come out to the *campo* on holidays and summer vacation back then," she said.

All over Chile women had used the exclamation "*Que valienté*," to describe me and my horse trips. I had heard this from women who had ridden home through snow up to their horses' bellies to save their sheep, from women who rode the same trails I did, in a blizzard, pushing a hundred goats, from women, like Hortencia, who had given up everything so their children could go to school. A life without hardship had left me bored and dissatisfied. I didn't see anything valiant about wandering around Patagonia on a horse for fun. Did simply doing something other than what you were born into make you *valienté?*

"Now my kids are all grown, so I live here with my husband. Our three grandkids come visit often. Life is good again," she said. "When I go to town the television is always on and the kids attention is elsewhere. Better the grandkids come visit me here."

Pictures of her kids growing up entertained us the rest of the night. Patagonia is a small town. One of Hortencia's photos was of Pancho and Cuchi, with a wagon-load of kids. My friends looked so young, their own kids yet to come. Time goes by whether you are paying attention or not.

The conversation broke long enough for sleep, and we picked up where we left off in the morning. When I left, Hortencia gave me enough bread and cheese for lunch, dinner, and the next day's breakfast. When I went to pay them for camping they tried to refuse. It was my turn to lecture. "You can't have a camping business and not charge people for camping," I reasoned. They had given me the gift of friendship and conversation. The camping I would pay for.

I left Luis and Hortencia's in a good mood. I wasn't sure of what lay ahead, but felt more capable of dealing with whatever that might be.

Not far down the road, a man in a brand new four-by-four jeep pulled up beside me. His face did not tell of years spent in the Patagonian sun. He was from Valdivia. He had just purchased a huge *campo* up the Rio Bravo.

"*Oh, que bueno*," I said, expressing my approval, even though I knew nothing about it and had no idea if I approved.

As it turned out, he had never seen this *campo*. If his *campo* was indeed where he was describing it, he wouldn't be driving there, even in that fancy jeep. His best chance would be to drive to the end of the road, take a boat across the lake, and hire horses to take him up valley from there. Finding either a boat or horses was highly unlikely this time of year. I considered for a second inserting myself and my horses into his wild scheme, but quickly decided against it. There had been enough craziness in my world lately.

Confident he could buy his way wherever he wanted to go, he motored on. I had forgotten to ask him what he planned to do with this *campo* he had never seen. I imagined living there was not in his plan.

"He probably plans on selling it for a lot of money in a few years," I said aloud after he was gone.

My next encounter was even more disturbing. A car suddenly stopped, and two men hopped out. I flinched, but they just wanted to talk. Maybe they hadn't ever seen a *gringa* on horseback before.

It took less than twenty seconds for the conversation to turn to the dreaded, "*Estás sola*?"

I didn't answer. They could see that for themselves.

"*No tienes miedo*?" the tubby one asked.

I tried my well-practiced line. "Afraid of what? There are no snakes, no dangerous animals, and the people are all wonderful."

"*Si, pero donde estás tu companero,*" the tall one asked.

The question, "where was my companion," struck a painful cord that was far closer to the surface than I expected after all these years.

"*Estás muerto,*" he's dead, I said.

They had no more questions.

I marched on, fuming and ranting.

"Is that a reason I should stop living?"

"Should I shut myself up in a house?"

"Should I go home to live with my mother, until another man comes along? That's what people here would do."

For the second time that day, I was talking aloud to someone who was no longer there.

Back on the *campo* I built a tiny twiggy-fire for hot water and ate the last of Hortencia's bread. Tears that had been just under the surface for days welled up but I didn't cry. I was too far out, too unstable, and too far from home to let that happen.

If there is truly one person for everyone, if soul mates are real, I was lucky, I had known mine. I had experienced the deep companionship of having a true partner. We had spent most of our twenties together, exploring the world's wild places, and building a cabin in backwoods Alaska. Later, he died climbing a mountain in Nepal. A decade and a half and a thousand adventures had passed without him.

Alone on the *campo* there was plenty of time to think and too much time to worry. If indeed soul mates meant there could be only one, I was doomed to travel alone.

But, I still had a life to live. I wasn't going to miss out on mine, especially because, at twenty-seven, my best friend already had.

Maybe I could go visit the family of the boy who had come by on horseback a while ago. He had seemed friendly. Maybe I could get to know them. In the wind and drizzle of an early winter evening, I started walking in their direction. I hopped a couple of fences and trudged across a long, open field. It was rapidly getting dark. I hadn't brought a head lamp. The sliver of a moon lolling just above the horizon would be setting soon.

I stopped. Was I nuts? Would the neighbors think I was crazy to come visiting at this hour? I stood in the middle of the field paralyzed by indecision. Again I saw myself as others would see me, a distraught, confused *gringa* standing in the dusk in an open field, unable to move in any direction.

The tears I had been fighting all day finally came. I missed Paty and Scott and the children they would surely have. I saw myself, years from now, as my neighbors would come to know me, a looney old lady alone on a *campo*. For all the things that I loved here, it was time to go.

If only I had been able to see into the future that night, what lay ahead would have amazed and comforted me. Six years later, this *campo* would again be home. My life would be filled with puppies, chickens, horses, friends, children, and, best of all, Fredrik, the man who would become my husband.

Chapter 11

Al Norte (Northward)

TWO YEARS LATER, I was getting ready to leave Alaska for Chile when I got an email entitled "Horses gone." The words glared at me from the subject line. What the heck could that mean? I opened the email . . . Tamango and Chucao had been sold!

Back in Alaska, two more winters of running the Alaska Avalanche School had passed. Somehow, someway Chile needed to fit into my life again. I negotiated a little more than a month off work in the early part of the winter. For me this was a ridiculously short time to travel to the other end of the world. I wanted to be in the saddle every minute of it. My friend Rachel volunteered to go down early to get the horses ready, something that had always been my job.

Rachel's communication left me shocked. What? How could this have happened? Patricio and Carolina lived on a *campo* in Patagonia, but they also lived in a world of quick, simple, communication. One email explaining that they were having a hard time keeping the horses and I would have gladly sent money to buy all the hay they needed.

I had trusted them. I had promised my good, sweet boys a secure place to live. I had heard from Carolina not three weeks earlier. She hadn't said anything about trouble with the horses. Later, I learned she hadn't known my horses were gone. As in many families, Carolina dealt with the home and the children; Patricio concerned himself with the animals and the farm. For many people in Patagonia, a horse is a tool, like a hammer or a tractor. Tamango and Chucao were my friends.

My emotions rushed from betrayed, to angry, to confused and back. I was mad, mostly at myself. What kind of person would abandon her best friends? Patagonia was changing. No, it had changed. In the early days, asking someone to take care of my horse had been offering them a free horse for a year. The automobile culture had altered that. Now I was asking people to take on an extra mouth to feed? After a long, long time my heart finally settled in at sad.

Rachel was already in Patagonia. We had an expedition planned. She was committed to making the trip northward to Palena, something I had dreamed of for years. I couldn't let her down. I had to resign myself to the lesson Chile had been trying to teach me for years. I needed to accept what is and move on.

By the time I arrived in Coyhaique, Rachel had found one new horse. Platano, a short, stocky bundle of attitude, had bounded over the fence at NOLS and eaten the boss's wife's vegetable garden one time too many. He was for sale.

When I arrived, all the horses were loose on the upper *campo*. Having no horse available for the round up, Rachel and I hiked uphill, optimistically carrying a halter.

At the highest point of the *campo*, a band of horses stood silhouetted on the skyline. Manes blowing in the wind, the entire Valle Simpson below their feet, they appeared wild, majestic, and impossible to catch.

A narrow trail along a rocky face was the only access to the plateau. Our plan was to pinch them off there. I worked my way to the outside of the herd. The wild bunch wanted no part of me and started running for the exit. Visions of an American Indian buffalo jump and horses running full speed over the edge of the cliff crossed my mind. This herd, of course, had way too much sense and knew their territory far too well for that. With one quick swerve they swept past Rachel standing in the trail and headed for the *campo* below. As the blur ran by, I got a glimpse of Platano. A light *bayo*, he was the color of a peeled banana with a dark stripe down his back neatly splitting him in half. We would never catch him now.

Rachel had an idea. Slowly, over the course of half an hour, she walked toward Consuelo, a dark mare with a long, wild mane. She eased a halter over Consuelo's ears. Consuelo was the subtle, but unequivocal, leader of the pack. All the others, including Platano, followed her quietly into the corral.

In the corral, Platano staked out his corner, pinned his ears back, and charged any horse that came within striking distance.

"This one has a personality," I said. Once again, I would be traveling with a whole new set of characters.

At least Arraquien and Rachel were proven companions. Twenty years younger than me, Rachel was one of my best friends. She and

I had done other expeditions together, including crossing Alaska's Harding Ice Field on skis. Small, cute, blonde, and amazingly tough—a winner of extreme mountain running races back home—she and Platano appeared to be a perfect match, at least physically.

We still needed one more horse. Pancho had offered twice to loan us his mare, Negra. I was less than enthusiastic about the idea of borrowing a horse. Making sure every animal made it home in good condition was always my highest priority, but deep inside I realized there were never any guarantees. Besides, Negra was young and inexperienced.

"It will grow her up a little," Pancho insisted. "I want to be a part of your trip. I can't come along. I have a family and a business here, but Negra can go."

The reality was we didn't have any other leads and every day we waited in town was one less day on the trail.

La Negra was five years old and pure black. I suspected she had never traveled far from her own backyard. Fat and shaggy from the winter, she wouldn't win any beauty contests, but that wasn't what we were doing here.

When Pancho's wife Cuchi laid her head against Negra's shoulder, a wave of guilt and doubt rushed in. This horse was deeply loved.

"Are you sure you want us to take her?" I asked Cuchi directly.

"*Si, porsupuesto*," she said.

I shuddered at the responsibility I was taking on.

"I will try not to bring her back pregnant," I joked.

Pancho laughed. "Why not? We are already expecting one by Cuchi."

I glanced at Cuchi's belly. She was indeed barely, but noticeably, pregnant.

"*Felicitaciones!*" I said.

I had known Pancho and Cuchi since they were a young couple fixing up the small cabin that now stood above their new straw-bale house. I couldn't imagine better parents. I would try to take good care of their beloved horse.

We now had three horses on three different *campos,* and they all needed shoes. We hired Christian Vidal. Christian was known as one of the best farriers around, and he had a truck. When we arrived at Carloina and Patricio's, Arraquien was tied to a tree in the front yard.

"Arraquien, my sweet, sweet boy." I leaned my head on his shoulder. Suddenly, the pain of losing my big strong Tamango and my swift little Chucao came flooding through my body. Tears welled up. I stood with my head against Arraquien's withers. The world swirled around me. Rachel and Christian were nearby. I didn't see them. I didn't hear them. It was just Arraquien, me, and my sorrow.

Slowly, I ran my hands down his legs and picked up his feet, they were bad again. A horizontal split ran across his left front hoof just under the coronary band. Am I the only person here who ever thinks to trim a horse's hooves? I fumed. I had left money with José to do exactly that. Then again, what could I expect? I was the one who had not been here to take care of my horse.

I tried to show Christian the concerning split in Arraquien's left hoof. He gave me a perfunctory glance and started collecting his tools. It wasn't the first time that statements I made about my horses had been dismissed as irrelevant by men in Chile. Still, if Christian wasn't concerned about the crack in Arraquien's foot, maybe it wasn't as bad as I thought.

Christian held the sturdy knife, that every *poblador* kept tucked in his belt, flat against Arraquien's right hoof and whacked it with a wooden mallet. Slivers of hoof piled up on the ground. The farm dogs sneaked in to steal chips to chew on. When the hoof was flat and a shoe held to the foot did not wobble, the nails were carefully bent to angle to the outside of the hoof and pounded in.

When he had finished with the right foot, Christian picked up Arraquien's left foot and saw, for the first time, the crack I had tried to show him a half hour earlier.

"*Que mala*," he said.

Just as I had thought, it was bad. A stone had worked itself all the way through Arraquien's hoof from the bottom. A fine liquid oozed from the spot it had popped out not far below the coronary band.

"Injuries like this grow out," Christian assured us, "but it takes a long time. If he were my horse I wouldn't take him on a long trip."

Those words crushed my heart, but I knew instantly, if Christian wouldn't take this horse then neither would I.

Everything was a mess. Carolina and Patricio were moving. Arraquien needed to go somewhere and it wasn't going to be with us.

Then Christian said, "I have a horse called Guanaco. You can use him. I will take your horse home with me."

It sounded like a generous offer, but I didn't know if I liked it. I had just lost two horses by leaving them with people I thought I knew well. I barely knew Christian.

"Once his foot grows out then you can have him back again," Christian assured me.

I was reluctant to trust anyone with my horse. On the other hand, if this trip was going to happen it needed to move in a northward direction and soon. We were already committed to buying a truck ride home for Negra. And one thing was for sure, Arraquien couldn't live here.

With the words, "*Bueno, gracias,*" we had two borrowed horses.

Guanaco turned out to be a tall tan *bayo* with a gorgeous set of white splotches dripping down his left hindquarters. He was leggy and lean, like his namesake, and matched me in the way Platano matched Rachel. Our *tropilla* was complete.

One miraculous morning well after the date we had hoped to depart, Rachel and I loaded Negra with all our gear, saddled Guanaco and Platano, rode out the *campo* gate, and turned decisively south.

To minimize travel on the *carretera* and avoid Coyhaique we would head first south and then east all the way to the border of Argentina before turning northward at last.

A few kilometers from the *campo* we ran into Sergio driving a tractor the other way.

The night before, at his kitchen table, Sergio had said, "These days everything is pre-determined. Even adventurers have a sponsor and a sat phone. No one does what you girls are doing any more!" My first mentor in Patagonia was proud of us.

Only a few miles after we waved good-bye to Sergio, Negra stopped. We tugged, begged, coerced, even swatted her butt. She wouldn't budge. What was up?

She was round as a barrel and the saddle kept threatening to roll under her belly. We adjusted her saddle. We rearranged her load. Nothing.

"I don't think she wants to go," said Rachel.

Negra had just caught on to what she was in for and was opting out.

"Yep, I think we have found our weak link," I replied, unexcited about dragging a reluctant mare for the next 450 kilometers. "Maybe things will get better in a few days," I said with an optimism I didn't really feel.

Eventually Negra followed us down the road with her ears laid flat against her head. Our little girl was pissed. After a couple more refusals, I was more than ready to camp. I missed traveling with my *tropé*.

That night we built a fire and cooked dinner under a troposphere of stacked lenticular clouds turning rose, salmon, corral, crimson, and ever deepening shades of maroon. As the sun slipped farther below the horizon and the fire slowly died, sleep took over.

We woke up on the edge of Argentina, old volcanic plugs towering above the plains were the only topography for miles. A long dirt road disappeared over the horizon, a sandy horse trail on both sides. It was Wyoming, with flamingos. We trotted and galloped on the dusty trail beside the road. The *pilchero* load held tight. Life was perfect.

Four days into our trip, we arrived in the small village of Ñireguao, exactly as planned. We had traveled the last day and a half through one of the biggest *estancias* in the region. In a landscape where you could see the dust plumes of a passing horse for miles, we had seen no one for days.

"Hello. Where do you come from?" a middle aged man greeted us in perfect English from the first doorway we passed. He had us in his kitchen in twelve seconds. Like many people who speak good English, he wanted to talk politics. But before we could answer his questions, he told us his own opinion. Twenty seconds into the conversation I knew I'd rather be somewhere else.

He had worked much of his life for Haliburton, a multi-national oil field service company that employs over 100,000 people. This man had worked all over the world. He listened to Rachel just long enough to hear that she worked for an organization trying to protect the world's oceans.

"That's awful, those people are ruining things," he proclaimed.

"Those people," of course, were us but before he could digest that fact he went on.

"This guy Douglas Tompkins, do you know him? He is setting up his own country. He is going to cut Chile in half."

I actually knew a fair bit about Douglas Tompkins and his project.

In 1991, newly retired from Esprit, Tompkins had bought a 1,749-acre farm accessible only by boat at the head of Fjordo Renihue. His plan to create a wilderness reserve grew, and the foundation he created, The Conservation Land Trust, managed to purchase 762,000 acres of pristine hardwood rain forest north of Chaiten. His project, Pumalín Park, sits at the narrowest part of a long, thin country; only sixty miles divide the vertically walled Pacific Ocean fjords from the border with Argentina. To his surprise his project became one of the most controversial land purchases in Chilean history. It seemed everyone had an opinion. Mine was not to be part of the conversation.

"Tompkins will sell a small strip of land for the road and make a fortune. He is trying to destroy our country," the man carried on.

Only a year earlier, *Presidenté* Richardo Lagos had granted nature sanctuary status to Pumalín Park, something Tompkins had worked on for years. But there was no use arguing. This man wouldn't make me change my mind, I couldn't change his and there was no escape. *Maté* and sweetbread were making the rounds.

His wife was the saving grace of the evening. A tough woman who I immediately respected, I cornered her in conversation.

After dinner the one-way conversation continued.

"We will put dams in Patagonia. With this we can get energy, with this we can produce many things and everyone can have money. They will run a power line all the way to Santiago."

This was the most preposterous thing I had ever heard.

The next day was my birthday. I was forty-seven, an event I wasn't exactly thrilled to celebrate. I just wanted to buy food and get out of town. The family from the night before had generously offered to let our horses graze an empty lot they had nearby. Food bought, we went to get the horses.

Remembering the pleasures of galloping bareback on birthdays past, I jumped on Negra without bothering with a saddle. One strong buck and I was air born. Still hanging onto her lead rope I landed on my back in fresh cow shit. Negra dragged me across the pasture at full speed, wearing my only clean shirt, which I had put on special for the occasion. Happy Birthday from Negra.

Walking through town with fresh cow dung smeared on my back and towing a reluctant mare, we met our friends from the night before. They wanted to take photos.

Somewhere in Ñireguao is a picture of me, standing starch upright, fake smile plastered across my face, trying to pretend that there was not fresh cow shit smeared all over my back.

Twenty-four hours in town had been plenty. We galloped away, *pilchero* in tow. We found a good camp just off the road and settled into what looked like a delightful evening. Just as I fell asleep Rachel hollered, "Stallion!"

A free ranging stallion was trying to mount poor Negra. Free horses mixing with horses tied with ropes terrified me. Granted Chilean horses are a lot smarter about ropes than horses back home, but with the powerful urges of sex involved, I foresaw ropes burning into fetlocks, entanglement, panic, and pain. Rachel saw it all at the exact same moment and popped Negra's rope free from the fence post. It was for moments like this that we always tied our horses with a slip knot.

Negra, with her own ideas and desires, yanked hard on the rope. Before the rope could seriously burn her hands, Rachel let go. The young lovers romped off together. I caught up with them at the first gate, fully engaged. Negra's rope still dangled from her halter, dangerously close to flailing legs.

I lunged for it. There's a lot of stretch in twenty feet of rope, but when Negra hit the end of it, I got knocked to the ground hard. Stupidly, I let the rope burn deeply into my hands before letting go.

Like mothers of a teenage daughter, Rachel and I ran screaming at the young stallion. Overcome by a protective instinct I didn't know I had, I picked up a six-foot log and hurled it at the young buck. He got the message and bolted. I calmed a still shaking Negra.

With no fenced area to put Negra in, I assumed the stallion would be back and that a long night was just beginning. Both assumptions were correct.

"How long does a mare's heat last?" I asked Rachel.

"Up to a week," she responded at three in the morning after our third chase-off of the night.

The next night in search of an uninterrupted nights' sleep, we spotted a fence that ran near a lake but didn't appear to connect all the way to the waters' edge. If we could convince the horses to get their feet wet, we could enter, camp stallion free and exit the next day.

Platano stepped into the lake and around the fence like he had done it a million times. He probably had. Negra was a bit harder. I had to get my own feet wet and pull her around the corner. Guanaco flat-out refused, bolted, and tugged Rachel off her feet and through the *calafate* bushes. Rachel hung tough and didn't let go of his rope. Eventually we were all on the inside of the fence.

Repeating the procedure the next day with Guanaco was even worse. This time, getting yanked through the woods, self-preservation kicked in and Rachel let go of the rope. Guanaco took off at a full gallop away from home. It was rare for a horse to go alone into the unknown, but I was beginning to accept that with horses crazy things happened every day.

We cordoned off the road behind us with rope in case he decided to storm the front lines and head for home. Then I trotted after him on foot. I crested a hill, expecting to see a thin strip of dirt road fading off into the *pampas.* Instead I saw fifteen horses, a *campo,* and the first closed gate I had seen in days. Guanaco was in with this unruly bunch and stirring them up even more. His rope still dragging, I again envisioned a massive knot of flying hooves and tightening ropes. Slowly, arm outstretched, cooing softly, I walked toward him. A dozen horses thundered past me, leapt the fence, circled around, and jumped the same fence again. Guanaco tried to follow them, but his rope literally fells into my hands. He was going nearly full speed when he hit the end. I braced for the jolt but I couldn't hold him.

For a moment I watched myself from the outside. A wild haired woman chasing a band of crazy horses on a rainy Patagonia morning.

Then, I was back in the moment and an amazing thing happened. Guanaco put his head down and walked toward me. Something had shifted between us. He put his soft muzzle on my shoulder, and we headed back. He was now my boy, and I would not have to chase him again.

By afternoon the weather had turned *puro Patagón.* The horses moved well in the driving wind and rain. We all understood, if we stopped we'd freeze.

Two days earlier we had hidden our sunburned noses from hot, dry, wind. Now we hid under wool scarves from the driving rain turning to granular sleet. The border of Argentina pushed us westward until perpetual dampness penetrated everything we owned. At night we checked ourselves for leaches. *Cachañas* had replaced flamingos as the sexiest bird in the neighborhood. At night we heard the *chucau tapaculo* singing out his name along with the soft huffing of the *huet-huet.*

That night we camped under a Yosemite size granite cliff. The plant names of the temperate rain forest came flooding back to me like old friends, *canelo, tepú, arrayán*. Oh, how I'd love to have this kind of vegetation without the incessant rain that makes it all possible.

The only option going northward was the *carretera.* The gravel hurt the horses feet. For two days we trudged north, like a parade of turtles. Our mounts seemed to despise road travel as much as we did. Snow-line crept down to within a hundred feet of us. More than ready to get off the road system, we considered heading up the Rio Turbio. Names are simple and descriptive in this land. The Rio Claro is clear. The Rio Pedregroso is rocky. The Rio Peligroso is dangerous. The Rio Turbio would be turbid. With all this rain it would be high.

The sun came out for a moment and we could see the valley above. The combination of fresh snow, verdant vegetation, and blooming, red *notros* looked like Christmas. It was still winter in the Rio Turbio valley. We would have to travel back eastward and cross the mountains in a dryer climate.

We fell in pace with an older man, a loaded *pilchero,* and a couple of dogs going our way. Jorgé was headed for his *campo* another few hours inland. The herd energy was strong, and we clipped along at a good pace.

Soon, it began to snow in earnest. Flakes the size of quarters fell on our heads. Jorgé's light brown woolen poncho and worn leather hat were soon covered in fresh snow. Rachel and Jorgé marched ahead of me, chatting, their hats growing whiter. A full blown Patagonia blizzard was brewing.

With typical Patagonian practicality Jorgé said, "I know some people with a barn nearby. No one is home but it doesn't matter. We can stay there."

A barn, a fire, and a roof over our heads for the first time in weeks, sounded wonderful. We dumped saddles just inside the door and turned five happy horses out to graze. Soon a fire was burning, clothes were hanging to dry, and *maté* was making the rounds.

Jorgé was sixty-eight. I would have guessed ten years younger.

"I once owned *campos* all over Aysen," he told us. "But I sold all of them. I miss my home on Lago Verde the most. It was a beautiful spot, *muy tranquilo*."

"What about where you live now?" I asked.

"I used to own it as well. Now I work for the guy I sold it to."

It was a common theme in the countryside these days, people selling their farms and living the rest of their lives working as caretakers for the people who bought them, while their children get jobs in town.

"Why did you sell all your land?" I asked him.

"*El dinero*," he said, brushing his thumb and fore finger together and looking me in the eye.

Land prices were rising, partially due to foreigners—people like me—buying land they weren't going to farm or even live on full time. The difference between the money you could make selling your farm and what you could make raising sheep for the rest of your life was hard to ignore.

A calico cat that hadn't had company in a while crawled onto Jorgé's lap. He put a hunk of meat on a stick over the fire and pulled out a chunk of fresh bread.

Eggs we had bought at a farm house right before we ran into Jorgé boiled in a tin cup beside the fire. The rich, dark yellow centers of fertile eggs were delicious. Well fed and content, we each settled into a place to sleep. One of Jorgé's dogs curled up beside me. Warmed by fire, the company, and the comfort of a culture where it was perfectly normal for two women to sleep in a barn with a sixty-eight-year-old man who happened to be traveling the same direction, I fell fast asleep.

The next morning the sun poured through the clouds. Two inches of fresh snow blanketed the green grass. During *maté,* the fog lifted and the mountains loomed up intimidating and white to the north. A few kilometers down the road, we said goodbye to Jorgé at a trail junction.

As we rode away he reminded us, "If you want to head north, look up my friend Sergio Calgan in La Tapera."

Midday we met a well-dressed family coming from La Tapera. I felt like a traveling junk show, in comparison to this freshly washed family. In Patagonia, people dress up to go to town.

"Locals do the route you want to do, but only in the summer," the father told us.

Granted, it had snowed last night, but it was already well into December. "When will summer begin?" I asked.

"Summer begins on December twenty-first," he said, wondering where we had gone to school. "But people use that pass mostly in January and February."

The family invited us to visit their *campo* over an hour's travel in the opposite direction. The idea of enjoying ripe cherries and fresh cow's milk rather than fighting our way over the pass did seem appealing.

"If we end up coming back this way we will definitely stop by," I told them, acknowledging for the first time that we might not make it over the mountains.

Tapera means ruin, a place where people once lived, but La Tapera was a real town, with a couple hundred people, a phone, a grocery store, and a *hospidaje* that sold hot meals. A big, blue school building sat on the edge of town, the following winter's heat, acres of split cordwood, stacked neatly behind it. The days of residential schools far away were over for these villagers. Most towns now had at least an elementary school. La Tapera's new school building housed seven students.

Our maps clearly showed the main road crossing the river just a few kilometers out of town.

"There definitely isn't a bridge across the Rio Cisnes until you are in Argentina," said the woman, serving us a heaping plate of chicken and mashed potatoes at the *hospedaje.*

We had confused an approximation of a planned route for reality. Our maps had been made a decade before the road existed.

Rachel and I started quietly concocting a wild plan that included sneaking into Argentina where there is no border post and trying to cross the range in a lower, and an even drier place. Giving up now, with most of the wild country still ahead, would feel like ending the trip before we started.

"I know a man who has a *campo* on the other side of the river," the woman said. "You should talk to Sergio Calgan."

Word that two girls on horseback wanted to cross the pass to Lago Verde had spread like wildfire. On my way back to camp that night, a stranger ran a block down the road to tell me that our plan was preposterous.

Assuming we could do something the local people thought impossible seemed arrogant and dangerous, but I had done it before. I needed to talk to this person Sergio Calgon.

When I arrived at camp, an extra horse was tied out front. Sergio Calgon was sitting on his haunches talking with Rachel.

"I cross the Cisnes every day. It is swift, and you must know exactly where to cross," he told Rachel. "You can cross with me tomorrow if you like."

Sergio didn't understand the lines on our map. He didn't need to. He held the intricate subtleties of the landscape in his head. As he spoke, he named the drainages and mountains along the way, and we pieced it together on the map. Most importantly, he did not out and out tell us we were mad.

"Come by my house this evening. You can talk to my father," he said

Wow, I thought, if Sergio knows the country this well, imagine what his father knows.

When we arrived, hours too early, his father was nowhere around. Sergio's wife was watching her favorite *novella* on TV.

Television had come to Patagonia in the 1970s. But, few people I knew had one in their homes. Women spun wool and knitted. On long winter nights, people told stories. I abhorred the constant chatter, senseless violence, and exaggerated sensationalism that poured from television sets world wide. I was shocked to learn that in my country people spend an average of thirty-four hours a week in front of the TV. My opinions aside, we were guests here and TV it was. We sat in silence, while beautiful, fair-skinned women paraded around immaculate apartments.

Sergio came in accompanied by another man his age.

"That route cannot be done, definitely not until summer," the stranger informed us.

Rachel and I smiled and nodded. We would wait to hear this from Sergio's father. Eventually, Sergio's father showed up, but before we got down to business, we were offered a glass of wine.

"*Bueno,*" I said, settling in for a long night.

As father and son bantered back and forth, reminiscing about journeys past, all of them of course, in the summer, Rachel and I were able to piece together a detailed description of the route.

Sergio's father was not as alarmed about us going so early in the year as he was about us going alone.

"*¿Pero estan sola?*" he kept asking.

I was thankful for Rachel's presence. I could only imagine his dismay if I were truly traveling alone. What he meant was, don't you have a guide—or at least a man—along?

I was tired of shocking people, yet the country ahead humbled me enough not to just slip quietly through town and take off, as I had sometimes done. Besides, it was far too late for that.

"We will hire Sergio to accompany us the first day," I blurted out without thinking or conferring with Rachel.

No price was decided upon, but a departure time of eight a.m. was set.

We were saddled and ready when Sergio arrived in the morning. I rode La Negra. Nicknamed "*La Reina del Mundo,*" Negra had earned the title "Queen of the World," because she demanded that we and the other horses treat her like royalty. I was going to need to push her hard to keep up with the guys. When we crossed the river, I wanted her to understand that she was traveling with the herd.

"We are going farther up river today because the river is extra high," Sergio informed us.

The night before Rachel had confessed that the river crossing scared her. I was nervous as well, but her confession frightened me. Rachel was small and compact, but amazingly strong, competent, and confident. If she was scared, there was something to be scared about.

The river was deep and fast, but at the crossing it ran smooth and glassy, with no waves or underwater boulders. Better just do it. The horses would feel, and take advantage of, any hesitation on our part. On the bank of the river Sergio reached for the *pilchero* rope. For once I let go of my ego. Happy to have only Negra to deal with, I handed him Guanaco.

The strong current pushed waves up around Negra's belly, soaking my boots. I didn't lift them up over the saddle the way the locals did. This was by far the biggest river I had crossed on a horse. La Reina plowed ahead without hesitation. The girl had potential. Tall thin Guanaco carried his load across with grace. Short, stocky Platano maintained his typical "so what" attitude. As the water broke around her thighs, Rachel's eyes were pinpoint focused on the far side of the river.

We had crossed the Cisnes above where the Rio Casaras came in, so we had another river to cross. Not nearly as deep as the Cisnes, the Casaras contained plenty of volume plus boulders to navigate. The horses plowed in like they were born to do it. They, I was learning, were capable of much more than I thought.

Rapidly, we climbed into the *lenga* forest, then descended through steep, slippery mud down the other side. Concentrating on keeping the saddle upright on Negra's rounded form kept me focused on the moment.

Two men and couple dogs joined us. Traveling with the pros, we moved at a completely unfamiliar pace. Negra was trying her little heart out to keep up with the big boys. So was I. My mind, as well as my body, was getting tired of pushing Negra to keep up. I could hear the men talking, but couldn't quite get close enough to understand. Then one of them turned to address me. "A man brought eleven cows over the pass from Lago Verde yesterday."

I was thrilled. The footprints of eleven cows would be easy to follow.

Sergio never handed Guanaco back to me. The *pilchero* load loosened a few times and much to my embarrassment he had to stop and tighten it, but I could tell he respected us. Unlike most of the town's people, he believed we had a chance of making it over the pass.

"I would like to work as a guide for tourists," Sergio told us.

He was patient and competent. He seemed to enjoy showing us his backyard. Maybe I could get him some business.

"How can people get ahold of you?" I asked.

"They can leave a message for me at the store."

"That will not work for most tourists," I told him, imagining clients from the United States calling the local grocery to book a horse trip in Patagonia. "You will need to get a telephone. My friend Pancho can help you set up your business," I told him, explaining about *Esquela de Guías*.

A simple splash across the last river, and we entered a wide, flat meadow with good grass, home for the night.

Sergio would leave us here. Awkwardly I asked Sergio for his fee. In many places in the world asking the fee for a service that has already been rendered is ignorant and an invitation to be over charged, but I was unconcerned. Whatever it was would be fair.

"*No, no, no es nada,*" Sergio responded.

Rachel broke in, "*No, la contesta es no.*"

We were going to pay him no matter what.

"No, if you are going to have a business you have to charge people," I said.

The guy drove a hard bargain. He settled for an extra lead rope, an Alaska t-shirt, and our biggest candy bar.

A cherry tree near camp caught my eye. Someone must have planted it. A little farther on I stumbled across a faded picket fence and a tiny house that looked for a moment like a doll house. I had found a grave. People had lived and died here, but who? Most likely the parents or grandparents of the men we had met earlier that day. Another structure stood mysteriously on the skyline. As I wandered closer, it became a bunch of tree trunks leaned together like a teepee. Why was it here?

Across Arctic Canada are mounds of stones called inukshuks, markers that communicate, here is a place: A camping place, a fishing spot, an island just over the horizon.

Of course, this was a marker. To a person on horseback in the valley below with their heads just above the *ñirre* trees, this pile of wood said, "People live here."

When asked why they built inukshuks in the North, the Inuit replied, "Because it makes the country less lonely." Unlike a lot of places we call wilderness—where city people go to try and find solitude—in truly wild country people are looking for each other.

Scrub *ñirre* broke into *lenga* just above camp. A hundred meters overhead, snow covered the ground. We only needed to gain 250 meters to get over the pass, we had tracks to follow, and someone was camped up valley. Maybe the townspeople had been just naysayers. We would move to the last green spot tomorrow and go for the pass the next day.

As we crept closer to Cerro Aguila, the spire that had dominated the skyline for days, our route appeared more and more intimidating. Rachel and I repeated out mantra, "anywhere cows can go we can go too."

Just at nightfall, we arrived at a small *puesto,* the last green spot this side of the pass. We expected we would find the man who had recently crossed the pass there, but Raúl had no idea that two *gringas* with laden horses were about to show up at his doorstep.

"Oh, no, you can't do that," he announced once he figured out our intentions.

"But, sir, you just did," Rachel said.

"Yes, but it was tough," came his answer.

I acknowledged that I was sure it was really tough and asked specifically about conditions.

"But you two cannot," he insisted.

"*¿Por qué?*" I asked

"*Porque soy Patagón.*"

I couldn't argue that point. He was *Patagón,* and we were not.

No matter what our crazy intentions, we were company and we were invited into his *puesto* for *maté* and fresh bread.

"*Vas a sufrir,*" he informed me.

I assured him I was quite accustomed to suffering, but inside I questioned if I was willing to let my horses suffer as well.

"A man fell in the river, lost his shoe, and lived with me for three days."

"A father and a son died. Nobody ever found them."

"Ever?" I asked, unsure how he knew for sure they were dead.

"Your horses will fall through the snow into the swamp."

This one disturbed me. Swamps terrified me more than anything.

"And there is a steep spot. My horse rolled over on me. I hurt my back," he said, pulling up his shirt to show his lower back and pointing to his kidney area. This was disturbing, an injury in that area could be serious, but locals never got off their horses. We would undoubtedly be walking.

With a little wine the conversation slowly turned around.

"We are only going to look. If the route is too hard we will be back tomorrow night," I promised.

"I will make more bread," Raúl said.

Then he gave us one small opening for confidence. "If by chance you make it through, could you tell my wife Magdelena in Lago Verde that I made it?"

The next morning dawned clear and calm. This was our day to cross, or return to Coyhaique. With a million promises to be careful and the absolute assurance that we would be back if things got too rough, we headed out.

At first the trail wasn't bad. I wondered once more if we had been the victims of excessive protectiveness. There was one last grassy meadow below the snow line and then firm snow between the *lengas*. A wide swath of cow hoofprints kept us on route.

Once we were above the timber, the sun started working on the snow and it got deeper, softer, and punchier. I worried incessantly. The thought of a horse breaking a leg on a snow-buried log, gave me a thick sickening in my stomach.

By noon we were walking. I led Guanaco. Rachel led Platano. Negra was wedged, off lead, between us. At 12:45 p.m. Guanaco turned his head, yanked the rope out of my hand, and trotted off in the direction we had come. Negra followed. One free horse was not a big deal. Our *tropilla* had become a family. But two free, pissed-off horses might go all the way to Raúl's or worse. I definitely didn't want horses galloping in these conditions. Walking slowly, patiently toward them, I coerced them back into the parade, but their vote had been registered.

Near the pass things began to get ugly. The snow was drifted, solid enough in most places for the horses to walk on, but soft and punchy in others. I looked over my shoulder to see Rachel, Platano, and Negra headed for what looked like a shallow spot in the snow. In an old, over-wintered, snowpack, deep snow is strong snow. Shallow places are often weak.

"Wait!" I yelled, but not in time.

Negra punched through. Dark muddy swamp water came up around her belly. Shit, this was it, we were falling into the swamp to die just as Raúl had said. I hated myself for ever wanting to try this pass.

Chapter 12

Ángeles y Diablos (Angels and Devils)

THE CHERRY TREES in Magdelena's front yard were in bloom and the garden was producing lettuce and cilantro. Summer in Lago Verde was weeks ahead of La Tapera.

"*Pasé*," Magdelena said even before she knew what our business was. When we told her we had seen Raúl, a big smile spread across her face. We did not mention our hardships crossing the pass.

Settled behind a big wooden table, her grown daughter served us soft drinks in tall glasses. Hand-carved wooden plaques adorned the walls. My eyes gravitated to an extraordinary carving of two horses galloping. Wind-whipped manes, perfectly defined muscles, only one who had spent a lifetime with horses could produce that kind of detail.

"My husband makes them to sell," Magdelena's daughter said. "He is Mapuchi, so our daughter is part Mapuche," she told us, picking up her two-year-old so we could see the indigenous heritage in the little girl's round face and straight dark hair. The child had the easy smile of a girl who knew of nothing except love and acceptance. Every so often she jumped onto her mother's lap to nurse for a moment. If I lived in this town these people would be my friends.

Magdelena's other granddaughter, six-year-old Estephania, returned from school, snuggled in next to me, and started practicing her English.

Next a young man popped in. He had heard rumors that two *gringas* had just arrived from La Tapera. He had come to see for himself.

"Two men from town just tried to cross the pass to La Tapera yesterday," he informed us. "They turned around."

Two *gringas* showing up the next day, that could be embarrassing. I understood, and I told him the truth. "They turned around because they are much more intelligent than us."

BACK ON THE pass, Negra had valiantly pulled herself out of the muck and stood, soaking wet, stone-still, in the middle of the semi-frozen river, ears flat against her head. Her red lead rope draped ridiculously over one eye, Negra gave us the old forget you. She wouldn't leave us but she was done following.

"We have to be well over halfway. It's better to go on than go back," I surmised, knowing darn well I might be lying to myself, Rachel, and the horses.

With an uncooperative Negra, we began to ferry loads as I had done on big mountains all over the world. We led two horses forward. Then one of us went back to drag Negra. Progress slowed to a crawl.

Late in the day, we found a steep, muddy downward trail. We could see the green valley bottom land below. The horses finally bought our story that it was easier to go on than turn around, and we traveled as a team again. My goal now was to keep large animals, with tremendous *ganas* to get to the valley below, from sliding out of control down the muddy slope. Passing a place with barely enough grass to last three horses half an hour, Guanaco threw an ears-back, knees-locked protest.

"Would you just trust my judgment on this?" I begged, knowing my track record on good decision making was seriously lacking.

A big grassy oasis with a corral and a *puesto,* the obvious stopping point for people crossing the pass, awaited us. Saddles came off. Noses went down. Ears came forward. While I re-lived visions of slipping horses lunging through snow and "what ifs" and "could have beens," played out in my mind; the horses spent the evening happily munching.

"THE PORTEZUELO CASINOVA is even steeper and higher than the one you just came over. You can't get over it on horseback," the visitor warned us.

Rachel and I were unanimous, this time we would listen to the locals.

"What do you know about the Rio Quinto?" I asked.

A route along the Rio Quinto would add over sixty miles to our travels and take us far into the wet, western rain forest, but there would be no high passes to cross.

"I have gone that way. No snow there," the man promised. "But, the trail doesn't get used much these days and the river crossings are really big."

Magdelena started setting up a spare room for us.

"We have to go. We can't leave the horses alone all night, but we will visit again tomorrow," Rachel promised.

That night I untied Negra while Guanaco was still free. Mountaineering had taught me to clip in before clipping out, to never leave yourself unprotected, but it had been weeks since we worried about our horses abandoning us. My hand only inches from her halter, Negra glanced at Guanaco for confirmation, looked me squarely in the eye, and trotted off. Just the other side of the river from camp was a huge pasture and twenty free horses. Guanco and Negra splashed easily across the river and joined the herd.

Damn it, I thought, feeling especially tired and stupid.

Just then a man came down the trail, obviously the owner of the *campo* we were camped on and the herd of animals mine had run off with.

"*Tienes algunos extras*?" I asked him if he had just acquired a couple of extra horses.

"*Si*," he said, chuckling at his good fortune.

The good-natured way everyone here took things like this in stride made me embarrassed at my earlier aggravation.

"No problem," he said seriously. "I need to round up my horses in the morning anyway."

The next morning when we arrived at the man's house, he was already out looking for the horses and his wife had just finished milking the cows.

Young and pretty, Minda was intelligent and seemed more worldly than most *campo* women.

"I grew up in Lago Verde, but I was a town girl till I met Carlos. I didn't know how to milk a cow or ride a horse or anything." She laughed.

"Lago Verde only has a school until eighth grade, so I went to high school in Chaitén. My daughter is going there now."

I was still trying to wrap my head around Minda being old enough to have a daughter in high school when the conversation turned to Chaitén, Pumalín Park, and Douglas Tompkins' foundation, The Conservation Land Trust.

In a place like Palena, where news travels primarily by word of mouth, rumors often run rampant. Fueled by fear and lack of knowledge, stories about what Tompkins was doing up there ranged from the creation of a new Jewish state to a nuclear waste dump.

To farmers who had spent a lifetime wrestling a living from this wet, wild landscape, the idea of buying land just to let it sit there was an alien concept. The same year Tompkins began buying land for conservation, Trillium, a logging company from Washington State, bought 625,000 acres in Tierra del Fuego. Nobody questioned Trillium's intentions for buying such a tremendous chunk of land. Their motives were understandable. They planned to log it.

Minda had never traveled into the richly diverse temperate rain forest that is Pumalín Park, few people had, but she too had an opinion.

"Chile can't afford to protect its own land. I am glad that someone is doing it."

Pumalín Park is home to the endangered alerce tree, one of the world's oldest living species. There are trees growing north of Chaitén that were old when Christ was born. The park is also home to the endangered *pudú*, an eighteen-inch-tall deer that lives entirely within the thick, dripping rain forest of Patagonia.

This band of mountainous forest at the narrowest part of Chile also contains Patagonia's only hope for a north-south road connecting central Patagonia to the rest of Chile. The complexity of building that road would match anything constructed in the fjords of Norway.

"I agree with the park, but I also think the road is a good idea. It will make everything cheaper here," Minda said.

"I have seen some of that country," I told her. "Even if a road could be built through that vertical world of twisting jungle it would be so tortuous to travel that it would still be cheaper for goods to come through Argentina or by boat."

The wilderness-lover in me didn't want to see this tremendous piece of Patagonian rain forest divided in two and the changes that would bring. But, I had to admit, there was already a road to my house.

"But, my opinion isn't as important as yours. You live here," I told Minda.

"Oh, no," she said. "Your opinion is important too, because you know the rest of the world."

"The world I come from has too many roads and power lines and aluminum smelters already. That is why tourists from all over the world want to come here. What you have here is precious," I told her.

"I am definitely against the dams," Minda said.

This was the second time I had heard this rumor about dams. Minda seemed so educated and socially connected. Could this be true?

"What dams?" I asked.

"They want to put dams on the Baker and Pascua Rivers and run a power line all the way to north of Santiago. It would come right through here."

"Who wants to do this?"

"A company from Italy, I think."

"That can't happen here," I said, wishing like hell that I was absolutely sure of that fact.

"No, it can't. We don't need it. We have a solar panel," Minda said, pointing out the window to a small array set up in the yard. "We will be getting a windmill soon. We can create all the power we need."

I wondered about a connection between the road and the power line? If a road was built, it might not help people here get goods more inexpensively, but it would make an easy corridor for a huge power line.

Leaving behind a quiet little town, beautiful gardens, blooming cherry trees on the street corners, and lots of new friends, heading out into wild county again, felt like escaping from paradise.

I woke up on our first morning, under a huge coihue tree to the sound of grazing horses and flowing water. Peace welled up inside me like the boils in the deeply churning river beside me. I was both intimidated and exhilarated by the towering glaciated peaks up valley turning pink with the sunrise.

The day was blessedly uneventful. No horses ran away. We didn't lose the trail. No saddles slipped under bellies. Huge silver trunks, from fires in the forties, were scattered across the landscape, mixing with the bright red and green of *notros* in bloom. Dotted with small *lagunas*, the country had an appealing eerie beauty. Ancient *coihue* giants watched us amble by, an irrelevant passing in their long lives.

By noon the next day, the horses stood beside a river choked with log jams. The trail had apparently been flooded out. Rachel and I scrambled around, balancing precariously on wet logs over running water. There was a trail on the far bank, but one that did not resemble the wide, trouble-free trail we had traveled yesterday. That trail headed up toward the snowy pass we had decided not to use. A small path continued in our direction.

We made our way around the log jam and headed slowly west. The deep purple and red flowers of the *chilco*, an exotic member of the fuchsia family, dripped from branches. The needle-shaped leaves of the *mañio*, soft white *luma* flowers, and the fragrant *arrayán* tried to crowd each other out. Everything had flowers and everything had thorns. There would be no traveling without a trail in this country.

The trail ended again where the river butted into a cliff. Positive the trail crossed the river at that point, we waded the horses belly deep through the flowing water. Finding no trail on the other side, we rode back through the river. We found no semblance of a trail on the original side, so again we pushed the horses back across the current.

Then all together, as if preplanned, the horses went on strike, refusing to budge until we knew where we were going. They had lost confidence in our ability as navigators. I was inclined to agree.

Rachel and I headed off in opposite directions on foot. I found an old board lying in the woods, proof that people had been there. A hundred yards away, near the edge of the river, I discovered a stump cut, decades ago, with an axe. Then I noticed, far downstream on the other side of the river a place where animals had climbed the cut bank.

Unwilling to march the horses across the river again unless I was sure, I entered the river on foot. The current pushed strongly against my legs. Rachel had no idea where I was. I realized midstream it was a dumb move, but I continued sidestepping carefully, facing upstream. On the other side were branches cut with a machete. I repeated my foolish move and arrived back at the horses wet to the waist.

That crossing was our first introduction to the fact that on the Quinto the trail not only crossed the river multiple times, the route often was the river, sometimes for long distances.

Next the trail disappeared into a muddy slough. I couldn't make myself kick Guanaco into a place like that, so I got off and stepped in myself. Wet to the waist, I could feel a solid bottom below. A faint trail took off from the other side.

"Remind me to check for leaches tonight," I told Rachel.

My brain was tired of searching for the trail. I wanted to let the reins go slack, let Guanaco find the trail for a while, but when I did, he just stopped. He was looking for leadership. If I wasn't going to provide it, he wasn't interested in playing.

At dusk the trail came to the river again. Downstream the river swept around a huge gentle bend. All I wanted to do was camp. We hadn't seen an opening big enough to camp in all day. The trail obviously entered the river, but there was no opening in the jungle wall as far downstream as we could see. Were we seriously supposed to take off walking down a river with no idea where we could get out? The bend looked swift and deep on the outside. Who knew what was beyond that?

Just then, yet another problem came trotting down the trail behind us. Three wild-looking range horses had come to check us out. We hadn't seen a fence in days. Who, if anyone, this long-haired *tropé* belonged to, we had no idea.

Circling behind the wild bunch, Rachel rode right into the pack, whooping and hollering. They took off downstream, right into the river. We followed them. A hundred yards downstream they climbed up the embankment in a steep spot we would have never chosen. We had found ourselves a group of local guides.

Rachel nicknamed our bunch *Los Ángeles.* Pushing them forward, whenever we lost the trail, we followed our *tropé* of angels. When it was almost completely dark, we came to a small clearing with pitifully poor grass, home for the night. Guanaco pawed the ground and stomped his feet in protest. There might be nothing better for days.

We tied two horses on the longest lines we had and left Negra, the least likely to leave, free to graze. To make ourselves feel better, we fed the horses handfuls of oatmeal from our own food supply.

Not long into the night I heard Rachel say, "The wild ones are back."

Darkness had transformed our angels into devils, and they were trying to steal our mounts. I launched out of bed into the darkest night I had ever seen. I could hear horses milling around in the woods, but by the weak six-foot beam of my head lamp, I could see nothing.

Rachel and I stumbled around in the starless dripping mist, looking for a black horse on a black night. The wild boys were riling up our two tied horses, but we couldn't scare them away for fear Negra would leave with them.

Finally, I saw the white star on Negra's forehead buried in the foliage. Terrified of my head lamp Negra bolted into the night. In complete darkness, we lured her in with the last of our own oatmeal and a bit of salt.

"*Ándate diablos!*" All our horses safely tied, we ran yelling and waving toward the wild bunch.

Twice more the devils returned, twice more we drove them back into the woods. In the morning our angels were nowhere to be seen.

At first light, we moved on. We had to get the horses to grass, plus it was now raining in earnest, and we had many rivers yet to cross.

A couple hours into the next day, we stumbled upon a *campo* with huge grassy fields and a couple of towering *coihue* trees. I couldn't imagine the work it must have taken to wrestle this land from the forest. What would it be like living with the ever-present threat of all your work being swallowed up by vegetation in a year or two?

Heads down, eating, the horses weren't going anywhere any time soon. Several old wooden buildings clustered around a cherry orchard—a house made of faded gray shingles, a barn made of planks cut with a chainsaw, and an old chicken coop. A few chickens and a gray-and-white cat were hanging around. The place was lived in. We hollered off into the woods, but found no one.

A *campo* was always a likely place to lose the trail. Grassland doesn't show the impact of passing hooves and dozens of trails head off in all directions.

"Maybe the trail crosses the river again," Rachel said. But there wasn't a worn path to the rivers' edge or an easy exit on the other side. Farther downstream the river would get even bigger, especially with all this rain.

"If we cross here we will have to cross again later," I stated, wiping away the awareness that probably dozens of ever deeper crossings lay ahead.

On foot, we explored a wide trail on our side of the river. It quickly turned into a tiny path. A huge *coihue* had recently fallen across the trail. Scrambling over to see what was on the other side, I stepped on a mat of suspended *quila*. Rachel watched my head disappear as I fell to the forest floor six feet below. Clawing my way up from the dark musty forest underworld, I hollered, "No trail here."

Rachel saw an ancient arrow etched on a tree. "This could this be a marker," she said as she scurried off into the woods. I just sat there distraught, staring at the map. The map did not show a river crossing near here, but it hadn't shown our other six crossings either. Some jungle travelers we were, we didn't even have a machete, let alone an ax, or better yet, a chainsaw. Rachel was gone a long time.

"It's a trail," she said when she returned, "but I sure hope it's not our trail." Overgrown to the point it was difficult to follow on foot, the route consisted mostly of faint arrows etched in bark.

"If this is it, I don't think we can do it," Rachel said.

Until then, I hadn't thought "can't" was a word in Rachel's vocabulary.

Back at the empty *campo,* we sat on a huge rock in front of the house and petted the cat. Nearly the whole day had gone by, and we were a few kilometers from where we woke up. Our only plan was to hope someone would come home and point us in the right direction.

"I think we should look at the river crossing again," I said.

Rachel was less than excited about crossing in an unknown spot. On every crossing we had done so far there were signs that other horses had entered there. The water on the outside of the curve along the opposite bank would be swifter and deeper than it was on this side. How much stronger?

Stranding on the river's edge with a basketball in the pit of my stomach, I ran the lead rope through Negra's halter and put both ends in my hand. If she drifted downstream I could at least set her free to swim unencumbered by a rope.

Guanaco stepped decisively into the river. Platano and Negra followed, as if they had known all along the trail was over there. The current parted mid-belly on Guanaco. Water filled my boots. I looked back. Rachel was wet to the thighs, a look of concentrated intensity, but not terror, on her face. The lead rope went slack. Negra was keeping up. So brave and cute with just her nose out of the water, she was fully swimming. Whooping with relief, we lunged up the embankment onto a well-used trail.

Occasionally, parting clouds gave us a view to the ridge tops. Half way up the mountains was a line above which the unburned vegetation was taller, darker, and greener. Up there humongous *coihue* trees towered through the mist, like figures in a fantasy book. The entire mass of snarled vegetation we were traveling through had regrown in the past sixty years. The real old growth forest was a couple hundred meters overhead. We would not get there this trip.

Without the people who built and maintained these trails, who constantly cleared and re-cleared the land, we could neither travel through this country nor find grass for our horses at night. That evening I smelled smoke. We were back in populated country. The trail steadily improved, but more river crossings lay ahead and every drainage we crossed added water to an already voluminous river.

That night we slept in an old *puesto*. Rain pounded on a metal roof while visions of flooding rivers and swimming horses haunted my dreams.

The next morning we crossed the river again, but to my delight the gradient had mellowed and, even though the flow was larger, we crossed with ease. We were gaining confidence in ourselves and our horses.

Not far downstream we met a man with a big beard, something unique in this country. He flashed us a bright smile with perfect teeth, something else not common in these parts. Who was this guy?

"*Pasé a la casa*," he said, inviting us to his house, "just down the way."

After what seemed like miles, I wondered if we could have passed his house. It would be unspeakably rude to simply travel on. As it turned out, his house was still miles ahead. This guy owned everything we had ridden through for an hour behind us and three or more hours ahead. His waterfalls plummeted hundreds of feet, cascading down rock walls beside *coihue* trees nearly as tall. Only rocky, snowcapped peaks divided his land from his neighbors.

"*Que linda la casa*," I said aloud when we finally saw the peaked roof of his beautiful three-room wooden house.

"The only things I brought in from outside were the windows and the woodstove," he said.

I tried to imagine packing such large panes of glass on a *pilchero* over this kind of country. Most *campo* houses had tiny windows, many had no glass at all.

A bathtub made from a hollow *coihue* filled the entire north wall. The level of craftsmanship in his tidy dwelling spoke of wealth, but not necessarily money.

"Did you grow up here in the *campos,*" I asked him.

"My parents had a *campo* up north near Osorno,"' he told me. "It is way too busy there now, not *tranquilo* like here."

This man intrigued me. There was not much of a "back to the land" movement in Palena. Nearly all the population movement was going the other way.

The kids who had once splashed in the big bathtub, were now teenagers going to school in Coyhaique.

"And your wife, is she in Coyhaique as well?" I asked, expecting to hear the common story of the wife and children in town while the husband takes care of the *campo*.

"*Ella se fue*," he said. "She left."

It took me a moment to understand what that meant. The expression on his face told me the rest.

"I'm sorry, sometimes that happens," I said.

Suddenly it all made sense: This cute house in the country, children growing up on the farm, a young couple's dream. Now the garden and greenhouse sat empty, missing a woman's touch.

Over lunch we compared the homes we had built over eight thousand miles apart. Waldero's house had a gravity-fed water system.

"I catch mine in a rain barrel off the roof, when there is enough rain," I told him.

"Are there times when there isn't?" he asked, unable to imagine a world without abundant rain.

"There must be water uphill of you somewhere," he questioned.

"Oh, there is, but it is on my neighbor's land."

"Your neighbors don't let you use it? Are they horrible people?"

I fumbled, trying to explain an entirely different sense of private property, a system I was afraid was headed his way.

"I have a solar panel for electricity," I said.

That would never work in his cloudy rainy world, but he was considering a waterwheel.

Whether in bush Alaska or the remote sections of Aysen; water comes from the sky, heat comes from trees, and everything you have comes directly from your own hard work.

When it was time to leave, Waldero decided to accompany us to the edge of his *campo.* We traveled on and on, crossing the river numerous times in places I would never have chosen.

Hours later he left us at the first real road we had seen since Lago Verde. Suddenly finding ourselves deposited on a dirt road, the jungle, that we has so recently cursed, seemed too far away. Road travel felt like watching a movie, rather than participating in life.

The horses seemed bored as well. In the morning Platano wouldn't move, in the afternoon it was Guanaco. The town of La Junta didn't intrigue or welcome us the way Lago Verde had. La Junta saw lots of visitors. No one needed to talk to us.

Crawling north on the *carretera* at a pace that would stupefy a tortoise, Rachel read the Spanish dictionary as we plodded along. It had been weeks since I had thought about the world outside Patagonia. Now, removed by a thin strip of gravel from the need to look and think ahead, I worried obsessively about problems thousands of miles away. Now and then, a shiny new automobile would pass us, slowing to stare. After two days of mindless plodding, I was aching to make decisions again.

The seasons were changing. The rain was warmer now and the threat of snow had disappeared. The Rio Frio ran beside us, deep and dark, with branches a dozen shades of green overhanging steep cut-banks on both sides. How we would cross the Frio I had no idea, but I was beginning to believe that we would find a way.

Villa Vangaurdia, a line of nearly identical houses, many of them abandoned, had once been a construction camp for the building of the *carretera.* As we swung our legs out of the saddle, a woman about my age called out, "*Pasé,*" from her doorstep.

Nangaya came from the world of homesteading and family, but she immediately comprehended what we were doing.

"*Que marvioso,*" she exclaimed.

She loved her country. That foreigners would want to travel it slowly on a horse was not a surprise. Inside over *maté* we learned her story.

"My youngest daughter is fourteen and in school in Chaiten, so I live here during the week. I have a *campo* eighteen kilometers up river. You can stay with my son and daughter in law when you get there."

How much could be left of her weekend after riding eighteen kilometers each way? I wondered. "How long does it take you to get there?" I asked.

"Oh, maybe four hours," she told us.

It would take Rachel and I at least a full day.

"My husband died two years ago," she said, "but my son and daughter in law help me out. I will stay on the *campo*."

Her voice held something I was just beginning to understand, something I find rare in my culture—the gentle acceptance of the way things are.

"When I was a girl, my father had to travel several days by horse to Argentina to buy supplies. I went to school for a few months in Chaiten, but then my father had to go back to the *campo*."

As much as I didn't want a road to traverse the wild mountainous country north of here, I understood that it was the *carretera* that made it possible for Nangaya's daughter to go to school. Nangaya had never been to Santiago or even Puerto Montt. She had never seen a place with too many roads, power lines, smokestacks, and dams. But this woman, who had gone to school for three months, like everyone else I had met, knew how to read and write. She knew where Alaska was and that it was part of the United States, not Canada. She also knew the names and medicinal uses of the multitude of plants found in the incredibly diverse forest surrounding her home.

"I will call Vladamir and Yolanda and tell them to expect you," she said, reaching for the handset of the HF radio that sat on her desk.

"The trail ahead is steep and muddy," she warned us.

What concerned me was the river. "How do we get across the Frio?" I asked.

"There is a bridge just down stream," she told us.

Sure enough, a red-and-white swinging bridge just wide enough for horses took us easily across the river. On the other side, the wide easy trail quickly deteriorated into a muddy mess. To my surprise, Negra stepped out front. Our sweet weak link, the laughing stock of the expedition, was growing up. So proud of herself, she plowed through knee-deep mud, leading the way for the boys.

Around noon the next day we met a neighbor on the trail.

"Go two more gates, look for four free horses and wait on the side of the river. They will come get you in a boat."

"We have to cross the river in a boat?" I asked. "What about the horses?"

"They will swim," he told us as if we were children.

I had heard about towing horses across rivers with boats, but I never expected to do that to my horses.

"Isn't there a trail on this side of the river?" I asked.

"*Si, pero muy feo,*" he said, making a sign halfway up to his thigh, which I took to be the depth of the mud.

The worst trails I had experienced so far in Chile had been referred to by the locals as *medio feo*. The idea of *muy feo* was indeed intimidating.

When we arrived at the river, Vladamir waved and rode off to exchange his horse for a rowboat.

After brief pleasantries, saddles were taken off and thrown in the boat.

"Is it dangerous?" I wanted to know.

"We do it all the time," he said.

That I knew, but I still suspected it was dangerous.

Rachel led our bravest horse, Platano, to the muddy edge. He willingly stepped into the biggest river we had ever crossed. Vladamir rowed a slight upstream ferry angle as Rachel held onto Platano's lead rope. Soon he was fully swimming.

Photograph by Nancy Pfeiffer.

Crossing the Rio Palena with the help of a rowboat.

Next it was Guanaco's turn. I was terrified but Guanaco swam with his full neck elegantly arched above the water. His blond head held high above the river, he looked like a giraffe. The ripples of his passing through the laminar flow made a deep V pointed at the other side.

Negra, the one I worried about the most, entered the river without a fight. She swam valiantly for the far side, but we were losing ground. Vladamir would have to row upstream at some point to make the landing on the other side. With only her nostrils above the water, her upper lip curled back, and she showed her bright red gums to the river. Negra looked like a hippopotamus. I wanted to let go of the rope and let her swim downstream with the current, but I was afraid there would be no exit for her on the far side.

When we pulled into calm water near the other side. Negra charged up the bank to join her companions. All three put their heads down and started munching Vladamir and Yolanda's grass, as if nothing had happened.

At twenty-two years old, Yolanda was one of the most competent woman I had ever met. She had, no doubt, ridden horses since she sat side saddle in front of her mother, the way her two-and-a-half year old daughter, Molly, did today. Yolanda could chop wood, throw hobbles on a stubborn cow, and shoe horses. Adept in her world, she was quiet and shy around people.

A beautiful two-story structure built by Vladimir's grandfather in the days when nothing came from anywhere else, awaited us. After years of drinking *maté,* I realized the advantage of a prescribed ritual to relax the meeting of strangers. In the simple passing of the gourd from hand to hand, everyone knew what to do.

I asked Yolanda about the trail to the small population of Rio Tranquilo, only a few kilometers away, where someday Molly would attend first grade in a one-room school house.

"I don't know, I have never been there," Yolanda told me. "Why would I go there? Molly doesn't need to go to school for another four years."

Born only six kilometers away, Yolanda lived in one of the smallest worlds of anyone I had ever met. I was glad we were going to be there a while. I wanted to get to know her. It would take time.

Rachel and Molly went out into the garden. Molly returned, beaming, holding a pot of dirt. The girl charmed me with her shoulder-length cropped hair, chubby cheeks, and broad smile, but she ran away and hid when I tried to join in her games. Kids always know if you need their attention more than they need yours.

After a tremendous lunch of mutton and bread, I suggested Rachel and I go chop wood for the family. I wanted—no needed—to be outside. After only a few hours indoors, I realized how accustomed to living outside I had become. There would be no sleeping in a tent tonight. We were to be tucked in the extra beds, left from when Nangaya had three children growing up in this house.

Yolanda scooped Molly onto her shoulders and strode out across the pasture to a pile of downed trees. She set Molly aside and swiftly chopped a few limbs from the scattered trunks and hacked them into chunks. Yolanda moved elegantly and seamlessly through her life in a way I could only step back and admire.

I chop wood every day in Alaska, yet the axe I swung into the Patagonian hardwood bounced off as many times as it penetrated. In Alaska we burn softer, easier to split, spruce that disappears quickly in the woodbox. And everyone uses a chainsaw to buck full-size trunks into stove-size pieces.

Guanaco needed shoes, and Vladamir agreed to help, but his hammer was on the other side of the river where he and Yolanda were building a house of their own.

In remote parts of the Palena region, homesteading was still possible. A family who was established in the area could build a house and farm a chunk of land. Eventually, the state would grant them deed.

"When I first arrived in Alaska in late 1970s a similar system existed," I explained to Vladamir. "But, that program is gone now. There are few parts of the world where people can just build a house and live."

Off to get the hammer, the five of us began a slow meandering walk with Molly leading the way. A bug crawling up a post stopped the procession for ten minutes.

From the edge of the river I noticed that the hillside behind his house had been recently burned.

"What happened there?" I asked.

"Our neighbors burned their land and it got out of control," Vladamir said. "People here sometimes burn large chucks of land so they can pick morel mushrooms the next year to sell. It is a bad idea to burn a forest just for that."

I was horrified. In the United States if a neighbor burned your land there would be lawsuits and fighting over money for decades.

"It's too bad, but it happened," Vladimir said, with that calm acceptance of things as they are that I just couldn't seem to reproduce in my life.

With hammer in hand, we returned to catch and shoe Guananco. By then I wanted to fall sleep more than shoe a horse, but I didn't have much to do except hold Guanacos halter as Yolanda lifted his feet and Vladimir swiftly and confidently changed his shoes.

The next morning Yolanda supplied us with food for the trail: A chunk of meat that would last for days, fresh baked bread, and herbs from the garden for tea.

The trail beyond their house turned from a muddy one-lane track to a wider, drier easy-to-follow path. We were past the most remote part, *el interior.* This time we would not be returning to the deep forest after a re-supply in town. I could feel the end. I longed to savor every moment.

The sweet smell of flowers filled the air. Easy valley bottom travel led us through fields of blooming pink, purple, and yellow lupin. An old ox cart rested on the river bank. Summer had finally arrived.

We passed the tiny white school house with green trim where Molly would someday go to class. A satellite dish was parked in the front yard. The Internet, and the outside world, would be waiting for her there.

The straight streets, square blocks of houses, and automobile traffic of Palena came as a shock. Signs proclaiming, "*Camino Ahora,*" *(Road Now!)* were everywhere. Just to the north the longitudinal highway, considered to be the spinal cord of the country, was only sixty-five kilometers from completion. Everyone had an opinion. No one was afraid to post it in their front window.

We were directed to camp at the rodeo grounds. Rachel and I celebrated the completion of the trip by galloping around the arena bareback on a sleek, muscular black horse. Was this the same horse who had refused to walk with us down the dirt road outside Coyhaique and deposited me so ignobly in cow poop on my birthday? I beamed with pride. Our three compatriots rolled in unison in the dust. They were done and they knew it.

Photograph by Fredrik Norrsell.

Having maté and discussing the future of Patagonia with local poblador Don Julio Romero. Don Julio told me, "I don't like all the changes, but in ten years all the problems of the world will not be mine."

Chapter Thirteen

Cabalgata Sin Represas (Horseback Ride Against the Dams)

Photograph by Fredrik Norrsell.

IN THE PRE-DAWN hours of the following November, I heard a truck backing up. Dragging myself out of a deep sleep, I fumbled my way out of my tent at the rodeo grounds in Cochrane just in time to see the horses being unloaded. A floodlight streamed into the corral, lighting the chaos as fifteen frightened horses, nostrils flaring, hooves flying, charged into the corral.

The dust they stirred up made it impossible to see. From the darkness beyond the floodlights I could not tell if Arraquien was among them. Some of the men were already separating horses inside the corral. I wanted to jump the fence and look for my horse, but I knew better. If I so much as stepped inside the gate, it would trigger widespread panic, not amongst the horses, but amongst the men.

Eventually, the white blaze on Arraquien's forehead showed up in the darkness, separating him from a half dozen other *colorado*s of about the same age. He looked none the worse from the journey.

Some of the horses were still fussing at each other, but the herd was beginning to calm down.

Another woman also watched intently from outside the fence. With long, rusty hair pulled back under a cowboy hat, she looked *gringa,* but something told me that she belonged here. I was curious. Who was this woman? Too tired and timid to find out, I headed to bed.

A dozen more horses arrived while I slept, and by morning five or six more tents had been erected on the rodeo grounds. The *Cabalgata Sin Represas* was beginning.

The unfathomable rumors that I had heard the year before, about dams and power lines headed for Patagonia, had been true. A multinational energy company, Endesa, was scheming to put a total of five dams on the Baker and Pascua rivers, flooding more than 15,000 acres in the heart of the province of Aysén.

And that was just the beginning. The project would include construction of a high-tension power line running 2,450 kilometers from Aysén to large copper mines in the north of Chile. This 120-meter-wide gash would pass through four national parks, eight forest reserves, thirteen sites prioritized for the conservation of biodiversity, and create the largest clear-cut in the world.

The people of Patagonia were adamantly against the project, but how do people who live on remote farms and in isolated villages gain a voice? They hold a *Cabalgata*, a 330-kilometer horseback ride, in protest of the dams. I would have the privilege of riding alongside the sons, daughters, and grandchildren of the people who settled this land.

The first people to wake up—or maybe those who hadn't yet been to bed—had built a fire in an abandoned stall and placed a tin pot of water at its edge. *Yerba maté* was poured into a gourd, and a *maté* session that would last most of the day commenced.

A man in a denim shirt and blue bandana leaned against a post and played old-time ballads on the accordion while another braided a halter. People in ever-growing numbers were arriving, setting up camp, and preparing their horses. I sensed the beginning of a ten-day *fiesta.*

Two young men, who had traveled to Cochrane from the village of Tortel, were carving rain forest scenery onto hardwood tablets.

"We are more natural boatmen than horsemen, but we are here today because of the river," the younger one said. "The river has always been our way of life."

Five years earlier, the Carretera Austral had arrived, almost, but not quite, to their village, a small cluster of houses interlaced by wooden boardwalks at the mouth of the Baker River. The new road brought the outside world to the edge of town, but everything coming in and out still had to be carried up and down several one-hundred-step flights of wooden staircases. In Tortel, the consumption of products from outside was still minimal.

After over ten years, Sergio and I would finally be doing a trip together. The pre-trip meeting was already in progress when we entered the tiny office of Cochrane's environmental group, *Defensores del Espíritu de la Patagonia*. The elders were seated on folding chairs near the front of the room. Others were sitting on wooden boxes, stacks of papers, and bags of grain. I quickly headed for the back of the room to lean against the wall with the young people. We were there to listen.

Don Cecilio Olivares, a local pioneer and landowner along the Baker River, sat facing us in a gray woolen suit coat, his huge bushy eyebrows jumping up and down as he spoke.

"I don't remember how old I am, I think about forty," he said with a subtle wink, "but I can tell you for sure, I was born in 1918."

I did some quick math in my head. This man was eighty-nine years old, and he would be riding with us.

"The first time I went to Coyhaique on horseback was in 1930," he told us. "It wasn't a big organized event like this. We just went. We brought along a hundred cows. It was fun." His memories made him chuckle. "There was, of course, no road to Coyhaique then. Chile was pure jungle, so we went through Argentina, not a problem back then."

An older woman entered the room, and a chair was immediately made available for her. I had seen this woman before, but where?

Eight years earlier, at a bus stop at the end of a road that had been in existence only a few years, an older woman had gotten off the bus, strapped spurs to her city shoes, clipped an extra strap to her handbag, turning it into a backpack, and mounted her horse. Her name was Señora Lelia de la Cruz.

"Cecilio is older than I am," Lelia told the crowd, "by at least three years," she added with a girlish smile.

Lelia de la Cruz was one of the first settlers in the region. The interconnectedness of Patagonia's social system became even more obvious when I learned that my friend Jorgé, who would be riding with us tomorrow, was her grandson.

If these dams went through, some of the best ranching land in the region and the homes of many of the people in the room would be under water. A sense that on this day, the baton of history was being passed from one generation to the next was palpable in the room.

A young man with a dark, tightly bound ponytail, Marco Diaz of the environmental organization Defenders of the Spirit of Patagonia, moved to the front of the room with his laptop.

"Chile doesn't own its water rights," Marco informed us. "Near the end of the Pinochet dictatorship, most of the country's water rights, including the Baker and Pascua rivers, were privatized."

This fact I had heard before. What had escaped me was that the complicated political events of the late 1980s could manifest, over twenty years later, so close to home. The power company Endesa now controlled more than eighty percent of the water rights in Aysén. With the apparently inevitable melting of Patagonia's ice fields, Endesa controlled some of the largest fresh water reserves on the planet.

In addition to the 10,700 acres that could be inundated in the Baker Valley, three dams on the Pascua River would flood more than 4,000 acres of southern temperate rain forest, including the home of Chile's largest remaining population of *huemul*. Outside Patagonia, only tiny slices of this incredibly diverse forest remain in the world.

"¿Quién gana y quien pierde con estos proyectos?" "Who will gain and who will lose with these projects?" Marco continued. Facts and figures flew by me in rapid-fire Spanish, but numbers told only part of the story. What I missed in the details, I understood in my heart. If this infrastructure were to go in, nearly every river in Patagonia would be in danger. A world hungry for cheap energy could descend upon Patagonia, and the life I knew here would change at a rate I never dreamed possible.

In the Aysén of the 1930s, large cattle companies had been pitted against family farmers. Like today, those who saw Aysén as an economic opportunity stood against those who saw it as home. But this time the magnitude of change was unimaginable.

Marco described our mission: "Over the next ten days we will travel north along the Carretera Austral, picking up anyone willing to join our cause. We hope to arrive in Coyhaique, over a hundred strong. We leave tomorrow morning at nine."

The next morning, at promptly nine a.m., we rode out of the rodeo grounds. Riders were dressed in their *gaucho* best: woolen *ponchos*, goatskins *chivas*, and black wool *boinas*. Don Cecilio, dressed in a dark wool sport coat, and his son, Aguilino, in a plaid shirt with a sporty white bandana around his neck, led the pack. On that bright morning, I had but the faintest inkling of how much the quiet, solid leadership of these two men would be crucial to our march.

Locals, cheering us on, lined both sides of the road from the rodeo grounds. I rode beside Elizabeth, a tough woman in her forties with a deeply chiseled face, a stylish black leather jacket, and riding chaps. She rode alongside her mother. I had watched them ready their horses, working with the simple expertise of riders long accustomed to the feel of leather in their hands.

Nacho, a sixteen-year-old from Santiago, rode alongside Don Abraham Fiuroa, a local rancher on a white mare. Don Fiuroa wore traditional goatskin *chivas,* a wool beret, and a pair of large plastic sunglasses with bright red rims. In the coming days I would often slip in beside them to listen to Don Fiuroa's stories. Nacho was missing high school this week. Instead, he was getting an education in the history of his country and helping to shape its future.

Our band of thirty horses and riders made several passes around the plaza as townspeople and members of the local media documented the event. School kids in dark blue uniforms poured out of double doors and waved wildly, leaning over a white picket fence. If this project were to go through, by the time these kids became teenagers, 5,000 imported workers could move into their community of 3,000 people.

Between 1974 and 1977, tens of thousands of workers unfamiliar with local customs descended upon the state of Alaska. A boomtown atmosphere, complete with high rates of crime and prostitution, arose nearly overnight. The population of the small town of Valdez burgeoned from 1,300 to 8,250 in just two years.

Thoughts of the debauchery that descended upon Alaska during the construction of the 800-mile trans-Alaska oil pipeline arriving in Cochrane scared me.

Before leaving Cochrane, we gathered outside a shiny new clapboard office building a few blocks off the *plaza*. A sign proclaiming

"HydroAysén" was plastered above its front door. HydroAysén, the name chosen for the dam project by Endesa, struck me as a cheap attempt at appearing to be a local company. Seeing this fancy new building, which looked so out of place in Cochrane, made the threat terrifyingly real. It was a Monday morning; people were working inside that tall, white building, but no one opened a door or showed a face through a window.

While we observed a moment of silence outside that building, I returned to third grade. I was a child in the sixties. Protests in the streets were common place. Ecology was the new buzzword. People were just beginning to talk about, "a problem with the environment." I was nine years old and horrified. There was—if I understood it correctly—a big problem on planet Earth. Somehow, our parents—who existed solely to love and protect us—had created this problem, and now we were supposed to fix it.

My elementary school friends and I attacked the problem with the enthusiasm of youth, but inside I was worried. "What if our third grade paper drive wasn't enough?"

Not only were today's nine year olds inheriting an unfathomably larger burden, I doubt they could remember a time when they didn't know this horrific problem existed.

We marched one last time around the plaza before taking off on our grand adventure. The *Cabalgata Sin Represas* would someday be a historical event. That we were pitted against multinational companies with billions of dollars was irrelevant. On that bright morning I was confident our simple, grassroots protest would win. It had to.

Just outside of town we rode into wide open scrub country. Recently leafed-out *ñirre* trees covered the landscape and filled the air with the delicious, sweet scent of spring. Our first view of the Baker River took my breath away. Wide and deep, its tranquil turquoise waters gave no hint of the power it held. The slow passage of silt-laden glacial rivers through Lago General Carrera, made the water of the Baker look almost tropical. It was not. It was clear, cold, and clean enough to drink.

On the banks of the Baker, Arraquien and I put our lips to the water and enjoyed a long, cool drink. The same simple ferry Nimbus and I had used to cross the river nearly a decade ago was returning to our side.

Photograph by Fredrik Norrsell.

Drinking from the Baker River.

Part of Chile's transportation system since the mid-forties, this river-crossing method uses no outside energy and does not slow the progress of the river. Fifteen horses at a time wedged onto the flat-bottomed *balsa* and stood nose-to-tail while the power of the river and a slight change of angle pushed the barge to the other side. The horses stood patiently as we drifted. I tried not to imagine the kind of chaos that would ensue if fifteen North American horses were wedged onto a tiny boat and pushed out into the river.

Somewhere near the ferry landing we picked up a mascot. A scraggly mutt with a lame hind leg limped along beside us, full speed, bound for Coyhaique.

"It's not just humans; horses and dogs don't want dams either," I joked with Jocelyn, a young veterinarian from Coyhaique.

We jointly named our new companion Baker. By day, he hobbled along willingly, and at night, he enjoyed bountiful bones from our never-ending stream of *asados*. For him, the *Cabalgata Sin Represas* was a grand adventure of his own choosing.

That night we camped on a wide bench above the Baker River. A woman with long light brown hair caught my attention. Her Spanish was impeccable, but held no hint of *poblador.* Allison Silverman had never ridden a horse in her life. She worked for the Natural Resources

Defense Council in New York City. I was glad she was there. The fact that big, international environmental organizations were involved in helping fight multinational corporations seemed only fair considering the value of these resources on a worldwide level.

At the same time Endesa was touting this as a project that would create local jobs, it was planning to construct massive housing complexes for its imported workers. Most of the money and all of the electricity generated by the dam project was slated to go elsewhere. This didn't surprise me. It's a common story all over the world. Twenty-nine temporary towns were thrown together for the building of the trans-Alaska pipeline.

Five kilometers upstream from where we were camped, world-class whitewater gushed through deep canyon walls. Not yet discovered by whitewater enthusiasts, the Baker had been run in its entirety only a handful of times. In the narrows at the end of the canyon, visible from our campsite, Endesa planned to put the first of its five dams. Road accessible and only thirty kilometers from Cochrane, this would be the easiest dam to build.

Endesa employees were already conducting exploratory drilling. Local environmentalists were livid. The company's "exploratory" tunnel matched exactly the blueprints for the actual bypass tunnel Endesa planned to use for the dam. An exploration permit had been issued. A construction permit had not.

THAT EVENING WHILE meat was on the grill, three generations of the Arratia family rode in from the Rio Colonia. Riding into camp on her own horse, four-year-old Romina, with her wide-brimmed leather hat and enchanting smile, stopped the show. The girl, with the dark, almond-shaped eyes of a sage, would mesmerize me throughout the journey. When people would get tired or grumpy, Romina would be there to remind us there was a tenacious child enduring the same hardships with a smile on her face.

With shiny, dark, shoulder-length hair and a sweet, shy smile, Romina's mother, Carmen, was also radiantly beautiful. Romina's grandparents, too, exuded a health and vivaciousness that made them seem much too young to be grandparents.

Riding with the Arratia family was the tall woman with reddish blond hair I had seen outside the corral. She rode a long-legged,

Photograph by Ignacio Grez.

Four-year-old Romina Arratia rides her own horse in the Cabalgata Sin Represas.

brown-and-white *tobiano* mare. With her riding chaps and wide brimmed hat she looked as *gaucha* as a *gringa* could be. Here was a woman who had chosen the path I had considered for years—originally from Switzerland, she had bought land and settled in Chile. How many times in life do we get the opportunity to meet the person we might have been?

Over the next few days I was fortunate enough to ride beside her and learn her story, and over the next few years, to become her friend.

She now owned a gorgeous *campo* and a dozen cows near the confluence of the Colonia and Baker rivers. Upstream from her home a glacial lake named Lago Cachet Dos, wedged between the Colonia Glacier and the steep mountainous terrain of the eastern Andes, was slowly rising. The following fall, the waters of Lago Cachet Dos would bore a tunnel eight kilometers long beneath the glacier, draining the lake in less than twelve hours. The flow of the Colonia River at its confluence with the Baker would run 120,000 cubic feet per second, putting her cabin and most of her good pasture land under four feet of water. These Glacier Lake Outburst Floods had happened before, but no one could remember when. Little did anyone know, that with the rapidly melting ice of the Colonia Glacier, the flooding of her land would happen seven times in the next few years. Nor had anyone planned for what such a tremendous influx of water would do to a downstream dam.

At its confluence with the Rio Nef, the Baker River thundered over one of the most impressive waterfalls I had ever seen. Aguilino Olivares' homestead was just the other side. A fantastic spread of land that reminded me of Montana, his home was accessible only by a powerful row across the Baker in a small boat or a burly belly-deep ford on horseback across the Rio Nef. Even though Aguilino and his family lived only a kilometer from the road, a trip to town was a big deal.

The confluence of the Rio Baker and the Rio Nef.

Photograph by Fredrik Norrsell.

The afternoon wore on long, hot, and dusty. No one felt much like talking. Two o'clock was solar noon, and the sun at its apex did not feel good. The ozone hole at the South Pole looms larger than in the Northern Hemisphere, and the burning rays of the sun penetrated my skin, leaving it scorched and painful.

Near the top of the hill, some tourists had stopped on the road to take our picture. They didn't speak Spanish and had no idea why we were there. I stopped. I wanted to explain.

"See that river over there. It is in danger. This whole valley could be gone," I told them.

"We rented this car in Pucón. We hope to drive the entire way to . . ." The driver left his sentence hanging. He had forgotten where they were going.

The length and details of their car trip did not interest me. The fate of this river did not seem to interest them. There were fifty horses on the road that day merely as a subject for their photos.

As we crested the final hill, Lago General Carrera stretched out before us. The turquoise waters of the suspended sediment of more than a dozen glaciers and the lush, emerald vegetation along the shore again made the scene appear tropical. Camp was just ahead. With grass halfway to their bellies and soft waves lapping the gravel shore, it looked like heaven to hot, tired horses. Aguilino and several other *gauchos* stripped their saddles and headed for the lake. As fast as I could, I dumped my saddle in the shade of a *coihue* and rode up behind them.

"¿Tu también?" Aguilino asked, glancing once over his shoulder.

"Si," I said. "Me too."

"Bueno," he said, honoring me with his trust.

The lake was surprisingly warm. Wet blue jeans clung to my legs. The water rushed up around Arraquien's belly. I felt a soft lunging motion. We were swimming. I wrapped my arms around his neck.

"Oh, que rica el agua," I exclaimed, feeling the water's sweet, delicious coolness.

On shore, seventy-two-year-old Elvira waited for me. She wanted to cool her dappled gray gelding, but didn't want to get in the lake herself.

"Elvira, I would be honored to wash your horse," I said.

A couple of evenings before, sitting under a gigantic *coihue* tree, she had told me of her life on the Colonia.

"I was raised there, I raised my family there, and when I die, they will put a wooden *tabla* there for me," she said. "If my land gets flooded, what will I do? I will have to go up on the mountain and live in the snow with the pumas."

For the next several days we traveled along the shores of Lago General Carrera. The forest changed from semi-steppe to temperate rain forest. Flowering trees, flaming-red *notro,* orange *calafate,* and white *uña del gato* filled the air with the sweet smell of spring on this late November day. The shores of this alluring lake provided the only north-south corridor through this country of east-west running valleys. If an enormous power line were to be built, it would go right here. A 120-meter-wide swath of cleared vegetation and an access road would stretch along the shoreline between us and the lake. A row of 210-foot-tall towers would march across the landscape, with long, thick wires cutting the view in half.

In Puerto Tranquilo, a town that made its living on tourism, we spent the night in the soccer field. *Patagonia Sin Represas* signs were in nearly every window. That night a multitude of visitors poured into the circle of light around our fire.

There was tremendous support for our cause, but only a few more people rode out with us in the morning. People had jobs, kids, and farms. Unlike me, they were not on vacation. It was lambing season and there was work to be done.

At Bahia Murta, the group gathered in front of the old church where Nimbus and I had stopped nearly a decade before. Father Porfirio, a distinguished man in a long, white robe, mingled with the crowd, greeting everyone as if an old friend. The group of almost seventy riders and townspeople, circled closer. Father Porfirio's silver-haired head towered over everyone. The crowd hushed. He had a special sermon for this day.

"En esta hora peligroso," he began. "In this hour of danger . . ."

"The region forgotten, the refuge of paradise," the group joined in.

"Quieren construer represas . . ." he continued. "They want to build dams, cutting your glory, flooding the valleys. Where we see beauty, where we see purity, they see money."

His final prayer, *"Cuida a tus hijos y hijas que defienden su obra,"* was for the care and blessing of the riders defending the work of God.

I hadn't been to church since I was a child. I was deeply touched. In Chile the Catholic Church holds a powerful voice. The church taking a strong stand against the dams was a compelling demonstration of the force behind the opposition. Afterward, riders and townspeople alike had testimonials of their own.

"*Los conquistadores* have arrived in Patagonia," a bearded man said, who, even after years of living in Patagonia, still spoke Spanish with a distinctly German accent. His Chilean wife stood beside him, nodding as he spoke. "They come bearing gifts for the schools—pencils, notebooks, even computers, but they come with *mal intención*. They have come to take the water."

Don Cecilio had a few words for us, as well. "Neighbors, *campesinos*, young people, grandchildren, take this into your memory; you have much responsibility. "*¡Viaje con calma, con tranquilidad, pero con firmeza!*" He encouraged us to march to Coyhaique with calmness and tranquility, but also with firmness.

Father Pofirio had a few more words of his own. "Not taking care of the land is losing the health of life. For the health of the whole world, for the goodness of the entire Earth, we need to defend this place."

There was value in us standing strong together that afternoon, but I couldn't help feel as if we were indeed preaching to the choir. Where were the people who most needed to hear these words? No one from Endesa and not one public official stood amongst us.

Before the crowd dispersed, the local women unveiled mounds of freshly baked bread.

At our next stop, the rugged spires of Cerro Castillo rose above the plains. It felt like the wind had been blowing through the streets of Villa Castillo since the day I had first arrived there, hungry, wind-chapped, and exhausted nearly a decade before. Bumper to bumper, cars and trucks rattled down the dusty road to the rodeo grounds. Folks poured in from nearby towns and farms on foot, on horseback, and in automobiles. As the sun sunk behind Cerro Castillo, rays of light penetrated the dust created by our arrival, and long pillars of golden light stretched toward the earth. To my delight, I saw a familiar face in the crowd. My friend, Lili, had arrived from Puerto Ibáñez with her horse, Feo.

"*Feo*" means "ugly." Old, dull-brown, skinny, and in need of shoes, Feo had an extra-long nose and the tips of his ears were missing. They had supposedly been frozen off one winter long before he had come to live with Lili. Feo was definitely nothing to look at, but today the men would give him a new set of shoes, and tomorrow, he would take Lili to Coyhaique with the pride and stamina of a much younger and more beautiful horse.

Lili, herself, looked gorgeous in her bright blue wind jacket and stylish scarf. When she recognized me, her smile shown through the crowd. I invited her to throw her things into my tent and be roommates. Nearly my age, she was one of the few Chilean women in the guiding industry. We had become instant and steadfast friends a few months before when we worked together on one of Pancho's courses for budding Patagonian mountain guides.

It has long been an embarrassing reality that, just like the situation we were fighting with the dams, most of the money created by guiding jobs in Patagonia goes to foreigners like me. Lili was an exception. Her unique life story led her to speak three languages, a huge asset on the international guiding circuit.

Lili grew up in the era of Pinochet. Although it is seldom talked about, a variation of her story is one shared by many Chileans her age. During her childhood, the government kept a tight hold on the opinions of private people. When she was nine years old, the police forced their way into her family's home, ripped an unauthorized poster off the bedroom wall, slammed Lili and her seven-year-old sister against the door, and went looking for their father. Shortly afterward her family escaped to Argentina and was taken in by nuns. Eventually, an opportunity to immigrate to Germany presented itself. Lili entered third grade in a foreign country without knowing a word of German.

As a young woman, she married an adventuresome German and had two children. Lili and her husband, Geraldo, dreamed of owning a farm, but buying farmland in Europe was impossible. Unless your parents were farmers, you never would be.

Five years before we met, Lili, Geraldo, and their youngest son had moved back to Chile. Here in Aysén, they were able to buy a piece of land so large it took an entire day to ride its perimeter. Their gorgeous *campo* reminded me more of Utah's red rock country than anywhere I'd been in Patagonia. However, arid land is hard to farm. A small parcel of rich valley bottom dotted with regal *maiten* trees had to produce most of the family's food.

The Patagonia Sin Represas poster proudly displayed on Lili's front door tells of the changes Chile has seen in the last several decades. Things were indeed different now or this whole procession could not be happening.

Lili and Geraldo enthusiastically took on the task of learning to be *campesinos*. Without having grown up on the land, they needed to acquire the multitude of skills and tools needed to survive in this windblown place. One of the reasons I admired Lili was that she, like me, followed her heart, first deciding to do something, then promptly beginning to learn how.

With her beautiful dark complexion, wavy black hair, and perfect Spanish, she was born *pura Chilena*, but the townspeople still spoke of her as "that German lady." It's a tough reminder of what it takes to be considered a local in a place like Puerto Ibáñez, where new people in town are rare.

Inside the community hall a crowd was gathering. A public defender was speaking to people about their rights. Imagine a stranger stepping out of a helicopter onto your land, and telling you, "If you don't sell your land to us now, the government will just take it later, for a much lower price." The average *campesino* has few resources for legal advice. Endesa, with its throngs of lawyers, is an intimidating entity.

Acoustics were awful in the cavernous building, and the microphone distorted the already indecipherable language of lawyers. However, I didn't need to understand all the words to get the message. In addition to passing through land designated as protected, much of the proposed transmission line would also run across the private land of people adamantly opposed to the idea.

"Chilean law states, if it is found to be in the best interest of the country, land can be appropriated for development," the lawyer informed us.

The whole picture was slowly sinking in. In a world hungry for power, if this project were to go through, industry worldwide could be clamoring to set itself up in Patagonia. The thought of Patagonia filling up with aluminum smelters and other energy-intensive manufacturing plants terrified me. But the faces in this room told another story. Young people, eyes fiery with determination, stood united with an older generation whose faces, although well weathered, showed no sign of being beaten. These tough, pragmatic people had fought for their land before and won.

The lawyer was politely reciting a list of policies and regulations. A long stream of procedures to be followed was not what the people in this room wanted to hear. They wanted to know how to save their land. Voices were becoming tense as heckling rose from the crowd. The subtle, indirect mode that Patagonians use to express conflict has always been a mystery to me, but anger was there in the room, just under the surface. I could feel it rising, about to boil.

At just the right moment, the band Maté Amargo took the stage. Accordion music filled the hall, and within moments the dancing began. The animosity in the air was whisked away and the room came alive with the ambiance of festivity.

The first song was a *cueca,* the Chilean national dance. Men and women twirled and coyly flirted as they peeked out from behind white handkerchiefs, never touching but always maintaining eye contact. It is said that the *cueca* is a stylized reenactment of the courting ritual between rooster and hen, with deep African and Spanish roots. As I watched, more old-timers stepped in. I longed to dance, but, unfortunately, the *cueca* and the *chamamé*, (the Patagonian two-step) had not been part of my upbringing.

Outside, men stood behind a line drawn in the dirt playing *taba,* a game that reminded me of horseshoes. The outstretched fingers of the first competitor held the anklebone of a young cow with two metal plates attached to its sides. The anklebone twisted as it flew more than six meters through the air.

"Clavada," an older gentleman hollered as the bone landed.

"*Suerte,*" another man called. The toss had scored a point.

I walked over to the *asado,* where eleven lambs were splayed out roasting over an open fire. After another great meal of roasted lamb, Lili and I moved into the tent. We had thirty-eight kilometers to ride the next day. We were supposed to leave at six a.m.

At five-thirty, I emerged from the tent and went looking for my horse. Barely awake, I stumbled into Don Cecilio, who had already saddled his horse and was helping the others. Once again, I had been outdone by a man nearly twice my age. Lili and I had heard the party going strong at four in the morning. Many had slept no more than a couple hours. To my utter amazement, a hundred people on horseback rode out, en masse, at six a.m. exactly as planned.

Our crowd had changed again. I no longer knew everyone's face, let alone name. Like an ever-shuffling deck of cards, I never knew who I would be riding next to or what stories I would hear. On the ride out of town I found myself riding alongside Pato, an artist from Coyhaique. This was the first time our horses had fallen into step with each other.

"I love doing art, but what I really want is to live on a *campo*," he told me. "But things are so expensive these days. My parents sold their land, and now I can't afford to buy a piece for myself."

It's the same story worldwide. Farmland is being bought up by people who made their money elsewhere and have no intention of farming or even living on the land. One reason I never bought land in Chile was that when foreigners like me bought land, often at prices locals couldn't pay, it left people like Pato looking for work in Coyhaique. I understood all too well that by not buying land, I wasn't changing anything, but at least I wasn't participating. Now Pato and I were in the same situation.

"I can't afford to buy land here now, either," I said.

We left the *carretera* and headed uphill. Spreading out six abreast, we moved through a pasture of newly green grass. At the top of the slope, we entered a short section of woods. The sweet fragrance of young *lenga* leaves filled the air. The first rays of morning light streamed through the branches, turning the air, itself, a brilliant green. The energy of being alive on such a spectacular morning erupted into hooting and cheering throughout the crowd. This was the best of life, and we knew it.

We were headed into country I knew well, La Horqueta and the Rio Blanco Valley. Three weeks earlier, with the gullies between these rocky spires filled with snow, these mountains had looked like Alaska. Today, the bare, twisted, gray and bronze rock was more reminiscent of America's arid West.

Mobs of horses streamed through fields of dandelions. At the Rio Blanco, a hundred horses flowed like water itself down a steep incline and across the river. Once across, I stopped to watch the horses behind me. Water splashed around the bellies of paints, roans, blacks, *zainos,* and *alazáns*. Men, women, children, and grandparents crossed the river with an easy, natural gait. I sat quietly on Arraquien until the last horse had crossed, letting the scene seep deeply into my soul. I felt a profound sense that I was witnessing history unfold. Like everyone else riding here today, and like, indeed, Patagonia itself, I would never be in this exact time and place again. These were truly precious times.

When we hit open grassland, several young men on horseback burst into a spontaneous gallop. Arraquien and I could not resist. At exactly the spot where I had thrown backflips and ridden barefoot and bareback on my (almost) fortieth birthday, Arraquien's bouncy trot smoothed into an easy lope. Delight poured through my body.

Fourteen hours and thirty-eight kilometers from Villa Castillo, we arrived at our camping spot. It was a tough first day for the people and horses that had joined us in Castillo. Lili stepped down gingerly from the saddle onto legs she wasn't sure would hold her. Six hours since lunch break, I was hungry and on the verge of grumpy. Everybody was tired, but not a single complaint was heard.

Lili and I slept poorly on a sloping campsite, listening to the wind batter the tent and getting up to move our horses to better grass several times in the night. The next morning a screaming dehydration headache threatened to split my skull in two. I munched a bit of dry bread for breakfast, and we started saddling horses in the coldest wind we had felt so far. I was secretly wishing myself back in my warm sleeping bag when a young guy from Tortel stood on a rock and hollered into the crowd, "*¡Esa es la Cabalgata Sin Represas! ¡No es un vacación!*" "This is a protest ride against the dams, not a vacation!"

People looked different today, wrapped in ponchos and scarves. Hoods pulled tightly around faces, we headed into the cold Patagonia wind, a reminder that winter had not entirely left us and would return all too soon. Cold hands held reins, shifting places frequently to warm themselves beneath woolen ponchos, but spirits remained high. This was the *Cabalgata!*

Twenty-eight kilometers later we could sense the grand finale coming. Eighty-nine-year-old Don Cecilio Olivares rode at the front of the pack, along with four-year-old Romina and her family. The herd energy peaked as we rounded the last bend. Just ahead was the NOLS *campo*, where we would spend our last night on the trail. We were only twelve kilometers outside of Coyhaique. The entire NOLS staff cheered us on from the corner of the property. Another *asado* was waiting. The horses broke into a spontaneous gallop as we neared the gate. No one held them back.

Thundering up the hill past Sergio and Veronica's house, I saw myself as I had been so many years before, a neophyte on a *yegu tobiano* closing the *campo* gate, swinging her leg up over a tremendous load of gear, and tentatively riding off alone into Patagonia. Today, like a character in an old Western movie, I galloped across the finish line. Victorious already. We had arrived.

While we waited at the NOLS *campo*, a meeting between the city officials and organizers of the ride was going on in Coyhaique. Rumors about our entrance into town had been running rampant for a week.

"We might not get permission to enter the city."

"They won't let us ride into town on the main street, Calle Prat. They will try to shuttle us down some back road where people won't see us."

Lili had been chosen to represent Puerto Ibáñez at the meeting. I trusted her to fill me in. The possibility of us traveling more than 300 kilometers to be denied the right to enter the city worried me. Was all this fuss really about a little horse shit in the plaza? Or, was some government official trying to keep us quiet, hoping that authorization of the dam project would get pushed through just as unobtrusively?

I knew one thing, after riding all this way to have their voices heard, these tough, matter-of-fact ranchers were not going to go home and let their land be flooded. At least a large portion of us would ride into Coyhaique the next morning, with or without permission!

Images of people gunned down during the Pinochet era for far less blatant protest than standing in the plaza with a horse flashed unbidden into my head. That was then, things were different now, I reminded myself. I am probably safer protesting here than in my own country these days, I told myself to ease my anxiety. Still, I was scared. What if things went wrong? Got ugly? Visions of Arraquien and I galloping down a back alley, outrunning the police, and slipping off into the countryside entertained my mind. At least I had a fast horse.

More than 120 people crowded into the dining hall at NOLS to wait for the word. Clusters of people chatted quietly in corners. Gone was the festive atmosphere that had traveled with the *Cabalgata* since Cochrane. It was time for business.

After what seemed like hours, Don Cecilio stepped up to the microphone. The room fell silent. The respect the crowd had for this man was palpable. He knew what we wanted to hear and went straight to the point.

"We have permission," he said. "Tomorrow we will enter by Calle Prat!" A collective exhale of relief flooded the room. The next day we would arrive in Coyhaique in style, on the main street, and with permission from the city.

Later, Lili filled me in on the meeting.

"*El gobernador de la provincia* was entirely against letting us enter by the main street," she told me. "But he is also a *Patagón*. He went to high school with many of the men involved in the march."

The men in the room had greeted each other with polite embraces before sitting down on opposite sides of the table.

"This will be a peaceful demonstration," Don Cecilio had assured the governor. "We come with families, women, and children. We are here to have our voices respectfully heard. We must also show respect."

Representatives of each of the communities we had passed through sat around a rectangular table and echoed his viewpoint, reiterating the importance of entering on the main street of commerce. The *gobernador* had sat with his arms crossed in front of his chest throughout the meeting, apparently unmovable in his stance, but in the end he granted permission.

Back in the dining hall, Marco Diaz of the *Defensores del Espíritu de la Patagonia* stepped up to the microphone.

"The city officials are worried about the disturbance of having horses in town. Yes, we will cause the people of Coyhaique a small disturbance tomorrow," he admitted, "but better that, than the disturbance of a 2,400-kilometer power line in the future."

The room broke into applause.

I didn't entirely agree. Rather than a disturbance, I believed we would be giving the people of Coyhaique a gift—their own heritage, riding into town on horseback, bringing the stories and songs of their childhoods and the chance to redirect their future.

Aguilino took the floor. Again, the room hushed. "Tomorrow, there can be no arguments, no strong disagreements, and no violence of any kind or our cause will be lost." Again, there was total agreement in the crowd. "To this purpose, we must leave our knives behind."

Everyone started talking at once. Heated discussions in all corners of the room made it impossible to hear. Carrying a knife carefully sheathed and stored on a belt is a rural Patagonian tradition. In the countryside a knife, used to shoe a horse, sever an overhanging branch, or carve roasted meat off a bone, was a necessity. However, it was illegal to carry large knives in the city.

"Knives are part of our culture," a voice protested from the audience.

"Yes, knives are part of our culture," Aguilino agreed, "but this demonstration is not about knives. It is about dams."

A heated discussion ensued. In the end it was left to the individual to decide. In the morning most knives would be left behind.

That evening, a friend reminded me of something I had not considered. I was in Chile on a tourist visa. No matter how much I loved the place, officially, that was what I was. As a tourist it was illegal for me to participate in any political activity. This protest ride could easily be seen as exactly that.

I thought for a moment of all I stood to lose. But my own risks paled in comparison to what Patagonia stood to lose. If I was taking a chance, it was one I was happy to take. I, like my neighbors, was not turning around now. The next day, however, just before entering town, I would carefully tuck my incriminating blonde hair up under my hat.

The next morning, blooming lupines lined the road for the last dozen kilometers of our ride. We passed Laguna Foitzick, where I had gone looking for a saddle for Nimbus so long ago. We rode by the blue cement shrine of *San Sebestián*, the patron saint of travelers, where the driver of every car I had ridden in over the past fifteen years had honked the horn. The open-faced shrine was big enough to walk into. Inside, I could see dozens of burning candles, a multitude of melted stumps, and generations of plastic flowers. It felt as if I were watching a familiar show through someone else's eyes.

Three abreast, rows of well-groomed horses extended over hills and around bends farther than I could see. Riders carried banners from their home regions: Rio Nef, Rio Del Salto, Puerto Bertrand, Villa Castillo. We moved not as band of trail-weary, beaten-down *campesinos* with hundreds of kilometers behind us. Instead, we marched with flags flying as if in a parade.

Several kilometers from the edge of town, a chubby ten-year-old boy in a red-and-gray sweatshirt became our first official greeter. He stood alone beside the road holding a handwritten sign above his head: "*Bienvenidos a Coyhaique, NO! a las Represas.*" (Welcome to Coyhaique, NO! to dams)

Outside of town, new houses had sprung up like the legendary *casas brujas* nearly overnight. Unlike the original settlers who had nestled modest homes into the hollows of the countryside to escape the Patagonia wind, these were opulent structures, poorly placed on the landscape, suburban homes sprouting up on what had recently been farmland. It was happening all over the world, a not-so-gentle reminder that the population of the planet had doubled in my lifetime.

As we entered Coyhaique, our reception was well beyond anything I had imagined. Calle Prat was packed. People stood waving on top of cars draped with banners proclaiming "*No Endesa*" and "*Ríos Libre!*" Pancho's wife, Cuchi, held chubby one-year-old Lorenzo in one arm and waved wildly at me with the other. Corey, his wife, Melinka, and their new baby girl, Mila, cheered us on from the other corner.

Gone was the horse parking lot at the edge of town. A giant Sodimac, the Chilean version of Home Depot, stood in its place. These days, even during the afternoon *siesta*, the square bustled with people in business suits. The pleasant small town I had come to fifteen years ago had somehow become a city.

Waves of dark heads filled the streets and flowed with us into the plaza as we marched down Calle Prat. Hundreds of tiny Chilean flags waved by riders and watchers alike reminded me that these people were not here to resist Chile. They were here because they loved their country and wanted to protect it.

We were not the only people who had traveled a long way to be there that day. Signs marked the gathering areas for people from outlying communities: Bahia Murta, Tortel, Rio Tranquilo, Mañihuales, Ñiregauo. I saw folks from Cochrane and Lago Verde. I caught glimpses of people I hadn't seen in years. My urge to stop and share a *beso* with old friends was pushed aside by the momentum of the parade. I could only wave wildly as familiar faces appeared and then disappeared into the crowd.

My spirit soared with the power of waving flags and yelling in unison, *"Endesa entiende! La vida ne se vende!"* (Endesa, understand! Life is not for sale!) But, while observing a moment of silence outside Endesa's HydroAysén office in Coyhaique, I cried silently into my sunglasses.

We circled the plaza once and pulled our horses to a stop while the entire crowd sang the national anthem.

"Pure, Chile, is your blue sky. Pure breezes cross you, as well. Your flower-embroidered fields are the happy copy of Eden," the crowd sang loudly and sweetly. I sat in awkward silence. I had not learned the Chilean national anthem in school.

We circled the plaza again and stopped in front of the municipality building to await the attention of local government officials. We were going to have a long wait. The *Intendente* of the region, Viviana Betancourt, had decided to travel 570 kilometers to Villa O'Higgins that day.

Don Cecilio, in his white-collared shirt and slate-gray suit coat, sat astride his leggy *alazán*. The Chilean flag leaning on his left shoulder, he spoke eloquently to local and national news reporters.

"We do not want to dam the Rio Baker. We don't want to destroy our fatherland. This place, where we have lived for generations, it is for our children. Why now? We understand that the country is short on energy but we cannot change this thing by destroying another thing."

Don Cecilio's wisdom touched closely on the words of Albert Einstein: "The significant problems we have cannot be solved at the same level of thinking with which we created them." One by one, people took the microphone.

A man in a business suit spoke up for the rural people. "The *pobladores* of Aysén understand that they live in a privileged place. They love the land and know the importance of protecting our natural resources for themselves and for their children."

I also understood a bigger picture. This land and this life have value beyond what someone will pay. At a time when people throughout the world are trying to figure out how to live more sustainable lives, an intact system of working family farms is an asset the planet cannot afford to lose.

All afternoon people told their stories, their family's stories, and the stories of the history of this place. Six horses abreast, Arraquien and I stood packed nose-to-butt with the other horses in the searing sun. By mid-morning the heat was oppressive. Off came my hat and out tumbled unruly locks of long blonde hair. *Gringa* or not, I was hot. What seemed like interminable hours passed without food or water.

Don Cecilio Olivares speaks to local and national news.

Photograph by Ignacio Grez.

Eventually a man came around with water for the horses, but few of these horses, accustomed to drinking free-flowing water from a stream, had any interest in drinking chlorinated water from a plastic bucket.

Several hours into our wait, I noticed a man in a green uniform staring directly at me. Three horses from the edge in either direction, I was trapped in the crowd. My fantasy of galloping off down some winding back alleyway should I be approached by the police vanished. There was nothing to do but avert my blue eyes. The man approached directly toward me through the mass of riders. Looking firmly down, I studied the pavement. But there was no denying it, I was *gringa* and I was here. I felt an unmistakable tap on my knee. Resigned to my fate, I turned.

The confused face of my friend, Orlando, looked back at me. Orlando was a park ranger. He wore the green uniform of all Chilean *guadaleparques,* which I had confused with the uniform of the *carabineros* (the police).

"*¿Orlando, comos estás?*" I asked, embarrassed, trying to pretend I hadn't just been hiding from him.

"*Tanto tiempo, amiga,*" he greeted me. "It's been a long time, friend."

It had been a long time, fifteen years. Orlando was a student on my first NOLS course in Patagonia. He still looked exactly as I remembered him. Memories of a time when I barely spoke Spanish, yet had desperately wanted to learn even a portion of what he knew about the Patagonia forest, flashed through my mind. How had we managed to miss each other in the same town for fifteen years? We promised to find each other later. We could find some shade and chat.

He disappeared into the crowd. I never saw him again.

In the plaza, the celebration that had been growing for ten days blossomed to include the entire town. The band, Maté Amargo, strummed its first chord on the makeshift stage, and traditional music and dancing filled the plaza.

Over the course of the day, the incredible privilege of sharing this historical moment, of riding alongside the people I respected most in the world, soaked in. But something else, something more uncomfortable was slipping in, as well. An idea I had been stuffing conveniently into the back of my mind for a long time kept bubbling to the surface. Someone needed to tell the story of this place.

Almost with a sense of relief, I felt this wasn't my story to tell. This was Patagonia's story. But, the idea kept haunting me. Maybe, because I came from a place that already had way too many roads, dams, and power lines, because I came from a place where life went on at an ever-increasingly unhappy and unhealthy pace, this was, indeed, my story to tell.

Late into the afternoon, we were still waiting for government officials to acknowledge our presence. Remembering the morning in Villa Cerro Castillo when, after a nearly all-night party, a hundred people and their horses rode out at six a.m. gave me hope. The fortitude of these people and their horses, and the fact that an incredibly complex event like the *Cabalgata Sin Represas* had been immaculately organized and run, gave me confidence in our ability to win.

Hot, tired, thirsty, and in need of a public restroom, I looked around for Lili. Five hours into our wait, we took turns holding each other's horses for a few moments, so each of us could take care of our most basic needs.

My companions chatted casually from astride their horses, apparently unconcerned about how much longer we would be standing there. Patagonians wait for the rain to stop. They wait for the river to go down. They wait for spring to come and their lambs to get fat. Doing business in Patagonia, as I had repeatedly learned, requires long periods of waiting. Nor did anyone, other than me, seem distressed by the fact that we had no idea what was going on behind the closed doors of the municipality building. I wanted desperately to be *Patagon,* to accept life's uncertainties easily and with grace, but the North American side of me had grown up in the age of information. Unaccustomed to being uninformed, I shifted constantly in my seat, fidgeting with my reins.

Late that afternoon, Viviana Betancourt, who had been appointed *Intendente* for the region by *La Presidenta* Michelle Bachelet herself, returned from O'Higgins and quietly slipped in the back door of the municipal building. Chairs reserved for the local elected officials, sat empty in the plaza. No one was stepping forward to shake hands with constituents on this day. We still held in our hands the document,

Declaracion Por Aysén, a simple seven-point list of requests and concerns we intended to pass along to the *Intendente*. We would remain until we did.

Seven hours into our wait, Aguilino, Don Cecilio, and a few key spokesmen from our group were allowed inside. Most of the riders had no idea what was going on, nor how much longer we would be waiting. The only thing I knew for sure was that when the sun sank below the snow-covered mountains the heat we had suffered all day would instantly change to bitter cold. I had a wool hat but had left my warm coat at NOLS.

After hours of careful negotiation, Viviana Betancourt walked out into the streets, where her picture was taken with Aguilino Olivares. The photo shows a redheaded woman with big glasses, smiling beside Aguilino and waving a Chilean flag. She had read and acknowledged our requests, but had made no promises that she would pass them along to *La Presedenta* Bachelet.

That evening, Sergio and I galloped side by side back to the *campo*. As we thundered past miles of purple and yellow lupines, I knew. I would write this story. I would begin this new journey the same way I had taken off across Patagonia, with no idea what I was up against, no formal training, and no clear-cut picture of what was ahead.

Photograph by Fredrik Norrsell.

Afterword

OVER THE COURSE of next ten years I traveled over another thousand kilometers of rugged Patagonian horse trail. Both from within Patagonia and from afar, I watched the history of a place I love unfold.

On May 9, 2011, the Chilean government, under *Presidenté* Sebastián Piñera, approved the damming of the Baker and Pascua rivers despite overwhelming public opposition. In the largest public protest since the Pinochet era, 90,000 people took to the streets in protest of that decision. Disturbing pictures of armored and helmeted police confronting rioting mobs in Coyhaique and Santiago flooded the world news.

On that particular day in May, an earthquake-damaged nuclear power plant was leaking in Japan, friction was growing worse between the U.S. and Pakistan, the validity of the Wishbone Hill coal mining permit near Palmer, Alaska, was still being determined, and a California-based Christian ministry was predicting the end of the world in ten days.

In August 2012, the plight of Patagonia took a turn for the better. Colbun—Endesa's Chilean counterpart in the hydroelectric project—withdrew, stating "non-support from the community" as one of its primary reasons. Endesa began looking for other partners.

On June 10th, 2014 re-elected Chilean President Michelle Bachelet cancelled HidroAysen's permits to dam the Baker and Pascua Rivers! Thousands of people in Chile and around the world celebrated. "Patagonia Sin Represas," (Patagonia Without Dams) was the largest environmental movement in Chile's history.

In November 2017 Endesa agreed to return the water rights to the Baker and Pascua river to the Chilean government.

In December of 2017 Sebastián Piñera was again elected president of Chile.

On the Rio Blanco, news was also initially good for Anna Louis. In August, 2003 on a visit to Puerto Aysen, Chilean President Ricardo Lagos dealt the final blow to the proposed aluminum smelter by stating, "This is not the place for an aluminum plant." The damning of the Rio Blanco was canceled.

Unfortunately, as long as we live in a world hungry for cheap electricity, the rivers of Patagonia remain at risk. A decade of turbulent times and several more proposals for dams in the Rio Blanco, Cuervo area has gone by. In 2016 another project was approved, but the power produced was slated to be transported by the HydroAysén transmission line, which was canceled in 2014. Today the permit is up for auction, and, once again, Anna Louis is wondering what will happen next.

In Palmer Alaska, friends and neighbors were able to bring attention to the fact that the Wishbone Hill mining permit had been illegally renewed for decades. In what is a familiar story worldwide, mining companies had been dodging regulations to develop or lose their rights for years. In 2016 a federal court ruled that the permit issued in 1991 should never have been renewed.

On December 8th, 2015, conservationist Douglas Tompkins died in a tragic kayaking accident on Lago General Carrera. His passing was felt worldwide. Kristine Tompkins continued working full time on their many preservation projects in Patagonia.

On January 29, 2018 Kristine Tompkins donated more than a million acres of conservation land to the Chilean government. On that day Chile's president Michelle Bachelet signed into law another nine million acres, protecting an area the size of Switzerland!

One of the greatest joys in writing this book has been spending a few hours each day living in Patagonia in my head. Time may move at a different rate in Patagonia, but it still creeps by. Sergio and Veronica still live on the NOLS campo, however their children, Humberto and Javiera, are now young adults.

In 2012, I again rode deep into the Rio Bravo valley where I visited Don Rial who still lives alone at the halfway point on the old horse trail to Villa O'Higgins. However, roads are creeping ever closer to his home. This time I was traveling with my husband, Fredrik Norrsell.

In 2013, while on another horse trip through Patagonia, I visited Agulino and his family—including twin baby girls Maria Luz and Maria Paz—on their *campo* on the Baker River. Agulino's father Don Cecilio Olivares passed away on December 30th, 2014 at ninety-six years old. The Baker River still flows freely outside their front door.

In December 2017 I again visited friends and rode horses in Patagonia. Arraquien is living happily in his new home, Estancia del Zorro, a 15,000-acre ranch where he works sheep and gives rides to guests. I also visited my old friend Elvira on her *campo*. Elvira's exact age in unknown. When she was born a child's birth was registered on his or her first trip to town.

The continued melting of the Campo de Hielo Norte has cause the Colonia Glacier to pull away from the rock walls of the valley edge allowing Lago Cachet Dos to drain continuously. Downstream *campos* are safe from flooding, at least until another lake forms upstream.

Cochrane, while still a sleepy little town, has a booming tourist trade. Young people from the region regularly kayak the rapids of Rio Cochrane proudly sporting Patagonia Sin Represas stickers on their helmets. The former HydroAysén office in Cochrane is now a kindergarten.

One of the biggest changes in the decade it took to write this book is that ten years ago we were fighting one dam, one power line, one coal mine at a time. One piece of wilderness was either being lost or, at least temporarily, held on to. An unfortunate shift has taken place, within a decade it has become well known that entire ecosystems, whole natural processes, and the earth's atmosphere itself is at risk.

Rural Patagonia offers us a pristine wilderness, a working system of family farms, a whole culture of people who genuinely feel like they have enough, and a grass roots environmental protests that worked—lessons we cannot afford to lose.

Acknowledgements

I took off across Patagonia alone on horseback, yet there was no part of this whole adventure I accomplished myself.

I would like to extend a heartfelt thank you to the fine people of Patagonia who befriended a neophyte horse woman who was alone—and often lost. The lessons they taught me—acceptance, tenacity, patience, contentment—ran far beyond shoeing horses and milking cows.

My first mentors in the ways of *campo* life, Sergio Vaquez and Veronica Romero, have become lifelong friends. Pancho Vio, has been an inspiration in seeing what the world needs and doing it. Scott and Paty Harris let me and my horses live on their beautiful *campo* on two separate occasions. Long after the coming of the automobile turned an extra horse on the farm from an asset into just another mouth to feed, the following people took care of my horses: Carolina Castro, Cristian Vidal, Lilian Henriquez and Gerhard Dallmann, Aguilino Olivares, Pancho Vio Giacaman and Cuchi Ramírez, Patricia Soto, and Sebastian and Alberto Galilea. Kindness along the way has been given to me by a list of people whose names that would fill another book. Thank you.

I would also like to thank my traveling companions, Paul Twardock, Harry House, Lindsey Holstrome, Cory Bunce, and Rachel James. In this day of preplanned experiences these folks were willing to cast off on a true adventure, where even the best made plans would likely prove futile. Liz Rumsey, Fredrik Norrsell, Dick and Gretchin Peterson, and Paty Soto accompanied me on many of the journeys that happened after the *Cabalgata*.

Over the years, many people helped horses become part of my life. I would like to acknowledge my first horseback riding instructor Heather Pelletier, my friend Olga Vonziegesar who took me on my first overnight horse trip and Trudi Angel, of Saddling South, who let me come along on a mule packing trip in Mexico just before I took off across Patagonia. I would also like to thank the Dryden/Winnestaffer family in Palmer, Alaska for allowing me to continue to have horses in my life.

There isn't enough gratitude out there for the multitude of people who work, sometimes day and night, to try and keep our world healthy. In particular, Kristine Tompkins of Tompkins Conservation, who has made saving wildlands and wildlife her life's work. Peter Hartman, regional director of CODEFF, (Comite Pro-defensa de la Flora y Fauna) and president of Aysén Reserva de Vida has worked tirelessly for decades to keep Patagonia wild. Daniela Castro, Marco Diaz, Carlos Garrido, and uncountable others supported the Patagonia Sin Repreasas movement and helped make the Cabagata Sin Represas the well-orchestrated and successful event it was.

Does every book have at least one advocate without whom the book wouldn't exist? For *Riding into the Heart of Patagonia*, that person was Debra McKinney. At a chance meeting around a New Years' bonfire, Deb—the author of *Beyond the Bear*—asked to see my book. She ended up helping me every inch of the way. A million thanks is not enough.

Another writer who has been a tremendous influence on my life is my friend Jill Fredston—author of *Rowing to Latitude* and *Snowstruck*. Whether in the field of avalanche science or writing, I have been trundling along behind Jill for most of my life. It has been a pleasure.

Other writing instructors and friends who have given me insight and encouragement were Andromena Lax of Alaska's 49 writers organization, Dennis Eagan, Rachel James, and Nancy Shanteau.

I would like to sincerely thank Claudia Wilde and C.A. Casey at Bedazzled Ink for giving *Riding Into the Heart of Patagonia*, that "Yes" that every writer dreams of. In the publishing world I, once again, found myself a neophyte. Bedazzled Ink took it from there and ushered me forward.

In a culture where it is not common for women to do things like take of across Patagonia on a horse; I would like to thank my parents, Sally and Jim Pfeiffer for raising a daughter who—for better or worse—believed she could do anything she darn well pleased.

My husband, Fredrik Norrsell, is my biggest asset in life. Although I did not meet him until after the stories in this book took place, Fredrik accompanied me on over five hundred kilometers of rugged Patagonian horse trail through much of the same country described in the book. It is primarily his spectacular photography you see here. I could never have imagined a better partner in life.

I extend a heartfelt thank you to my friend Tammy Moser who allowed me to complete my final edits on her wonderful farm in Hawaii, and to NOLS Patagonia for taking me in off and on for decades. Everything I learned about Patagonia I learned in a second language. I would like to sincerely apologize for any mistakes I have made.

Resources /Recommended Reading

Bridges, E. Lucas. *The Uttermost Part of the Earth*. New York: Dover,1988.

Dixie, Lady Florence. *Riding Across Patagonia, A Victorian Equestrian Adventure*. n.p.: The Long Riders' Guild Press, 2001.

Swale, Rosie. *Back to Cape Horn*. London : Fontana, 1988.

Muster, George. *At Home with the Patagonians*. Charleston, S.C. : Nabu Press, 2010.

Murphy, Dallas. *Rounding the Horn: Being the Story of Williwaws and Windjammers, Drake, Darwin, Murdered Missionaries and Naked Natives—a Deck's-eye View of Cape Horn*. New York : Basic Books, 2009.

Tshiffley, A.F. *Southern Cross to Pole Star Tschiffely's Ride*. London, England: Head of Zeus, 2016.

Graham, R.B. Cunninghame. *South American Sketches*. Norman, Okla.: Univerisity of Oklahoma Press, 1978.

Darwin, Charles. *Voyage of the Beagle*. New York : Cosimo Classics, 2008.

Johannes, Wilbert. *Folk Literature of the Tehuelche Indians*.Los Angeles, Calif.: UCLA Latin American Center Publications, University of California, Los Angeles, 1984.

Galindo, Leonel. *Voces Y Costumbres del Campo Aisenino*. [Coyhaique, Patagonía Chilena]: Fondo Regional de las Artes y la Cultura Coyhaique Chile, 1992.

Galindo, Leonel. *Aisén y su folclor*. [Coyhaique, Patagonía Chilena]: Fondo Regional de las Artes y la Cultura Coyhaique Chile, 2004.

Bridges, Lucas. *The Lord of the Baker*. [Chile] : Douglas Nazar, 2009

Chester, Sharon. *A Wildlife Guide to Chile: Continental Chile, Chilean Antarctica, Easter Island, Juan Fernandez Archipelago*. Princeton, N.J.: Princeton University Press, 2008.

Smeeton, Beryl. *The Stars My Blanket*. Victoria, B.C.: Horsdal & Schubart, 1995.

As a lifelong adventurer and outdoor educator, Nancy Pfeiffer has traveled from Antarctica to the Arctic Ocean. Life as a mountaineering guide has given her the opportunity to experience some of the world's highest summits, yet it is the landscapes and cultures encountered along the way that intrigue her most. Her published works range from poetry to scientific research, and explore subjects from the joys and frustrations of building a house as a single woman to mountaineering for paraplegics. Since graduating from Colorado Mountain College in 1979, Nancy has energetically pursued life without picking a major.

As a novice horsewoman, Nancy took off across Patagonia alone on horseback. Over the next two decades and three thousand kilometers of rugged horse trail, the hospitable people who live there took her in, and Patagonia slipped silently into her soul. As if watching a beloved child grow up, Nancy bore witness to the subtle, yet disturbing, changes barreling down on Patagonia. Nancy now lives with her husband Fredrik Norrsell in a cabin outside Palmer, Alaska, where she enjoys hauling water, chopping wood, and high-speed Internet.

CPSIA information can be obtained
at www.ICGtesting.com
Printed in the USA
FFOW03n1558070518
46451219-48382FF

9 781945 805677